Jesus Goes to Washington

Jesus Goes to Washington

His Progressive Politics for a Sustainable Future

DOUGLAS J. MILLER

WIPF & STOCK · Eugene, Oregon

JESUS GOES TO WASHINGTON
His Progressive Politics for a Sustainable Future

Copyright © 2013 Douglas J. Miller. All rights reserved. Except for brief quotations in critical publications or reviews, no part of this book may be reproduced in any manner without prior written permission from the publisher. Write: Permissions, Wipf and Stock Publishers, 199 W. 8th Ave., Suite 3, Eugene, OR 97401.

Unless otherwise noted, Scripture quotations contained herein are from the New Revised Standard Version Bible, copyright © 1989, Division of Christian Education of the National Council of Churches of Christ in the USA. Used by permission. All rights reserved.

Permission granted for the Earth Charter, 2000. Downloaded on October 8, 2012 from: http://www.earthcharterinaction.org/content/pages/Read-the-Charter,html.

The definition of "liberal" adapted and reproduced by permission from *The American Heritage Dictionary*, Second College Edition. Copyright © 1991 by Houghton Mifflin Harcourt Publishing Company.

Wipf & Stock
An Imprint of Wipf and Stock Publishers
199 W. 8th Ave., Suite 3
Eugene, OR 97401

www.wipfandstock.com

ISBN 13: 978-1-62564-042-0

Manufactured in the U.S.A.

To the late
Honorable Walter H. Capps
who embodied it all:
preacher
professor of religion
prophet
politician
progressive
principled

Contents

Acknowledgments | ix

    Introduction | 1
1. Jesus and Ecospiritual Politics | 7
2. His God Who Sustains | 24
3. His Progressive Politics | 40
4. Conservative Opposition | 57
5. Holiness as Political Compassion | 74
6. Welcoming and Affirmative Action | 88
7. Prayer and a Living Wage | 105
8. Sustainability vs. Destitution | 120
9. Ecospiritual Insight and Judicial Activism | 134
10. Sustaining a Healthy World | 146
11. Sustainability Is International | 157
12. What Would Jesus Do in Washington? | 169

Appendix 1: The Earth Charter | 185
Appendix 2: Reconciling Past and Present | 194
Appendix 3: Jesus Speaks at Different Moral/Spiritual Levels | 197

Bibliography | 201
Index | 209

For a study guide go to: www.theprogressivejesus.com

Acknowledgments

SO MANY VOICES WENT into making this work possible. I would like to thank David Paul who helped edit as did Birdie Newborn. Many read parts of the manuscript and added critical, but very helpful comments including Dr. Bill Nelsen, Rev. Myrna Tuttle, Dr. Sylvia Casberg, Jerry Roberts, Anne Semans, Dr. Nzunga Mabudiga, Rev. Luis Cortes Jr., Dr. Wes Brown, Dr. Jim Dunn, Dean McClure, Dr. Steve Kindle, Dr. Jarmo Tarkki, Judy Mikalonis, and Stephany Evans. I also appreciated the encouragement from Dr. Jonathan Reed, Dr. Hal Taussig, Rabbi Rick Shapiro, Rev. Tom Geshay, Dr. Ron Davis, and Rev. Craig Rennebohm.

Thanks are also due to those who have given me valuable feedback after my talks on the subject. I have incorporated many of their insights and their objections forced me to rethink some ideas.

Most of all I would like to thank Sandie, my loving partner and primary supporter through the whole project. She read the manuscript many times and her comments were invaluable. My daughter Christine also helped immeasurably. My granddaughters Bella and Roxanne were great inspirations, especially as I thought about their futures.

So many Progressives have impacted me through the years by their writings and actions, too numerous to mention, but thank you all.

Introduction

> O come, O come, Emmanuel
> And ransom captive Israel,
> That mourns in lonely exile here,
> Until the Son of God appear.
>
> —From an old Latin hymn

THIS BOOK EXPLORES HOW Christian spirituality and its political ethic address the looming crisis of our time—persistent human misery amidst Earth's woes. Our global predicament is fed by massive moral failure. Thus, every effort in achieving a just society and a renewable biosphere will languish without changing our fundamental values and translating that into political will and action at the individual, local, national, and international levels. For this, a viable moral narrative must prevail, compelling a new ethical and spiritual paradigm grounded in "sustainability," i.e., in enhancing the ongoing human community compatible with upholding Earth's ecosystems.

One of the landmark documents of this century, the Earth Charter (appendix 1), urges a "shared vision of basic values" to restore a "sustainable global society." Setting the ethical standards for a viable long-term future, it challenges the world community to respect Nature, promote human rights, establish economic justice, and practice peace.[1] Acknowledging the power of religious beliefs, the document stirs us to marshal every moral and spiritual force—past and present—to achieve these ends. Thus, we invite you to journey into the heart and mind of the most influential person in history,

---

1. From the Earth Charter's Preamble. Go to www.earthcharterinaction.org for its rationale and history.

Jesus of Nazareth, and meditate on how his spiritual politics champions the moral and political change needed today. We shall uncover and explore the common core values he taught to sustain vulnerable human beings and heal a fevered Earth.

Our present society, unfortunately, is fractured over what values need changing. This fissure has erupted into the most volcanic reality of American politics today—the fire fanned under the labels "Liberal" and "Conservative." We shall attempt to shed some light from the ancient past on these two political contenders as they vie for our public souls. Long ago, Jesus, too, debated over political values, leaving us a legacy of the loftiest moral convictions. He summons us to be united, as Democrats and Republicans, as Independents and Greens, as religious and secularists, in achieving them. Significantly, the higher humane values Jesus advanced were deeply rooted in an ancient Land ethic. Because of the crisis we now face, this broader moral panorama is more compelling than ever. Boldly stated, any quest for an elevated spirituality will tie environmental, social, and economic ethics tightly together and fashion a viable political ethic of sustainability. In this day, our vision and morality must not only be unrelenting, but also comprehensive, lest we look back and shudder at the wreckage. In truth, then, the ripening of an *all-inclusive morality with the greening of faith* is the most compelling and transforming spiritual movement of the twenty-first century.

On the negative side, the same values that oppress peoples are the same ones that afflict Earth. Sadly, America is not an idle offender in generating human and ecological calamity, even though we consider our country to be the shining city on a hill destined to enlighten the world. It has lost luster due to extremist forces beclouding its enshrined Creator-endowed ideals: justice, liberty, and the pursuit of well-being for all—hope's highest prizes. Tragically, its "exceptionalism" has translated into the "divine right" to impose its will freely. And on a personal level, has not America's ceaseless din of barking hucksters too often hoodwinked us into mortgaging our souls for junky landfill-destined trinkets and playthings? Finding our transforming spiritual center as broken persons in a fractured world and beleaguered Earth is a serious call in these troubling times.

We have recently witnessed the folly of war coupled with a willingness to kill civilians, torture prisoners, and suspend basic rights. Then we watched the ransacking of economic justice and the widening gap between the super-rich and nearly all others, driven by a blind faith in unregulated market forces, the philosophy that greed is good, and high-horse CEO swagger. We've seen our leaders deport the highest humane values for paper-boat virtues. Add to this the corruption in high places, negative attitudes toward minorities, and deep internal divisions. Yet ominously, a lack of urgency for the Planet's increasing ruination has only confirmed America's moral bankruptcy. We grieve over the affronts and indignities—the anonymous horrors billions face daily. Along with these ethical pileups, we see a popular upsurge in a mangled, muddied Christianity that reinforces fear, divisiveness, selfishness, exploitation, heedlessness, and prejudice—the lowest bids for the soul of a person and a nation.

With faith in America's goodness besieged, and prevented from airing frustration to those in power, many have felt helpless, isolated—like sojourners in a strange land, in sad spiritual and political exile. They, too, experience moral hollowness and the need for redemption. This work is an invitation to champion a new vision and embark on a new course to recover those values that bring out the best in faith and in politics. Once recovered, we boldly and passionately critique a flawed political ethic and unleash the transforming energy of a deeper spirituality and its attending morality for the sake of a better humanity and a viable Planet.

For many Americans, the "Obama phenomenon" signaled a new and daring direction—the dawning from a long nightfall. His historic election and reelection represented a resounding cheer for a rekindled American idealism, uniting the hope of millions that a transformational politics—an epochal shift in governing that fulfills our deepest longings—would be possible. His animating vision and victories symbolize a spirit that some believe could reorder society amid all its infirmities. Yet, will he energize and mobilize citizens into the far future for the dramatic change needed? Indeed, can leaders alone provide the moral and spiritual compass to navigate through difficult and dangerous shoals or will they inevitably run aground in the shallows of "what works"? Purposed pragmatism could be an angel or a devil, serving virtue or vice; it never escapes a hierarchy of values. Accordingly, unless and until we *change our value sets* and enliven higher ideals, we will not acquire the personal or the political will necessary to save a languishing world.

No one has affected the spiritual consciousness of so many millions as Jesus of Nazareth. As the founder of Christianity, his waters run deep and wide in Western culture and he stands as a powerful envoy in humankind's contest for a viable future. With moral grandeur, he reached into his peasant and religious traditions and offered hope amidst despair. He stands as a blast from heaven and a guiding light to fulfill humanity's deepest spiritual needs—to find personal dignity, to embrace the worthiest values, and to experience the eternal and sacred in others and in Earth. He gives voice to those who cry out to engage their faith and values around issues for the common good. Given the interconnected ecological, economic, and health crises, he inspires persons of faith as well as powerful nations to step up and blaze the way for holistic transformation. Jesus speaks to us today as he spoke centuries ago to the longings, but withered hopes, of Galileans exiled from the Land. He called for people to change, even to repent, but from what to what? Unpacking the answer to this question for his time will provide a clearer picture of Jesus' message for us.

Christians try to shape their lives by asking, "What would Jesus do?"[2] In all our actions we strive to exemplify his quality of character, taking sustenance in the "Christ-centered values" he taught and modeled. They display the best in Christianity and the other major faiths, the genius of Western political traditions, and the noblest moral impulses and human ideals.[3] His basic moral markers, which we shall examine in some detail, are not always loudly sung by Christians. They are often muffled by self-serving claims, and thus, endangered and exiled.[4] Yet they remain valid and compelling for all people, whether religious or not. Serious followers of Jesus must return to his high standards, esteeming them, mapping them into their consciousness, and offering a clearer and more united witness for them. Then we need to sow them within all cherished institutions—family, religion, and business. Another of our institutions is government. Whether one cherishes it or despises it, most agree that it needs fixing. We shall be seeking answers to the question of what would Jesus do if he entered Washington to "cleanse" it, as he did Jerusalem.

By restoring time-honored values, Jesus hoped to end Israel's internal exile so that it could fulfill its divine destiny to bless the nations. Traditionally put, he yearned to *save his world*—a world that resonated with humanity's ties to the Land, but how humans, out of greed, indifference, and violence, exploit others and Earth. Yet, his story also speaks to our possibilities (our rescue and reform). Jesus lived and died so that all may sit at a common moral table, with equal grandeur, without pre-conditions. By dovetailing spirituality and Land policy, he initiated a mighty movement—a new spiritual politics he called the "Kingdom of God" that would dignify Earth and everything within, on, and above it—the ignored and exploited by imperial powers.

Universal and relevant, his legacy hears the choking voice of gassed air and polluted oceans; the cries of men, women, and children exiled by

---

2. This question was popularized by Charles Sheldon's classic *In His Steps*, subtitled, *What Would Jesus Do?* The work found residence in the Social Gospel movement of the late eighteen and early nineteenth centuries and the question pushed people to imitate Jesus in their social, political, and economic lives.

3. Raskin, *Liberalism*, 243–48.

4. Carter, *Endangered Values*, 2.

foreclosures, job losses, bankruptcies, hunger, inadequate health coverage, neglect, discrimination, war, deadly toxins, and the thousand other ways Earth and its inhabitants are humiliated on a daily basis. He strove to light the lamp of hope amid fear and despair. He resolved to lead the broken back home to be the salt of Earth and the light to the world. In so doing, he brought the face of a compassionate God to a suffering biosphere. Stirring the sacred empathy within, he shows us how to recover our pawned souls, to return home, and claim our spiritual purpose and our common moral creed. He makes clear that our destiny manifests a political factor—to transform broken governments and save a retching Planet.

We shall explore a serviceable spiritual politics amid the ways some well-intentioned religious people misconstrue the relationship between politics and religion.[5] For instance, the Christianizing of America by the Religious Right is often just a cover for sectarian conformity that leaves other major faiths out of the mix, demands traditional roles for women, pushes away people who happen to look different, denies climate science, or supports ill-fated military ventures. This avenue, which purports to corner the market on spirituality and values, does contain fragments of truth, but partial truths often distort Christianity, leading to grave misadventures. Thus, we are compelled to engage in the thorny values debate—to confront deficient moral and political ideals, while urging a broadened and more wholesome ethical and spiritual discourse.

To recognize that Jesus hoped to redeem the way nations govern is not to deny that he stormed history as the divine Son of God to "atone" for our personal sins—a fundamental Christian belief. Embracing theological orthodoxy and accepting the reliability of the Bible when properly interpreted does not, however, require us to hold regressive views on the burning social, political, and ecological issues of our times.[6] On the contrary, solid biblical reading and study leads in the opposite direction. More people recognize this as they watch Christian leaders flout some of Jesus' basic teachings like championing a militaristic foreign policy, supporting government actions that favor the rich over the financially strapped, and treating the environment with indifference. Ideally, this book will make clear why all Christians should unite around and help emerge a new transformational politics of hope that will guarantee a healthy and sustainable biocommunity into the distant future. We stand at a moment in history when it is time to fuse political power with spirituality in ways that enhance care for everything,

---

5. See Lerner, *Left Hand of God*, 41 for the phrase "spiritual politics."

6 Dr. Carl F. H. Henry, a well-respected Evangelical scholar, appreciated my conservative stance on Scripture in his *Confessions of a Conservative*, 330.

knowing that everything is vulnerable and subject to destruction. The world is ripe not only for a new spiritual *awakening*, but also for a spiritual *movement* that could sweep through local governments, up to the halls of capitols, and around the globe.

Though Jesus is universally esteemed and worshiped by many, he remains an enigma. As you travel through the following pages, you will experience a new reading of Jesus, begging a paradigm shift in understanding him. We want to discover him by spiritually journeying into his mind and heart, into his very soul. Yet, the Jesus story, as part of the human story, is planted in Earth's story. This requires accompanying him along the dusty roads of Palestine, seeing the Land indignities he saw, hearing the cries he heard, and observing his response. As we encounter his faith in a nurturing Creator/God, his policies for a coming Kingdom "on earth," and his confrontation with his opponents, hopefully a more authentic and compelling Jesus will emerge. In his attempt to show us "the way," his faint whispers resound into the twenty-first century and tender an ennobling narrative to walk the path of renewal and sustainability that could uncover the best in each one of us, in our nation, and in our world.

1

Jesus and Ecospiritual Politics

> If one person gains spirituality, the whole world gains.
>
> —Gandhi

A THEME PERMEATING THIS work is that human beings are destined to thrive and their flourishing depends on a healthy Planet. This calls for a viable spirituality in which the Universe and others exist apart from their instrumentality or even their being enjoyed, although it includes these to some degree. Indeed, the Cosmos and humans serve something much greater—the Universal or the Infinite, who many call God. In this understanding of spirituality, we exist purely out of gratitude to the Creator, to Earth, and to the Other from whom and for whom we came into being. The biblical writers see God's glorious "handiwork" and "image" expressed throughout Creation's stunning marvels and processes—and they stand in awe (Ps 19:1; Rom 1:20.). For many, spirituality is tethered to pondering the dazzling beauty and the unfathomable mysteries of human life and the Universe. Consequently, grateful people mourn when they see Earth and its multitudes suffering due to human arrogance and ignorance; when every affront tarnishes God's glory. We are in great need of salvation. The urgent call is for a broadened spirituality in which the traditional Christian notion of redemption must expand to include fixing our broken socioeconomic structures and healing our injured Planet.

In Jesus' symbolic world, derived from his Bible, Land/Earth played a crucial role, being the prerequisite for fulfilling all basic human goods. (In Hebrew, "Earth" and "Land" are interchangeable, so statements about the Land carry implications for the Planet.[1]) Through the Land, people found their identity. It mediated their economics and politics; it linked them to their past and their future; it brought security and sustenance; it connected them to their God and shaped their religion.[2] Land, then, was more than just a commodity. It cultivated vital moral/spiritual meaning that governed community interactions and aspirations, through which all key values—moral and nonmoral—flourished. The Land, as promised by God, would flow with milk and honey, providing for the well-being of all as expressed by the term "*shalom*" or, broadly, "the common good." The people saw themselves as citizens of the Land first; they readily spoke of the *Land* of Israel.

Thus, Israel's spirituality, rooted in the ground and the peoples' relationship to it, was an *eco*spirituality. When Land decisions exploited the people (for example, when farmers were squeezed off their ancestral Lands by the rich), it precipitated a national spiritual crisis that ultimately led to exile (Isa 5:8). To restore Israel meant restoring a just and fair Land policy. Being an agency of moral sanction, all Land/Earth was sacred, holy, and to be acted upon with reverent respect. Given their ties to Earth/Land, humans, too, were considered sacred and to be treated with grandeur (Gen 2:7). Following in this same spiritual tradition, Jesus inaugurated an earthly Kingdom of God that moored human dignity to life-sustaining Land relationships. Christians, as guardians of human worth, are summoned to a spirituality that cannot ignore the Earth in whatever we do. The greening of the Christian Faith and all faiths is surely a most compelling spiritual quest today. Why is this the case?

Imagine turning on the morning news and the anchor blandly reports, "20,000 dead" and then quickly turns to the next story, describing with animated passion and in lurid detail, the marriage break-up of a celebrity couple. The next morning you hear the same, "20,000 dead" and then some other trivial story. And the same is repeated day after day, year in and year out. In reality, this 20,000 figure is the number of people who die *every day* worldwide due to the ill-health caused by poverty. These are wrenching, miserable, painful, and avoidable deaths.[3] Unfortunately, this massive human death count is never a lead story. Caught in a relentless poverty trap, the poor remain voiceless. These desperate are mostly victimized by domi-

---

1. Brueggemann, *Land*, xiii.
2. Ibid., 2, 13, 200.
3. Sachs, *Poverty*, 1.

nating systems that squeeze them in an ever tightening vice and leave them to eke out a meager day-to-day living. Like the poor, dishonored, and landless in Jesus' day, they ride the precarious and vicious downward spiral of trying to survive. The numbers are staggering, but the situation is not much better for Earth.

As early as 1972, a group of MIT scholars grimly reported that the modern world would face an ecological crisis, if not a catastrophe, by 2100.[4] The researchers advised that "political and moral resolve" were indispensable for reversing the "deteriorating world situation," but their alert went unheeded for many years.[5] More recently, Jim Hansen of NASA's Goddard Institute for Space Studies has warned, "We have only a short time to address global warming before it runs out of control."[6] The U.N.'s Intergovernmental Panel on Climate Change states that global warming is "unequivocal" and only urgent and immediate global action will stave off its devastating effects on humanity.[7] It is now clear that other eco-subsystems—ocean acidity, ozone depletion, soil and water degradation, deforestation, chemical pollution, and exploding population—are reaching or have passed carrying capacity thresholds or tipping-points. Among other disasters, these systemic erosions converge in crop failure, signaling a most critical issue in our day, and one Jesus faced—food production and distribution. Like all crises, this affects mostly the poor, but soon will impact the not-so-poor. To extend our metaphor, Earth, too, is being forced into exile—held in bondage to domination, indifference, and waste. Spiritual people take seriously the overwhelming evidence that the fitness of the environment is worsening, based on a science that is as exact as putting a human on the moon.

The very factors that now feed the Planet's ailments, as noted in the MIT report, also birthed the circumstances of deteriorating life in Jesus' day—inequality and selfishness.[8] Jesus vigorously addressed these "sins," providing the moral and spiritual ingredients that shape the solution to our looming troubles. His views of God and Creation, his ideas about the political economy, his notion of justice, and his belief in restoring good governing all represent building blocks for developing a comprehensive and universal spirituality grounded in our relationship to everything in, on, and above Earth. For Christians, Jesus provides "the way"; but what is the path he compels us to walk?

4. Meadows et al., *Limits to Growth*, 190–97.
5. Ibid., 193.
6. Hansen, "Threat to the Planet," 16.
7. Pathauri and Reisinger, *Climate Change 2007*, 30.
8. Meadows et al., *Limits to Growth*, 191–92.

OUR SPIRITUAL JOURNEY WALKS THE PATH OF SUSTAINABILITY

Politically speaking, America today lies battered and bruised by divisiveness and cynicism, enmeshed in a nasty ongoing war of words. Read the current political best sellers; listen to the babble on talk radio; or watch the acrimonious debates on our most popular "news" channels and see how woefully divided we are. We struggle over which political ideas ought to reign and which are flawed. Battle lines have been drawn between competing value systems, and Christians, caught in the war zone, are likewise deeply split. Although the clash generates political noise, the undertone is ultimately spiritual—a "spiritual warfare," as some call it—between the many visible and hidden powers that influence our choices and shape our destiny. Gaining a measure of victory rests in a time-tested spirituality that bears witness to transcendent humane values.

The quest for a deeper spirituality has been called the most significant megatrend in our day.[9] Interest in the spiritual life of Jesus skyrocketed Deepak Chopra's *The Third Jesus* to a number one best seller. But what is spirituality? Why is it so important? And what does this most spiritual person, Jesus Christ, really teach us about a transcendent life, not just in a collection of his short sayings taken in isolation, but within the context of his everyday interactions with downtrodden Galileans? And how might his recollected truths break the trance that renders people so hard of hearing and so short of seeing?

Spirituality is about closeness to and dependency on God, yet a lifelong up and down quest. It begins when we first realize that because of fears, false hopes, and misnamed pleasures, we live distant from our God-determined destiny. Our soul has been captivated by and held captive to a larger world in exile—burdened with delusion, disillusion, and destruction—and so far from home. We grapple for transcendence and hope, for more than just everyday rawness, ravage, and revenge; we long for a transformed self, a better world, and renewed Earth—the ingredients of hope. The glory of a more Evangelical Christianity has been its insistence upon restoring a personal relationship with God through Jesus Christ—a relationship severed by Adam's calamitous pride and aggrandizing selfishness. Yet, Evangelicalism often ignores the truth that our oneness with God means bonding with all Creation; that neglecting and despoiling any part of it degrades spirituality.

The familiar psalm 23 expresses it comprehensively and most beautifully: "The Lord makes me lie down in green pastures; leads me beside still

---

9. Aburdene, *Megatrends 2010*, 4.

waters; restores my soul; leads me in the right paths." Today, the right soulful path to viable pastures and untroubled waters means traveling a *moral path of sustainability* for Earth and all its inhabitants. What does Jesus bring to this quest?

Jesus imparts five truths that elevate our closeness to God and births a new understanding of spirituality. First, Mark begins his gospel by describing Jesus' mission as "the way," a designation so suitable that the early Christians adopted it to name their movement (Mark 1:1–3; Acts 9:2). He teaches that spirituality is a journey to unite us with a loving nurturing God expressed by a family metaphor, "Father" or Parent.[10] Second, for Jesus, spirituality is not an otherworldly or escapist path. It always finds its "home" (*oikos* or eco) traversing Earth, and thus, its path is an ecospiritual one. It enters into our everyday transactions; into all that is important as well as into the mundane, into all the wonder and into the ordinary, into all that sustains us and into the wreckage scattered around us. Third, the ecospiritual way is always a way of life—affixed to ethics; straightening our crooked paths and transforming our narcissistic values and behavior into the quest for holiness, inclusion, communion, equality, devotion, insight, wholeness, reverence, and unity—all linked to loving our neighbor and our Earth as we love ourselves. As a way, it leads to true life. Next, walking the ecospiritual path exacts vigilance and exercise (spiritual discipline). Lastly, Jesus relates these truths about the ecospiritual way to the unsavory arena of politics, especially Land politics with its social and economic outcomes. For him, the transforming power of love determines local, national, and global policy. This book unpacks these five dimensions of the ecospiritual journey and its wisdom that Jesus taught and modeled.

For Christians, our path is one of love—first and foremost. The goal of this book is to capture this noblest moral impulse within the Judeo-Christian tradition and apply it in politically transforming ways. Nothing outflanks love, no religious rite, not even faith or hope. It is the hook from which every action hangs, the summary of all laws, the be-all and end-all of every virtue, value, and principle; it is the lifeblood of Christianity and the only hope for humanity and the Planet (1 Cor 13:13; Mark 12:33; Matt 22:40; Rom 13:10). Our ecospiritual formation aims at whole heart intimacy with God's pure love (*agapē*) to model its unlimited goodness in human affairs and in relationship to Creation. This extravagant love, however, is a gift of grace or generosity, "poured out" by the Holy Spirit on us, transforming our self-centered love (*eros*). We need only be open to God's presence to

---

10. I am sensitive to gender-bias language, but occasionally use the term "father" in reference to God, especially where Jesus intended the designation to undercut human patriarchies.

receive it. Openness, then, allows us to be touched and is a key component of ecospirituality. Love opens blind eyes to discern all the false addictive loves that govern us, providing insight into the hidden forces of domination that surround us. It opens our deaf ears to the sobs of tattered dreams and vulnerable ecosystems. It opens our closed hearts to enfold the unwelcomed and neglected. It opens our silent mouths to speak the inconvenient moral truths that need heeding.

This love that defines the heart of God and looks outward translates into moral values—compassion, fairness, peace, generosity, faithfulness, gentleness, hope, and self-discipline—appropriately called "fruit" of the Spirit because they nourish our withered souls and communities and a languishing Planet (Gal 5:22–23). Also included is joy (wonder), the true happiness that comes through loving the beauty that's everywhere. The ecospiritual person is always mindful of these virtuous "things above" and visibly practices them in everyday life as a sacred responsibility (Col 3:1–14). Thus, the path leads to developing our conscience and moral character. Jesus expressed it as replicating a heavenly Kingdom, but one coming on Earth where these virtues grow.

The evolution of human consciousness makes us aware that we exist as earthbound and that we must present ourselves to one another as part of the larger biotic community. This points to a new way Christians understand God's rule and a more expansive way we do ethics. The viability of the Planet and beyond must be taken into account in moral decision-making and action. As spelled out in the Earth Charter, sustainability rests on four moral pillars: respect for Nature, universal human rights, economic justice, and a culture of peace. Christian Ethics, along with all ethical systems must blend these four interconnected ingredients. Following Aldo Leopold's early lead, a comprehensive ethic can no longer neglect Earth's own systemic integrity—its balances, diversities, interdependencies, ingenuities, stability, sustainability, and natural patterns and processes.[11] Evolution, natural selection, death, decay, and even pathogens are also parts of the functioning ecosystem; and a viable ethic will struggle with issues these factors raise. Given the priority of neighbor love, a Christian ethic now extends the age-old question, "Who is my neighbor?" to include respecting and caring for Earth's own dynamics and how they bear on social, economic, and political issues that sustain humans into the far future.

The most important ethical truth holds that God's generous love is universal. It blankets everyone and everything, even that which fights against and rejects God. The pinnacle of the spiritual life, then, is to love all

---

11. See Leopold, *Almanac*, 237–95.

(including plants, animals, even enemies). Such love ends all divisiveness by bringing to Creation, its processes, and all its creatures their basic good as surely as God makes the sun to shine and the rain to shower on them (Matt 5:45). These beautiful biblical expressions see God as a force of Nature and celebrate Earth's marvelous gift of sustainability. Love also searches out the stranger—those strange to us—the downtrodden and the different (even in kind) who suffer neglect and wrath. On our ecospiritual journey we transplant the heart of God into a bleeding world and suffering Planet and are as exact in our devotion to these as we are to God (1 John 4:7–21). This truth points to the most glorious feature of Christianity: that Jesus Christ, who revealed God's loving face to us, models and empowers this ecospiritual way.

Jesus longed for the day that love might reign over everything. Embodying pure ecospirituality with a quality of character beyond compare, Jesus tapped into God's eternal truths of self-sacrifice, hope, and empathy. He never acted from the lower realms of self-interest, fear, and mistrust. The true nature of God shaped his ethic of love for all people, friend or foe, high or low—in the deepest ways. We emulate good news by following the way of Jesus, although we struggle to keep pace. The goal of ecospirituality is to accompany him so closely that we imitate him. Actually, we desire such intimacy with him that his very character becomes our own. His way is, in truth, the way of new life. How does this happen?

We are enlightened, counseled, and empowered by his Holy Spirit who leads us to do the right thing, which Christians speak of as being "conformed to the image of Christ." This image will come into clearer focus and bring grandeur to our discipleship when, along the way, we catch sight of Jesus; when we see him speaking deep wisdom to abused victims, taking children in his arms, touching unclean lepers, eating with sinners, healing hated Samaritans and Gentiles, honoring shamed women, dignifying the desperately poor, and living and teaching sustainability—all deeply spiritual and loving actions that would turn his world and ours upside down. Hopefully, our experience of Jesus' spiritual presence will ignite that same fire of love within us and our faith communities so that we might make a difference as sojourners on Earth.

Everything Jesus said about flourishing and suffering blazes our ecospiritual path, permitting us to see ourselves, others, and the Planet more clearly. Taking a page from Isaiah, Jesus, at the very beginning of his mission, connects the pouring of God's Spirit on him with bringing good news to the poor, the blind, and the oppressed, including the Jubilee Land restoration and rest laws (Luke 4:18–30). When we embody Jesus' spiritual outpouring, we are enlivened to experience his intimacy with God and feel his deepest yearning—his love that flowed so naturally to those in need. When our heart becomes his heart, he opens our eyes to the greatest spiritual truth under heaven—that *human beings and Earth are one huge household* with God as our Father/Mother and we as God's children. Now we journey together like brothers and sisters who really care for one another. In walking the Jesus way, we are stirred to be God's tools for building this all-inclusive family—very good news to a nation divided, a world broken, and a dying Planet.

Our ecospiritual path, however, is constantly subject to pitfalls, reflecting the truth Jesus spoke, "The spirit indeed is willing, but the flesh is weak" (Mark 14:38). The human spirit can soar so high, yet descend into the deepest, death-shadowed valleys. Like Pilgrim in John Bunyan's classic *Pilgrim's Progress*, our journey is filled with crises—temptations, obstacles, dead ends. We easily abandon our intimacy with God to fall in love with lower values and half-truths that Jesus likens to gaining the whole world but losing our souls (Mark 8:36). We inevitably seek the triune god of endless riches, status, and domination that jeopardize the very existence of so many and so much on this Planet. The ancient world molded these flawed values into moral and political ideals that defined the reigning ethic. Today, many espouse the same principles and are beguiled into worshiping, wealth, materialism, group egoism, ecological destruction, and military might. All these feed on such ruinous vices like greed, pride, envy, contempt, neglect, and revenge. These insatiable "works of the flesh" reflect our most primal passions and survival instincts—hoarding, domination, and fighting. Christians call this egotism "original sin," mirroring Adam and Eve's fall, Israel's exile, and the never-ending haunt of history. Self-centeredness and its offspring, religious individualism, poison our souls and loosen our bond with God, with others, and with Earth. They cast us into a moral dungeon that deadens our empathic impulses and deafens us to God's never-ending call.

We adopt the biblical image of *exile* to describe the spiritual calamity the Planet and its inhabitants face today. Exile implies alienation from one's Land. All the prophets and movements in Israel, including Jesus, were dealing with the devastating results of being driven from paradise, from the fruitfulness of the Land, imperiling life itself. While the exile metaphor speaks to our personal journey, it retains a basic political focus. Nevertheless, we may be exiled by so many of life's malignant overlords. These include fear, cynicism, addictions, poor health, the drive to get ahead, dysfunctional homes, crushing debt, oppressive work, no work, prejudice, narrow religious vision, environmental indifference, flawed values, spiritual stagnation, or any of the other embers from hell that blow our way. We are also routed off course from our true destiny by the impersonal "hidden persuaders"—the imperial powers in board rooms that shape our need to consume more and more, in governmental bills that strangle our rights, in media outlets that try to direct how we should think, or in pulpits that strong-arm our beliefs.

Yet, the summons of God to seek our divine-like destiny stirs deep in our souls. The first step in the Christian's ecospiritual journey is to hear Jesus speaking amid the din of this murky world's seductive and vicious cycle of want, obtain, want more, and take—the proven formula for a social and ecological apocalypse. He calls us to come to ourselves, like the prodigal son in his famous parable, to remember our created destiny, to change direction, to humbly shed tears of repentance, to root out this age's flawed ethic, and to follow him back home. It means being reborn into the full image of a loving God. In true transformation, the ways of broken systems lose their grip and fade, even though they remain alluring. This turnabout in values brings a restored conscience controlled by the varieties of divine love that Jesus taught and lived: compassion, fairness, generosity, unity, freedom, tolerance, diversity, Land care, non-militarism, and internationalism—values that march hand in hand and undergird a viable ethic for a sustainable future. We shall explore them further, since faith in and dependence upon Jesus is evidenced by subjecting every part of our daily life, both grand and minute, to these moral treasures.

Detaching ourselves from the seductive values that dominate culture is challenging. The cross of Jesus stands as a graphic metaphor of the rigor of the ecospiritual way—the same sacrifice, the same reproach, the same dying to destructive gain. Because being more God-like is always drenched in failure and humility, our Christian path exacts constant vigilance aided by the following exercises:

1. Humbly realizing our mistakes and being transformed by abandoning faulty values and embracing loving ones.

2. Humbly setting our hearts on holiness, welcoming, prayer, devotion, insight, wholeness, reverence, unity and tying them to neighbor and Creation mindfulness.

3. Humbly seeing our place within the biocommunity and immersing ourselves in the naked misery and frailness of everything earthly—hearing the groans, identifying the wounds.

4. Humbly meditating on and learning from reason, Nature, Scripture, and especially the life of Jesus, to see how God dealt with exploitation and suffering, while listening to the great cloud of witnesses (teachers and moral examples) that have gone before.

5. Humbly utilizing our empowerment and enlightenment, we then journey within faith and non-faith communities to take the appropriate loving actions that allow others and Earth to flourish.

Jesus practiced all these disciplines; and we grow in him by walking beside him, experiencing his oneness with God, seeing the vision God gave him, feeling his compassion, hearing his striking speeches and parables, and viewing his mighty acts of empowerment and healing—all ways in which he made his time and place more sacred. Hopefully, by encountering Jesus in his world, he will come alive within us as we engage our world; much like he did in Mother Teresa, who practiced all the traditional spiritual disciplines—prayer, fasting, Bible reading, meditation—but whose devotion towers because she did these within the slums of Calcutta.

To repeat: a return from exile means walking the holy highway back to a stronger union with God and fulfilling the destiny for which we were created—to bond with Earth and others. For Christians, this new ecospiritual vitality unites us with Jesus when we meditate on his life and death, embrace his vision, and abandon ourselves to his love-informed principles and virtues. All Christians, all churches, all religious communities strive to cultivate his values in keeping with his famous Nature metaphor that we are known by our fruits (Matt 7:16). The fruits, however, are not just private and for individuals only, but stand as *civic* principles and virtues, playing a significant role in the meaning and purpose of politics—to guarantee a sustainable future. How might Jesus contribute to this goal through public action?[12]

ECOSPIRITUALITY, POLITICS, AND THE SUBSISTENCE ETHIC

Jesus' most revolutionary insight confirms that the habitation of the human spirit lodges in the ups and downs of ordinary life within families, villages, and territories like Galilee and beyond. He knew that the conditions of our soul—spiritual dying through despair or reviving through joy—are profoundly affected by our daily struggles to survive. Inevitably, these harsh realities include *political* forces. In Jesus' world the economic, social, moral, legal, and cultural artifacts were shaped by religion, but subsumed under politics. If any one pillar collapsed, the society's whole structure would become rubble. As scholar Gerd Theissen observes, "In antiquity, nobody

---

12. Hardin, "Tragedy of the Commons," 1247.

could imagine politics without religion."[13] In essence, politics was embedded in spirituality and the spiritual life engaged politics. Many Americans find this link hard to accept because our traditions separate religion from politics, and consequently, spirituality from public life. Such a division could never occur in Jesus' day. The interlock between religion and politics reaches far back to humanity's "primal traditions." Long before and during the time of Jesus, religious leaders shouldered political rule and kings claimed priestly status or some kinship to divinity that justified their mostly oppressive rule.[14]

The union between religion and politics cannot be overstated in assessing the ministry of Jesus. What seems, at first sight, like a purely religious conflict between Jesus and his opponents resounded with political undertones. Spiritual ventures such as faith, morality, and worship always conveyed political meaning—pointing to a *national* God, a God *of the Land of Israel*. God expected faith, but a *political* faith—a faith in Israel's institutions and its special Land-linked destiny.[15] Jesus harbored this political faith when he announced a new all-encompassing ecospiritual reality, the Kingdom of God. Thus, we can only fully appreciate the *spiritual* significance of Jesus of Nazareth within the context of his *political* vision and vice versa. But what do we mean by politics?

Political scientist Harold Lasswell classically described politics as grasping and using power to *take* from others.[16] That's certainly the flawed base from which all nations, including Rome, exercised power. Jesus experienced this formula for human governing, and it deeply troubled him. More technically, politics is using power and authority to formulate, administer, and enforce (or critique) laws and public policies, underscored by social and moral norms.[17] Succinctly, politics deals with power, values, and laws.

Power, the capacity to control others, overshadows any discussion of politics. Political power, however, may don various mantles: from violent subjugation to the threat of violence, to outright rebellion, to subtle forms of resistance, to thought control, to voting, and to cultural elements such as patriarchy, patronage, honor codes, and ritual. It also includes the "soft power" of rational, moral, and spiritual persuasion.[18] Political power and authority formed the backdrop for Jesus' earthly mission, but he chose the

13. Theissen, "Political Dimension," 225–30.
14. Becker, *Escape from Evil*, 4–5.
15. Kaufmann, *Religion of Israel*, 345.
16. Lasswell, *Politics*, 7.
17. A synthesis derived from various common and political dictionaries.
18. Theissen, "Political Dimension," 226.

more subtle means to transform and drive politics, including the softer power of proclamation and conversion. Yet, he vied for authority with his announcements of an alternative governance (a Kingdom coming). Added were his compelling political teachings, legal formulations, and his "hidden" and overt critiques of the power brokers. Jesus plowed within the huge and fertile political field between the extremes of passivity and violent revolution. He was a nonviolent political agitator, but, in a security-obsessed empire, such people were often fated for execution.[19]

Ultimately, politics has to do with *values*, especially moral values. Aristotle had classified ethics under politics, which meant that values, principles, and virtues went hand-in-hand with law (see appendix 3). Jesus did not simply want to "throw the bums out" only to replace them with other scoundrels. Rather, he announced an alternative political structure—a domain grounded in values such as reciprocal cooperation, selfless sharing, forgiveness, wonderment, and restoration of the Land/Earth. He formulated legal pronouncements around these that christened his *Basileia* (a gender-neutral Greek term for "kingdom") of God.

In response to the brutality surrounding him, Jesus, a peasant, would draw upon the spiritual and moral tools that all peasants and oppressed peoples before and after him cherished—an ecospirituality grounded in the "subsistence ethic." This ethic (1) treated the Land/Earth as holy and assured its sustainability through renewal; (2) guaranteed the right to basic survival needs the Land provided; (3) demanded give and take (reciprocal) transactions to eliminate hoarding, to equalize imbalances, and to provide subsistence needs; and (4) looked to a future reversal of miserable and degrading conditions.[20] Essentially, the subsistence ethic guaranteed the moral and legal right to the basic necessities of survival and the obligation of those who possessed more to share with those in need. As found early in Scripture, the ethic mandated humans to be "keepers" of their brothers and sisters and of the Garden they inhabit (Gen 2:15; 4:9). *The subsistence ethic is absolutely essential for understanding the political mission of Jesus.* The present path to human and Earth sustainability takes root in these ancient ideals. The notion of "subsistence" carries heavy moral and political weight today. We face a future where sustainability, given the Planet's limited carrying capacity and the mandate to end poverty, dictates shedding luxuries for bare necessities or, as voiced in the Earth Charter, for "material sufficiency."

---

19. As opposed to Aslan, *Zealot*, xxx, who considers the only options for Jesus as either a zealous "revolutionary Jewish nationalist" or a "peaceful spiritual leader with no interest in any earthly matters."

20. For an in-depth analysis of the subsistence ethic see Scott, *Moral Economy of the Peasant*, 13–55.

Jesus looks within Israel's Covenant/Constitution and the prophetic traditions to reinforce subsistence ideals in the civic realm. For instance, Torah law summarizes reciprocity and equality in the love your neighbor as yourself command. By leading with the phrase "Hear O' Israel," Jesus confirms that this canon of love (providing subsistence needs) speaks primarily to *national* policy (Mark 12:28–31).[21] Here individual spirituality bespeaks a transformed Israel reconstructed around *political* love. Jesus uses his persuasive power and lawmaking authority to promote his loving sustainability politics.

Fundamentally then, ecospiritual politics is about moral values and their power to effect broad change through law. Because these values address political communities tied to the Land, we speak of *ecopolitical ethics*. Unfortunately, most of today's discussions about Jesus' "ethic" fail to fully appreciate this broader matrix. Whereas we all recognize Jesus as a great moral teacher, only a few have noticed that his ethic was a Land-based subsistence ethic that addressed broken and exploitive political/legal structures. Out of his intimacy with God, he attempted to "redeem" the nation/Land by passionately opposing prevailing values and reversing onerous farm and sea policies. For him and his detractors, most squabbles boiled down to conflicts over *competing political moralities and their spiritual foundations*.[22]

The heart of ecospiritual politics heralded by Jesus (and later listed by Paul) translates into civic love, civic wonder, civic peace, civic fidelity, civic kindness, civic generosity, and so on. Such values remain relevant for us and are brought to the political table to share with people of other faith journeys, even with those who reject religion, all for the purpose of enhancing the common good. Whereas these political fruits often spoil over time as they did in Jesus' day, he has shown us in dramatic fashion how to render them fresh again. They create and sustain a viable political community (his "Kingdom on Earth") as one large family, as an interconnected biosphere weeping and rejoicing together. Our nation desperately needs to headline enduring civic values to bring out the best in us to deal with the global crisis. Following in Jesus' footsteps to rekindle political ethics is the *greatest urgency of Christian spiritual development today*.

JESUS—A POLITICIAN?

Though Jesus speaks to the yearnings of the human heart, sometimes his message seems strange and hidden. Why did he talk so earnestly? What

---

21. Mark begins with the famous *Shema* of Deut 6:4.
22. I shy away from the term "ideology" since it tends to be pejorative.

problems did he address? Why did he frighten those in power? With four Gospel histories written about him, we might expect a clear and unmistakable picture. But who was Jesus, really? What drove him? How should we understand his earthly mission? Was he really obsessed with law and politics as we suggest?

Some might think it out of tune that Jesus concerned himself with the unsavory world of politics and are tempted to wrench him from the political realm, de-politicalize his teachings, and claim that he, unlike his opponents, announced a trans-earthly or nonpolitical governing. This view concedes that he fulfilled the role of the Messiah, but not that of a *political* Messiah.[23] Garry Wills, in his best-seller, *What Jesus Meant,* asserts that Jesus did not come to bring us a new politics, that he provided no political program whatever; and in fact, he avoided politics altogether.[24] Here Jesus' Kingdom message converts into moral abstractions, or into mere metaphors for entering a heavenly (other-worldly) sphere, or into describing a person's psychological state. At best, "Kingdom ethics" becomes strictly private ethics, and consequently, the sociopolitical and ecological impacts of his mandates lose force, except by implication.

Jesus once posed the identity question to his followers: "Who do you say that I am?" (Matt 16:15). In Peter's highly spiced political reply, "You are the Messiah, the Son of the living God," Jesus is christened Israel's royal leader. He spearheads a political reform movement to bring a new spirit-filled/shepherd-like governing to a regathered Israel (Matt 2:6). He knows that when Israel's *civic* life is revitalized, it can then fulfill its destiny of enlightening the nations on sustainability. Fundamentally, Jesus' core mission was both personal *and* political transformation. The events surrounding his birth, early life, and his death—Herod's slaughter of the new-born, Roman taxation, the angels' message about peace, Mary's song, his connection to a prophet who stood at the brink of his beheading for meddling in political schemes, his own arrest, trial, and crucifixion—all point to his political matrix. At the very end, people saw him as a prophet mighty in word (legal renderings) and deed, hoping that he was the one to "redeem Israel" (Luke 24:21). These political references proved to be in character, keynoting his single-minded political purpose. Gerd Theissen claims that, given the resounding political ramifications of Jesus' eventful beginning and fateful ending, we cannot dismiss everything in between as nonpolitical.[25]

23. Beyerhaus, *God's Kingdom*, 15, 32.

24. Wills, *What Jesus Meant*, 13, 43, 51, 55, 90. Also Aslan, *Zealot*, 125, 144, where he says Jesus had "no practical program, no detailed agendas, no specific political or economic recommendations." All Jesus possessed was zeal.

25. Theissen, "Political Dimension," 230.

By ignoring or downplaying the political dimension of Jesus, we miss the central point of the Gospel stories, distort his most basic aims, wither his contemporary relevance, and rest our commitment to him on flimsy footings. Jesus, who Christians consider more attuned to God than any other, felt no call to be a schoolmaster spouting pious platitudes. Thus, he can no longer be entombed in a box labeled "religion only." Rather, his spirituality unfolds most fully when his politics, which reaches out to the people of the soil being crushed like field clods, takes center stage. By uncovering Jesus' politics, we can better appreciate the beauty of his modern vision—a vision nourished by pledging the fulfillment of humanity's most noble aspirations for both personal and ecospiritual growth, while shaping public discourse and action on the underlying moral dimensions of the globe's most pressing concerns. With the human community and its terrestrial lodging being pushed to menacing tipping points, looking to Jesus now means we look to see how the integrity of Earth and its inhabitants (including the voiceless) ought to be mutually addressed. Then we are equipped and begin to work for the changes needed.

We might downplay a political Jesus by over-emphasizing his divine nature to the detriment of his humanity (even though the church confesses his full humanity as equally important). Yet, the Apostle Paul once quoted a hymn that beautifully expresses how Jesus "emptied" himself and became a human being (Phil 2:6–8). When we examine his human side, we find that in all points Jesus resembled us, including holding political views like you and me—and getting fired up when government screws up. Ironically, his divinity is affirmed by his political aspirations, since kings, including his chief rival Caesar, claimed to be gods. Yet, we may wince at the thought of Jesus being a politician and, even more, a very skilled one. Jesus scholar N. T. Wright has summed it up: "Attempts to make Jesus nonpolitical were always bound to fail."[26] Jesus was so enmeshed in politics that later Christians would surname him *Christ* (Anointed, Messiah), the defining political notion for the Jews. When we examine Jesus' life closer, we confirm his political role in first-century Palestine, enabling us to pinpoint him on a political spectrum that relates his mission to modern day concerns . . . and divisions.

As we shall see throughout, Jesus' every thought and action carried political weight directed toward sustaining struggling people. His vision for easing the downward slide of peasant farmers and fishers translated into plank-by-plank political solutions to the bruising effects of misrule—prejudice, inequality, poverty, inadequate health care, Land seizures, nationalism, and militarism. Jesus never intended to speak truth in a vacuum, but to

---

26. Wright, *Jesus*, 221.

speak specific truth to specific power (although often disguised). And his responses are remarkably relevant to our political scene today.

My central argument, then, revolves around trying to *re-politicize* Jesus in a meaningful way, lest exploiting interest groups, fear-mongering propagandists, or "cultural warriors" co-opt him for their worrisome causes. When these forces prevail, Christianity translates into "civil religion."[27] Here faith primarily functions like a hapless caboose pulled along the fast track of social whim, legitimizing fashionable, but flawed, public values. The crucial question, though, is *how* Jesus is re-politicized, lest extremists on the right and the left use him to bolster their gnarled ideals. Jesus opposed the harsh political ethic of both the governing authorities in Palestine and of the militants who wished to kill those very authorities. He was neither a radical revolutionary, nor a right-wing reactionary. When we connect him to either of these political moralities, we misunderstand his vision then and now.

In whatever way Jesus is described—whether as a spirit-filled charismatic, a movement-maker, a wisdom teacher/rabbi, a prophetic voice, a miracle worker/healer, a mystic, or all of these—he is only fathomed within the precincts of his political aims and agenda.[28] A political Jesus is not the whole Jesus, but a neglected dimension that shapes the whole. His parables, his legal renderings, his healings, and his symbolic actions, present a dramatically vivid portrait of his remarkable career as a down-to-earth political visionary within a world languishing under imperial occupation. He advanced an agenda that disclosed a political thrust, mirrored a specific political perspective, and promoted practical policy solutions. Seeing Jesus as a political figure actually enhances him as a "spirit person," a great and wise teacher, and, for many of us, the true Son of God who saves us from our despotic tendencies. Indeed, by acknowledging his politics, we broaden and deepen his spiritual legacy, then and now. Bringing it home, just as our spirituality includes a political dimension, so also our political devotion shapes our spirituality. Without politics, spirituality languishes; and without a spiritual renaissance, so do politics and ethics.

Jesus' moral narrative sprang out of a broader Jewish story—an important fact in light of later Christian tendencies to pit Jesus against the "Jews." Being part of the many lively reform movements within Judaism that spawned political parties like the Pharisees, the Sadducees, and the Essenes, he unflinchingly sparred over disputed visions of Israel's independence and destiny. As a Jewish *political partisan* with a specific constituency and sweeping agenda, he hoped to introduce a new way of governing and unite

---

27. Bellah, *Broken Covenant*, 165–86.
28. Borg, "Galilean Jew," 11.

the nation around the ecospiritual values he discerned to be compelling. He headed a political movement in which he engaged in political campaigning, presented a political platform, collided with other political parties, spoke in political parables, prayed political prayers, acted out political symbols, and initiated political demonstrations in the capital (Jerusalem). The authorities finally arrested him as a political agitator/claimant-king and crucified him—Rome's way of dealing with political troublemakers. Seeing the basic facts of Jesus' life in these political terms provides an overcoat for our understanding of his purpose.[29] By his words and deeds, Jesus campaigned as a flesh and blood politician with a humanizing and transforming mission, desperately needed then as well as today.

Jesus grew up soaked in the cultural, spiritual, and political realities of being a Galilean Jewish peasant, deeply affected by menacing imperial policies administered by local surrogates. The subsistence ethic of his peasant roots was reinforced in his Jewish tradition and its view of God. It also resonated in an impassioned desert prophet, called John the Baptizer, who deeply impacted his vision, fueled his spiritual fire, and helped shape his political ideas. Let's look briefly at how the moral wealth of these factors swayed him and guided his mission, especially as they fashioned his most famous notion, the Kingdom of God.

---

29. Sanders, *Historical Figure of Jesus*, 10–11.

2

His God Who Sustains

> Look at the birds of the air....
> Consider the lilies of the field....
> Seek first the Kingdom of God and its justice,
> and then all your needs will be met.
>
> —Jesus

JESUS SET FOOT IN a little but strategic corner of the world as a remarkable spirit-filled person in sublime union with God. He would launch a new Basileia—a new Kingdom, not one "of Israel," or "of David," or even "of Jesus," but "of God." What he believed most central about God, determining everything he said and changing the course of history, was shaped by subsistence realities. Jesus saw God from the peasant's "little" traditions outlook in response to the "official" traditions of the benefited elites.[1] Why is this important? First, as previously noted, peasants connected their notions of God and religion to the Land, its creation, its use, its bounty. Second, this Creator God would be depicted as nurturing and sustaining like Earth itself, like a parent. God is full of love, tenderness, compassion, generosity, and mercy and ready to help, forgive, and forget. The official renderings, however, portray God as distant and mainly concerned about rules and laws, always demanding strict obedience, full of

---

1. Horsley, *Galilee*, 152.

wrath when people disobey, and ready to severely punish at a moment's notice—a strict, parent-like God, the God of the rulers. This God turns a blind eye to prejudice, poverty, oppression, inequality, and war.

How these *central images of God* are prioritized makes all the difference in our perception of morality, spirituality, and politics and how we approach critical issues now.[2] Welding the Creator God to the nurturing/sustaining God had profound impacts on Israel's understanding of human/Earth relationships that still resonate today. Although not rejecting the stern-faced aloof God, Jesus seizes on God's empathic creative side, as the Hebrew Scriptures leads him.[3] Yet, the wellspring of his Bible was the peasant ethic that had seeped into Israel's earliest traditions.

THE NURTURING GOD WHO LIBERATES

The story began with the Exodus, Israel's master story and etched deeply on our Western political notions. A marginalized, enslaved people in Egypt rebelled against newly imposed labor conditions that undermined their subsistence rights. Misery-ridden, they began to conceive of the divine in an uncharted way, inspired by a powerfully new moral and political energy—the cry to be *treated with dignity*. This new reality meant a new name for God—*Yahweh* ("The Lord"), though not really a name, but more of a shout for joy (like "yaw hoe" or, in English, "you're here"). This new reference to God, presumably derived from the Hebrew verb "I am," implies both the *emotional presence* and the *liberating, sustaining activity* of the divine.

Yahweh is described as a *feeling* God who "hears cries," "sees miseries," and "knows sufferings" (Exod 3:7). These verbs assured the people that God does not disinterestedly observe woe. At the very core of God's character resides *empathy*—more specifically, *compassion* for the spiritual and political plight of those whose very existence is jeopardized. When Moses asks to see God's glory, God responds with the words, "I Am Who I Am," and adds, in synonymous parallelism, "I will show compassion on whom I will show compassion" (Exod 33:19). Here, showing compassion becomes divine essence and translates into the immediate righting of all injustices (Exod 22:27).[4] As John Crossan rightly concludes, "What we celebrate is a God of radical justice, known to us only as social, political and economic

---

2. Lakoff, *Moral Politics*, 43–176.

3. In opposition to Aslan, *Zealot*, 122, who claims Jesus knew only a "blood-spattered God."

4. See also Deut 13:17; 1 Sam 23:21; Ps 103:13, 145:9; Isa 49:13; Hos 11:8.

justice."⁵ Further along in the story God also becomes known as *ecojustice* since even the frogs, the locust, and the climate rise up in rebellion against Pharaoh's destructive imperialism. Pharaoh now knows "that Earth is the Lord's" and it, too, metes out justice (Exod 9:29). For the biblical faith, who God *is* becomes what God *does* for people oppressed by Land misused. The "glory," or essence, of God points to the historical and ecological stream of God's "goodness" (Exod 33:18–20). Put simply, where love and justice reside, God is; when they prevail, God rules and preserves (Ps 14:1, 5). In practical terms, God's essence is rooted in subsistence/sustainability. A new ecospirituality of both presence and justice is born on behalf of all Creation's survival.

God's moral activity was embedded early in the ecospiritual consciousness of the nation through worship. One of Israel's first confessions of faith, referred to as "The Credo,"⁶ reads in part:

> When the Egyptians treated us harshly and afflicted us, by imposing hard labor on us, we cried to the Lord, the God of our ancestors; the Lord heard our voice and saw our affliction, our toil, and our oppression. The Lord brought us out of Egypt with a mighty hand, . . . and with signs and wonders; . . . and gave us this land, a land flowing with milk and honey (Deut 26:5–9).

Since ritualized creeds articulate a people's essential truths, these earliest words set the standards for Israel, defining its God, comprising its spirituality, determining its Land and civic ethic, infusing the laws and statutes of its Constitution, and shaping its destiny.⁷ The Credo prioritizes and praises an empathic, nurturing God who "hears" and "sees" the desperate and refuses to endure their "affliction" (lack of justice), "toil" (lack of shalom), and "oppression" (lack of freedom). Put positively, God wills justice, well-being, and freedom—core *political* principles upon which the subsistence ethic depends and a modern ethic of sustainability is built.⁸

Note that this ancient confessional explicitly celebrates the Land's generosity. Its core principles are linked to the guarantee of a Land that will "flow with milk and honey," wrapping the people in its fertile sustaining bosom. When injustices prevail, then the Land loses its productivity, as the prophets never hesitated to point out (Jer 12:4; Hos 4:1–3). Furthermore, in referencing "hard labor," the Credo memorializes the fact that Land/labor

---

5. Crossan, "Jesus and the Kingdom," 28.
6. Rad, *Theology*, 122.
7. Ibid., 124–25.
8. Gottwald, *Tribes of Israel*, 616.

injustices gave birth to the Abrahamic Faiths and why Jesus was sympathetic to those working the Land. (Thus, Christians should be especially friendly to the labor movement and champion fair labor laws.) For the ecospiritual person, then as now, this earliest creed defines true worship of God as living in a proper moral relationship to the Other and to the Land.

Each generation of "losers" would look to this early creed for hope, worshiping a God who takes care of the lowly as celebrated in this psalm of community praise (also in Hannah's and later in Mary's famous songs):

> God is high above all nations . . .
> Who looks far down
> On the heavens and earth.
> God raises the poor from the dust
> And lifts the needy from the ash heap
> To make them sit with princes . . . (Ps 113:4–8).[9]

The Lord is venerated as the empathic One who looks down on Earth, confronts the political powers that misuse it and its inhabitants, and elevates those ground into the dust to sit equally with princes. A God-inspired justice now means *special treatment* for the dirt-caked worker by reversing conditions of exploitation and forging real equality and sustainability through political empowerment. This broadened "inversion" conception of justice with its world-upside-down tradition, central to the subsistence ethic, will hew the cornerstone of Israel's Constitution and the Jewish faith. Jesus would often cite this first/last reversal-of-fortunes theme to enhance his political vision and advance his renewal movement. This ideal also crowns a modern ecospiritual politics where abused people and ecosystems possess the "right" to be restored.

THE NURTURING GOD WHO CREATES

Much more is expressed by the notion of a nurturing/sustaining God. God not only gives birth to a people brought out of Egypt's oppression, but also to an Earth brought out of desolation. The Hebrews linked these two events by projecting the liberating/sustaining God concept back to Earth's birth. Here also begins two competing moral narratives that will duel up to the present. One story line describes, in literal detail, humanity's (Pharaoh's) imperial misuse of Earth as humans chose to take and take. This morality translates into a strict biblical mandate to "have dominion over" Nature, and "subdue" it (Gen 1:26, 28). Humans are encouraged to exploit Earth's

---

9. See 1 Sam 2:8; Luke 1:46–55.

resources, giving little priority to good stewardship. The result: massive poverty and ecological deterioration.

Scientist Lynn White chillingly traces this ethic in a seminal article: "The Historical Roots of Our Ecological Crisis" (1967).[10] White charges that the *biblical faith itself* has contributed to the world's ecodegradation. Our plight, he argues, springs from the belief in a transcendent God who creates, but stands apart from Creation—in contrast with the ancient *nature* religions that revered the sun, the moon, and Earth's assets. Yahwehism broke the power of sacral mystery within Creation, leaving Nature with no *intrinsic* value, only *instrumental* worth. For White, this theology extinguishes eco-affection and holds the Planet hostage to the aggrandizing forces of capitalism that are content to let the market govern its pillage.

White's assessment dismays those of us who believe that the Creation accounts convey another storyline with its profound human truths, including *ecological* truths. What are the major bench marks of these ancient narratives and how does Jesus strengthen them? Evidenced by his enthusiasm for the Child of Humanity (Adam) title, Jesus believes that his mission of restoring Israel's destiny to bless the nations also includes restoring Creation's original purpose to sustain them (Mark 10:5–6). The mandates gleaned from Genesis provided fodder for his calling.

First, the Creation story recounts God's struggle to bring habitable order out of the mythical monster "chaos" (indicating imperial ruin) with its unruly seas, environmental upheavals, and Land ravage. The sequential "days" of creation reflect an ordering that produces Earth's restored fruitfulness with its viable ecosystem: the sequential interplay of light, water, Land, life, death, and decay (Gen 1:1–25; Job 9:8).[11] To Earth belongs shalom, the systemic integrities (stability, interdependency, balance, etc.) that form the building blocks of a cogent sustainability ethic. In fact, "God created to make," implying that God intended Earth to be viable into the far future.[12] When Jesus calms the sea, where turbulent waters symbolize political and ecological upheaval, he himself engages in this ordering of unruliness (Mark 4:35–41).[13] His followers marvel that his authority extends even over the wind and the water. On another occasion, Jesus walks on the sea, again illustrating God's power over the forces of Creation (Mark 6:45–52). Jesus calls on divine authority to maintain order, ensuring that calm and well-being

10. White, "Historical Roots," 1205.

11. Isa 45:18 puts "chaos" over against "inhabited." See Meier, *Marginal Jew*, vol. 2, 914.

12. A literal translation of Gen 2:3b. See Bernstein, *Creation Theology*, 1–54.

13. Myers, *Binding the Strong Man*, 186, 197.

(shalom) be restored within the human community and within Nature—as in the early days of Creation.

In addition, since God *spoke* Creation into being, it is God's ordered word. Thus, ecospiritual people hold God's *divine laws of physics and biology* with the same awe and authority as they hold God's universal moral laws. The environment, then, signals ecomoral purposes—to bond with it and reverently wonder at its beauty and intricacy, to respect its ordered processes, and to sacrificially steward its (economic) resources. God gives Earth a stamp of approval, calling it "good" (intrinsically) at *all* stages of the creative processes, including its habitats and inhabitants (Gen 1:25, 31).[14] By divine fiat, then, people are handed the most important ingredient of a sustainability ethic—that Earth and its creatures have inherent value, with their attending "rights." Though human rights may at times override, they are not exclusive.[15]

A second ecospiritual truth Jesus derives from Genesis is that God reigns as Earth's ultimate owner, not humans. In his famous "give unto Caesar/give unto God" saying, he defends God's ownership of everything as attested in the Psalms (Ps 24:1; 89:11). David's final praise states, ". . . for all that is in the heavens and on Earth is yours; yours is the kingdom, O Lord . . . and it is in your hand to . . . give power and might to all" (1 Chr 29:11–12). Here he links ownership of Earth to God's Basileia authority granted to those who govern well. God's title to Earth implies that humans stand in moral obligation to it—to treat it in line with its God-intended integrity. The Earth Charter calls this a "sacred trust." God's sway means defeating all Land abuses and the injustices they create—a Land ethic undergirding Jesus' Kingdom notion and what he uses to challenge his opponents who have unfairly foreclosed on the peasants' farmland and commercialized their main fishery.

Third, God, as Earth's owner and out of infinite love, brings forth plants and animals from the "dust," including humans (Adam, meaning "Earth-connected"). The Land participates in and is the medium of all life. That human beings have been ordered from "lowly" dust, yet shaped in the divine image, further enhances our veneration of Earth and its essential link, not just to our biology, but also to our spirituality. This point resounds with ecological and political significance. It suggests evolution's role in human development. We are connected to those complex physical and biological forces that have been at work in the Universe through eons.

---

14. See Job 38:26–27 where God cares for the desert even though it is "empty of human life." Ps 104 also celebrates God's goodness toward the wild.

15. For a philosophical discussion about Earth's intrinsic goodness see Regan, *All that Dwell Therein*, 184–206.

Thus, no longer can theologians hold to the false dichotomy between a God of (human) history and a God of Nature. Rather Nature also has a glorious, evolving history that began billions of years ago with exploding stars, and *humans* are a part of that history. Over time and through natural selection, we emerged from and thus are akin to the many diverse life forms, thereby undercutting blatant "speciesism" (the good of other species counts only as they contribute to human good).

Because humans and other animals exist in community, as family, in bio-solidarity, the biblical faith respects animals, saving them during the Flood, "covenanting" with them afterward to guarantee their right to exist, granting some the legal right to Sabbath rest, and the right of "wild" ones to agricultural gleanings. The test of Rebecca's worthiness to become Isaac's wife turned on her sharing water, not only with a thirsty servant, but also with his camels (Gen 24:14, 8:21; Exod 20:10, 23:11). Naming the animals confirms their worth and dignity and our responsibility to protect them. Any attempt to extricate ourselves from our terrestrial and biological history means treating Earth's processes and creatures (including other humans) as alien. Then, possibly, they become objects of neglect, exploitation, and even destruction. Humans are sacred, Nature is sacred, but the tie between the two is *most* sacred.

In the Bible, raising the human being from the dust also suggests royalty or dominion as in the psalm quoted before. The Land and others are to be ruled in the "image" (another allusion to royalty) of God's rule; i.e., with shalom and justice and not of Pharaoh's exploitative rule.[16] God entrusts Earth to humans as royal tenants or householders to "subdue" it, to "till" it, to "keep" it, and to name its animals (Gen 1:28; 2:15). "Subdue" is spliced to "fruitful" and implies taming Earth for plowing or agriculture. "Keep" conveys caring for, preserving, and safeguarding the Land with its suggestive ecological obligation to heed Earth's delicate fabric. The term also crops up to describe our responsibility to be a brother and sister's "keeper," linguistically linking the sustaining of others to Earth's sustainability (Gen 4:9).

Just as a nurturing-Parent/God creates a tillable, nurturing Earth, as captured in the expression "Mother Earth" (*adamah* or "Earth" is feminine in Hebrew), we should in return, keep, love, respect, and care for Earth like we would our own parent. In a wider sense, we model St. Francis of Assisi who considered all of Creation as family members: "O brother wind, air, clouds, and rain . . . . O sister water . . . ."[17] Think of the consequences if everyone bonded so intimately with Mother, from whose breasts we all

---

16. Green, "Gardener Returns," 270–73.
17. Sleeth, ed., *Teachings on Creation*, 1–102.

suckle, that we treated everything in, on, from, and above her as siblings. The Earth Charter's metaphor of Earth as our home adds spiritual weight to these paternal notions and their sustainability implications.

With this same appreciation for Creation coupled with subsistence ideals, Israelite citizens were entrusted to be "keepers" of small plots, but for the benefit of all citizens, spawning the gleaning statues and laws holding essential utilities (like watering holes) in common (Num 26:55–56).[18] God's statutes permit emergency selling of the Land/Earth, but under the condition that "the land shall not be sold in perpetuity, for the land is mine; with me you are but aliens and tenants" (Lev.25:23–24). The Land remains subject to "redemption"—as stipulated by the Jubilee laws. Under these ancient policies, all the prophets, including Jesus, rail against concentrated wealth acquired through Land-grabbing by the one percent.

The Jubilee laws also mandated that the Land not be "overworked." A "Sabbath of complete rest for the land" must occur periodically (Lev 25:45; Deut 5:14–15). Sabbath Land laws, following from God's seventh day rest during Creation, affected both the political economy of Israel and the ecology of the Land, giving rise to the debt cancelling and restorative laws. These statutes helped eliminate poverty while recognizing the intrinsic worth of Earth and its right to be rejuvenated. However, like today, through the maneuvers of the oligarchy, these laws and rights were often ignored or eliminated, and wretchedness reigned (Mic 2:1–5). Distorted Land policies became Israel's curse, subjecting it to the sword, and leading to its exile. Yet the prophets' eloquent poems predict that weapons of war will be hammered into plows and pruning shears; the Land will return to its original purpose—idyllic and sustainable farming (Isa 2:4). Jesus' insistence on sharing scarce food symbolically points to this same policy: the exiled small farmers and fishers deserve the return of their parcels and the sea, a major plank in his concept of the Kingdom. The dream lives on in the ecological faith of today's more enlightened politics that sees humans as tenants of the Land and affirms the public's (including the world community's) rightful stake in sustainability for the common good.

Jesus draws a fourth implication from the Creation stories since reclaiming Earth as our heritage is never enough. While Earth nurtures and sustains (Eden is a Garden) and the Creator encourages us to enjoy it and celebrate its fruits, God also mandates that we compassionately and wisely *limit* our use of it, symbolized by the tree of forbidden fruit at the Garden's center. When Adam and Eve's imperial temptations of prideful greed and heedless accumulation infringe on Nature's laws and transgress the "limits

---

18. Vaux, *Ancient Israel*, vol. 1, 165.

to growth," Paradise is lost. Earth becomes "cursed" and our enemy. Adam's royal-like overstep amounted to profaneness—a rejection of God and the subsistence principles. Because of humanity's extensive impact on the environment, some scientists suggest calling the present geological timeline the "Anthropocene Age." The designation is sobering, as humans continue on a course that plunges the Planet back into the very chaos out of which God nurtured it.

In the end, as the writer of Genesis predicted, a ravaged Earth will defeat the exploiters and return us to the "dust" from whence we came. Nature's laws mock and chastise imperial arrogance and recklessness, turning blessing into judgment—the fate of Pharaoh (Gen 3:11–24). Jesus portrays this implication of the Genesis storyline in his tale of the Rich Fool, whose over-abundance and eat-and-be-merry ethic yields spiritual and physical death. Because our Earth/Land always remains vulnerable to imperial designs, each of us, our corporations, and our governments play the fool by not heeding the effects of our consumptive impulses and unfettered resource extraction on a fragile and limited environment. Our Earth will end up barren; we will be felled by our own wrecking ball.

Next, the Creation stories chronicle another ominous consequence of Earth's exploitation—a dark tale that history has never stopped unfolding. In vying to corral prized resources, human beings will end up as enemies, not only of Earth itself, but, like Cain and Abel, of one another. When Cain sarcastically asks the question "Am I my brother's keeper?" he brazenly violates the subsistence ethic. He lays another foundation stone of the ongoing imperial corporate morality and its human and ecological ruin—that being our brother or sister's keeper, and consequently the keeper of the Garden, is a matter of *calculated choice* (Gen 4:1–12). Without truce, without terms, Cain chooses to spill kindred blood. Whether we are a brother and sister's keeper remains an open question to this day and, consequently, imperils our ability to live peaceably with one another. Adam's missteps then, packaged as the loathsome brood of seeking glory, gold, and gore become the primal ingredients of a persisting imperial ethic—the original sin against God, against others, and against Creation. This ethic (promoting status, wealth, and militarism) has slithered its venomous way through history, striking each new generation as it did the first. Jesus would passionately expose its flawed spirituality and confront it head-on.

The last and most important truth in these Creation stories is the emergence of another political narrative grounded in human and ecological sustainability—that being our neighbors' keeper is not a matter of choice, but a moral and legal duty. To love your neighbor as yourself would find its place at the heart of Israel's Constitution and Jesus' message. Given our kinship with all creatures, "neighbor" includes the whole biocommunity: you and me, Land, air, water, plants, animals, the whole Garden. They all possess a right to the *upkeep* of their ongoing integrities and support systems—the most compelling mandate of the Creation stories for a viable sustainability ethic today.

This ecospiritual interpretation of Genesis, spurred by the Exodus story, mirrors Jesus' view of the Land and its effects on human flourishing. The first few chapters of Genesis stand as a precursor to the modern creed that knits social justice to ecojustice, as reflected in the Earth Charter. Actually, these stories teach a valid *science* of ecology and serve to counter Lynn White's critique that the biblical faith spurs the Planet's plunder. Put simply, Earth is an ordered ecosystem that sustains life and will degrade if misused. It also teaches *ecospiritual/moral* truths about a paradise-like shalom, about our non-anthropocentric kinship with Earth, about obedience to the divine laws of ecology, about ravaging greed and its deadly aftermath. It also tells about upkeeping Creation for its own sake and the sake of our brothers and sisters of all kinds, and sounds a call for Land restoration. All these themes permeate Jesus' political vision of God's Kingdom and his activities on its behalf. The Creation stories stand as powerful driving forces engaged in an unremitting struggle against destructive imperial impulses lodged within each of us, in statehouses, and in board rooms.

In summary, the following Seven Cardinal Earth Virtues derived from the Creation narratives bathe our Planet and its inhabitants in dignity and nourish a Christian political ethic:

1. *Goodness.* Earth's intrinsic worth means that it and its inhabitants possess moral/legal rights that enter the court room alongside any attempt to exploit them.

2. *Connectedness.* Earth's inhabitants and forces are interdependent. It is a biocommunity and, like all communities, is grounded in loving justice.

3. *Sustainability.* Earth's creative and destructive processes are necessary for the ongoing viability, integrity, and renewal of human communities and its ecosystems. When justly approached, it sustains its habitats and its inhabitants into the distant future.

4. *Wonderment.* Everything in the Universe and every person and creature possess beauty and complexity and are forever awesome from the micro to the astral levels.

5. *Truth*. Giving names to humans and everything else implies knowledge and bestows dignity in the most intimate, extensive, and thoroughgoing ways, which the sciences and the humanities help provide.

6. *Limits*. The carrying capacity of Earth, its ecosystems, and its inhabitants impose limits to their use, mandating simple living and precaution, with constant preservation, renewal, and consent.

7. *Service*. Humans must live responsibly toward one another and Earth, distributing resources fairly to meet basic subsistence needs while keeping Earth as natural as possible and the polluters bearing the costs of cleanup.

These Earth virtues interplay with and contribute one to the other. For instance, our ever growing knowledge of the Universe confirms its interconnectedness and increases our wonderment, but also compels us to respect its limits and renew its systems. The values also bond to a social ethic in that intrinsic goodness, interconnectedness, sustainability, etc., undergird our moral commitment to other humans.

Whereas the return of the Land to its proper treatment underlies Jesus' Kingdom notion, it would be stretching the point to say that he deals with all the social and environmental concerns of the twenty-first century. Yet, who can deny that his affirmation of the Creation stories and their values, his understanding of God as Creator and Sustainer, his views about the Constitution's Land policies, and his notions about subsistence and the political economy speak directly to the issues we face today? Under imperial rule, Earth and its people had become nothing more than a commodity, an "agri-business"—the means to feed a conqueror's citizens and sustain its armies, enforced by violence. As we shall see, Jesus' talk of a coming Kingdom grounded in the moral will of God introduces reverential concern for the Land and challenges imperialism with its destructive effects on communities and Earth.

A new way of governing has emerged that will shape Western civilization. An empathic and creative God identifies with downtrodden people and cares for them by creating a legal document supported by "steadfast love" (1 Kgs 8:23; Neh 1:5, 9:32). The fact that the idiom "steadfast love and covenant" is so common in Scripture, confirms that this love unfolds as *civic* love—guaranteeing the community's survival.[19] In return, the nation must give its whole heart, soul, and strength in devotion to this God by heeding the Constitution. As Israel's story unfolded, however, its judges, priests, and kings—like fallen Adam—forsook their new understanding of God, its civic

---

19. Wallis, "*Ahabh*," 105–7.

morality and legal base, and introduced imperial designs, sending Israel into exile and spiritual turmoil.

A PROPHET OF GOD FROM NAZARETH

Because Israel's leaders ignored their Constitution, one of the most influential spiritual developments in the history of humankind flowered—the prophetic movement.[20] The prophets were spirit-filled, "anointed," and "sent" as the mouthpieces of God, compelled to speak from God's overwhelming presence in line with God's moral essence (Isa 6:8; Jer 26:12). Their look to the future formed the backdrop for predicting the consequences of violating subsistence rights. Morality reigned supreme within their hearts and words, but it was a morality that looked to the nation's destiny—an ecospiritual politics centering on the moral/legal values that guarantee basic necessities as enshrined in the Mosaic Charter.[21]

One by one, the prophets rail unmercifully against the well-to-do who, dripping with piety, exploited the masses. The prophets' view of God compels them to speak such diatribes. Isaiah expresses this theology plainly, "But the Lord of hosts is exalted by (political) justice and the Holy God is shown holy by (social) righteousness" (Isa 5:16). Amos, a farmer, also confirms God's connection to justice when he dramatically co-opts the priestly ritual of a parallel three-fold call to worship, "Seek the Lord and live," "Seek the Lord and live," "Seek the Lord and live" (Amos 5:4—6:14). By changing the third injunction to "Seek *good and not evil* that you may live" (italics mine), the prophet, like Moses and the ancient creeds, equates "the Lord" with "good" or what is good for all; i.e., the common good. For Amos, God is sought, not at the designated places of worship, but by pursuing justice in the gate (the court) and bringing redress for the farmers whose fields and crops had been seized. Amos expresses this political morality in the most poetic way: "But let distributive justice roll like a raging river, and social justice like a never-ceasing spring." The nature imagery here is not mere coincidence, being repeated by Isaiah who likens God's internationally recognized justice to a planted garden sprouting forth what has been sown (Isa 61:11).

Given their vocation, the prophets call God, "O Just One," and see God as "ethical energy" who desires nurturing-type laws (Isa 26:7).[22] Following

---

20. Gottwald, *Politics of Ancient Israel*, 224–25.

21. Kaufmann, *Religion of Israel*, 345. See also Eichrodt, *Theology*, 278. "It is the moral sphere which for the prophetic preaching is of decisive significance."

22. Theissen and Merz, *Historical Jesus*, 380.

the Genesis story of the Land cursed due to imperial overstep, the prophets relentlessly hammer away at the "curse that devours earth," that "wastes" it, "withers" it, and "makes it desolate," that causes it to "mourn" because of national transgressions (Isa 24:1–13).[23] For the prophets and other Bible writers, the reign of God translates into restoring earthly governing for the common good, i.e., reestablishing the subsistence ethic. Likewise, when Jesus speaks of the Kingdom *of God*, he means little more than the Kingdom of the Common Good.

Jesus of Nazareth sees his calling as a lawgiver/prophet, in the mold of Moses and Elijah—both of whom affirm his mission in the Transfiguration story (Mark 9:2–8; Matt 17:1–8).[24] When Jesus enters into Jerusalem, the whole city asks, "Who is this?" The crowds respond, "This is the prophet Jesus from Nazareth in Galilee" (Matt 21:11, 46). Like the prophets of old, the people expect him to defy the onerous imperial order; and like the prophets before him, it ends in martyrdom. His disheartened followers describe him as "a prophet mighty in word and deed before God and all the people" (Luke 24:19). In line with the prophets, Jesus refers to himself as "anointed" and "sent" to bring good news of a coming Kingdom of God, i.e., to renew the Constitution by straightening the way made crooked by imperial schemes and then to lead a new exodus.

Jesus' prophetic vocation would be broadly shaped while under the spell of a dessert prophet, John the Baptist, noted for his sparse living. John does what all God's prophets tried to do during perverse times— ready a remnant for God's coming reign that would live and promote the ancient principles of subsistence, the prelude to freedom (Mark 1:1–14; Luke 3:1–22; Matt 3:1–17).[25] For John, standing and lineage no longer guarantee entrance into a new coming Kingdom, and so he calls the elites to repent for violating the social, economic, and Land laws embodied in the Constitution. Appropriately, he demands "fruits" worthy of repentance and when the people ask about what proper fruit God requires, John urges them to share an extra coat or some food with the needy, the essence of peasant ideals. He exhorts the soldiers and tax collectors to cease using their authority to extort money, directly challenging the rotten fruit of imperialism's exploitive designs. Jesus later expands on these same subsistence traditions in promoting his political program.

---

23. Also Jer 12:4; Hos 4:1–3; Joel 1:9–12.

24. See Wright, *Jesus*, 166. Also Luke 4:24, 7:16, 9:19; Mark 6:4, 8:28; Matt 13:57, 16:14.

25. See Chilton, *Rabbi Jesus*, 49.

John's fiery no priest, no sacrifice, no Temple baptism is politically radical. By denouncing the political ambitions through marriage of Rome's proxy ruler Herod Antipas, already suspicious of any wilderness/Promised Land symbolism, John is labeled a revolutionary and it costs him his head. He subverts the prevailing "kingdom ethic" and his message becomes deeply attractive to the peasants hungry for change, including Jesus, his most famous follower—one who would also face the wrath of corrupted authorities.

John's baptism of Jesus marks a turning point in Jesus' ecospiritual and political consciousness. After emerging from Earth's cleansing and life-sustaining waters, the Holy Spirit of God comes down on him as a dove, an honor appropriately mediated by one of God's winged creatures. A voice declares that he is God's beloved and pleasing son—the designation of all Israel's leaders from David onward.[26] In the true prophetic tradition and in the tenor of Spirit-possessed leaders during the time of the Judges, Jesus receives an infusion of God's very being. He now acquires an urgent vocation, a special moral authority, and divine status and power, spurring him to challenge the imperial order and re-vision a God-inspired way of life in line with peasant values. Unlike John, however, he embarks upon establishing the Basileia of God in Capernaum and "the other cities," i.e., locally within the hamlets of languishing Galilean farmers and fishers (Luke 4:43). In these places, he restores honor to those considered the least in God's Basileia—the tax collectors, prostitutes, and sinners—proclaiming them even greater than John. By eating with them, he anticipates the ancient creedal promise of Earth's fruitfulness while highlighting the inclusive shalom of God's new politics.

From his Jewish understanding of God, Jesus acted as a harbinger of humanity's highest ecospiritual and political aspirations. Some of the modern world's greatest political movements have drawn inspiration from his example. Gandhi looked to Jesus to ground a nonviolent philosophy that lifted his nation from the degradation of colonialism to independence. The Abolitionists and the leaders of the American Civil Rights Movement were compelled by Jesus to grant civil rights to millions. Might Jesus also lend support to other issues and dilemmas we face in this new century, and could his vision help transform our moral and political landscape? Ironically, we witness how some Christians are unwittingly drawn to a mistaken view of Jesus, feeding a political morality of human and ecological neglect, even ruination, that thrives unchecked. For this reason, some remain skeptical about dragging God and Jesus into politics.

---

26. See 2 Sam 7:14.

ABOUT MIXING POLITICS WITH RELIGION

All this talk about ecospiritual politics and drawing lessons from Jesus' political ethic could be interpreted as just another attempt to introduce religious dogma into governing. We have recently witnessed unabashed efforts to define America as an exclusively Christian nation and impose religious-specific convictions on the public. Often these beliefs reflect outworn and cold cultural creeds, scorn the rights of women and minorities, promote literal and harsh interpretations of the Bible, disdain science (especially climate science), brush aside general knowledge, and ignore statistical facts. Nonreligious Americans—and many religious people as well—are deeply troubled about emerging Christian Fundamentalists who hammer away at the Constitution's wall separating church and state. But a rigid, cold-hearted, literalistic, apocalyptic religion is not the only alternative for us who claim that faith shapes our politics. Certain basic values of religion such as love, caring, kindness, gratitude, tolerance, generous justice, and joy—offered to critique or establish public policy—also commend universal acclaim as core human values and appeal equally to those of a more "secular" mind. The fact that Christians derive their political ethic from Jesus' ecospiritual politics does not mean we should commandeer the political process simply in the name of some narrow religious belief. Rather, we labor to serve the public good through *common values*, with the separation of church and state remaining firmly intact.

Bringing the faith factor to bear on a civic ethic need not leave sinister political results in its wake. A valid ecospiritual politics could lift humanity to its greatest heights *apart from religious dogma*. Our religious base, however, could help us to hear the echo of higher values from the past and see their application now, while inspiring us to act. It also assists in knowing the ruinous political, social, economic, and ecological sins that need changing to save devastated people and Planet. Then religion could be part of the global solution. If Jesus were elected to serve in Washington, he would not go as a preacher of narrow religious creeds, but as a politician committed to the universal values he taught and for which he died.

All in all, despoiling people and environment are spiritual matters—sins against God, Jesus, Earth, and all its inhabitants. Our purpose is to show that Jesus brought us a new spirituality—an ecospirituality of hope—and his ancient words still resonate today. Although the music he played may seem somewhat strange to us, its melody is recognizable and enriching for those who wish to celebrate his truths. Following in the footsteps of Jesus, the goal of Christian ecospirituality bespeaks a wondrous journey through Creation that, in the legacy of God's sustaining love, treks with the downtrodden while reducing both our footprint's carbon and its size. Dostoyevsky expressed it most beautifully, "Love all of God's creation, both the whole of it and every grain of sand. Love every leaf, every ray of God's light. Love animals, love plants, love each thing."[27]

Spiritual persons understand this love as commitment to restore people and Planet by linking the spiritual landscape of ecology and sociology to the science of each, especially now, with looming poverty, extensive rights violations, and irreversible eco-damage. Signs of hope are emerging within the religious community. Apparently, Pope Francis has a heart for both the poor and Earth as did his archetype, St Francis of Assisi. Bill McKibben, a renowned ecologist, suggests that the last hope to reverse the ecological crisis might rest in the hands of Christians, especially Evangelicals with their emerging interest in Creation care.[28] What impact will the religious community have upon the well-being of people and Planet? As we shall see, Jesus shows us the way, but will we, his disciples, be up for the task?

We have explored the "of God" within Jesus' most famous political slogan, but what did he mean by "Kingdom," and why did it spark such controversy, even to the point of death?

---

27. Dostoyevsky, *Brothers Karamazov*, 319.

28. Bill McKibben in a speech at the University of California at Santa Barbara, Sept. 2, 2010. See Sideris, *Religion*, 446–64 for a survey of ecotheology.

3

His Progressive Politics

And the government shall be upon his shoulders. (KJV)

—Isaiah

THE SCENE WAS A Veritas Forum, a conservative Christian lecture series at the University of California in Santa Barbara. A contentious presidential election loomed a few days away. Philip Yancey, a well-known Evangelical Christian, had just finished speaking to a packed auditorium.

The first questioner raced to the empty microphone and blurted out, "I hear everywhere that Evangelical Christians should hold politically Conservative views, but I feel uneasy linking my faith to Conservatism. I'm more comfortable with Liberal values. Yet, where are the Liberal Evangelicals? Can a born-again Christian be a Liberal?" The audience, mostly Conservative Christians, sat stunned. I wondered how many others in the auditorium wrestled with that student's questions. How many simply assumed that Christianity equates with Conservatism? On the flip side, a recent study confirms that a growing number of young people are rejecting religion because they see it aligning with Conservative causes.[1] Another study suggests that the more we read the Bible, the more we lean to the Left.[2] Perhaps it's time for Christians to examine their political ethic and ask, "Did our very founder, whom so many of us love, adore, and worship—Jesus of Naza-

---

1. Putnam and Campbell, *American Grace*, 3.
2. Franzen, "Left-leaning Text," 32–33.

reth—promote values that resonate more with modern Liberal ideals than with Conservative ones?" Jesus shares an ancient vision to bring heaven's light to an Earth in darkness. Why did his dream cause such uproar then and what is its political legacy for us? The evidence leads to a conclusion that may surprise you.

IT'S ALL IN A CAMPAIGN SLOGAN

The high and mighty ruling class left Galilee soaked in bitter tears.[3] From an unnoticed hamlet in Palestine, Jesus suddenly bursts on the scene with an ecospiritual vision to restore Israel's political life in line with his view of a nurturing Creator. Like every good politician, he introduces a pithy catch phrase to highlight his unique message: "The Kingdom of God."[4] However, this campaign slogan (mentioned over 90 times), proved to be more than a mere public relations ploy.[5] His view of the Kingdom addresses the everyday realities of Land policies and their *political* implications. Biblical scholar N. T. Wright rightly warns that to remove politics from Jesus' Kingdom of God notion "falsifies and belittles it."[6] While the self-proclaimed god-king Caesar and the Messiah-wannabe Herod Antipas ruthlessly rule Galilee, Jesus vigorously campaigns there with his Kingdom rhetoric that races to the heart of the matter. In dramatic fashion, he headlines an alternative grassroots national policy built upon what God expects for good and right rule.

Jesus' Kingdom (Basileia) message spotlights God's all-encompassing reign over Israel and beyond.[7] The very name "Israel" means "God rules."[8] "The Lord will rule over you," Gideon insists, after refusing the peoples' clamor for him to be king (Judg 8:22–23). Certain psalms, known as enthronement psalms, celebrate the acknowledgement of God's reign by all the nations. Moreover, God's kingly rule is thoroughly "green" as the heavens are glad, Earth rejoices, the sea roars, the fields and all within them exalt, and the trees sing (Ps 96:10–12).[9] God's majesty provides for every creature

---

3. Horsley, *Galilee*, 216–22.

4. See Meier, *Marginal Jew,* vol. 2, 244, Apparently, Jesus surfaced as the first to use the phrase, although the idea of God's kingly reign was widespread. Matthew's substitution of "heaven" for "God" reflects the Hebrew reticence to speak the name "God."

5. Sanders, *Historical Figure*, 10. He calls Jesus' use of the phrase an "indisputable fact."

6. Borg and Wright, *Meaning of Jesus*, 219.

7. Chilton, *Pure Kingdom*, 31–44.

8. Rad, "Israel," 356.

9. Also Ps 47, 93, 97, 98, 99.

and "renews the face of Earth" (Ps 104:20–32). Jesus emphasizes the sovereign reign of God over all creation in his famous prayer: "Thy kingdom come (in synonymous parallelism with), thy will be done on Earth . . . ." As noted before, the will of God points to the rule of God's moral/legal intent—the compassionate-justice-for-all God who "sees," "hears," and "knows" all imperial caused pain. This Kingdom, then, refers to the transforming power of *spiritually formed political values* embodied, not only in human hearts, but also in good laws and policies.[10] When Jesus announces this Basileia—grounded in fusing ecospirituality with national life—he, like John the Baptist, creates a serious political movement.[11] It signals a returned-from-exile community, good news for the people (and for us), but bad news for Rome's leaders and collaborators.

Since the Basileia comes on Earth, it unfurls as an actual political entity with a designated leadership, a charter, and laws governing communities. Jesus invites people to "enter" it, even to "inherit" it, terms alluding to the ancient Promised Land (Mark 9:47, 10:15, 23, 25).[12] The Kingdom is about legal "entitlements" to soil and sea, to bread and fish and healing; it loves enemies. It intertwines with all daily affairs.[13] Jesus sends his volunteers into Galilean villages to break ground for the Basileia and claim its citizens (Matt 10:5–15; Luke 10:1–16). It highlights what God expects for the good of the people on the Land, but fashioned for those who have the "eyes to see and ears to hear." Yet how should we see this Kingdom of God in our time?

Today we find the concept of a kingdom both outdated and gender-specific. For us, "kingdom" translates best to "government" or the more active, "governing."[14] The phrase "of God" implies theocracy, which also lies outside our experience (although some worry that America has been sliding toward it[15]). As previously noted, for the people of the Bible, "God" means "good," as when Amos substitutes the word "good" for "Lord" in the traditional three-fold worship formula. Through a burning bush, Moses is shown God's new name, "I Am Who I Am," which God defines as "I Am Generous, I Am Compassionate" and refers to that as "my goodness" (Exod 33:19). Jesus likewise calls God good (Mark 10:18). The First Epistle of John

---

10. Malina, *Social Gospel*, 71.
11. Wright, *Jesus*, 296.
12. Also Matt 5:20, 7:21, 18:3, 19:23–24, 25:34; Luke 18:24–25.
13. Robinson, *Jesus*, 70–71.
14. Storkey, *Jesus and Politics*, 112.
15. Phillips, *American Theocracy*, 99–264; he speaks of "imperial Christian overreach" in the past, 99.

is more specific: "God is love" (1 John 4:16). The Basileia of *God* is truly the Government *of Good*—a governing grounded in divine-like sustaining love.

For Jesus then, and for us now, "Kingdom of God" translates best to "Good Government" or "Good Governing," where "good" points to cooperative goods or fruit of the Spirit like love, joy, peace, wonder, generosity, etc., achieved within a Land context. Essentially, the Kingdom of God means *governance for the common good*. Everything Jesus says and does bespeaks his main concern: to take Creation, persons, Israel, and ultimately all nations, out of their long exile by softening hard hearts and transforming governing into what God's full reign intended—*to fashion legislation for the sustainability of all*. Of course, Rome, the empire built on the rule of law, will bristle at the mere whiff of this outlawry. Another Kingdom? A different spiritual politics? Competing Land laws and values? Rome, like any corporate power, wants none of that in its colonies.

Yet, Jesus' slogan is doubly seditious. By calling it a Government *of God*, he strikes at the heart of the imperial morality—its divine basis. He repudiates the imperial cult that named Caesar a god, legitimizing the emperor's authority, and consequently, his very political existence. But more, Jesus' Government *of Good* undercuts Rome's "business as usual" ethic that entitled those at the top of the social pyramid to glut themselves with produce seized from those at the bottom. Jesus believes that God will finally reverse this travesty and reconstruct all nations to govern well, no longer based on inequality, coercion, and Land exploitation. Because Jesus' constant reference to the coming Good Government will unnerve Rome and its puppets in Palestine, he intrudes deeply into the political fray, and dangerously so.

Speaking to the deepest yearnings of downfallen people, Jesus, like modern politicians, bases his campaign for governing on a platform of change. We can identify and summarize eight planks, or ecospiritual fruits, of the Good Government (Kingdom of God) that Jesus attempts to renew and that resound to the present:

1. *Renewing Creation and the destiny of all peoples.* Jesus, like the prophets, believes that God-inspired Good Governing would restore Creation to its original Eden-like state. Accordingly, he publically adopts the ancient leadership title Child of Humanity (literally, Son of Adam). The phrase often meant simply "human being" and looked back to the Creation story, but assumed its royal themes. The title's highly spiced imperial tone is echoed in the book of Daniel, which warned that a Kingdom led by this Child would replace the major political powers of the day (Dan 7:9–14, 23–27). His realm reaches beyond Israel to include all "the people of the holy ones of the most High;" and they

shall, like Adam, exercise "dominion." Their dominion, however, will be of the nurturing type, not imperial based. As the Child of Adam, Jesus sees himself as a factor in the "renewal of all things," including the renewed Garden predicted by Ezekiel: "The land that was desolate will be tilled . . . and . . . become like the Garden of Eden" (Ezek 36:34–35).[16] Peoples will be reconciled with each other and with Nature (Isa 11:6–9).

For Jesus, the renewal of a scarred Creation also follows from Abraham's promise, developed by Isaiah, that God chose Israel to be a great light, illuminating every corner of Earth and transmitting the truth about how people and Land ought to be treated. The light is ecospiritual, yet beams a political ray that enlightens and empowers the path to sustainability (Isa 51:4). After Israel's rebirth, nations will learn that good laws are grounded in a divine-like universal ethic. When leaders see the light, they will "walk in God's ways" of expansive justice and lasting peace (Isa 1:17–18, 2:3–4). With the coming Good Government, Jesus holds out the elusive goal that people from the east and west, north and south will sit together in harmony and eat the promised fruits (Luke 13:28–30).

2. *Renewing the Constitution's subsistence laws.* The plight of rural farmers and fishers, plunging ever deeper into a social and economic black hole, calls for decisive action. Jesus looks to the subsistence principles embedded in the Constitution—with its Ten Commandments, Land laws, and debt codes, along with the Psalms and prophets—to stabilize village life. By his spirit-inspired egalitarian interpretations of the Mosaic Charter, Jesus trumpets an "activist" legal approach designed to unravel the devastating Land disenfranchisement of his day. Jesus and his followers traverse the towns, calling for repentance from the insidious imperial ways while teaching people the laws and policies of renewal politics. His reformulated statutes, many recorded in the Sermon on the Mount, will—if etched into the national consciousness—save the rural peasants, eventually restore farmland and sea rights, end Israel's exile, and humanize all legal systems.

3. *Renewing compassionate justice.* For Jesus, moral goodness is the primary characteristic of the new ecospiritual politics. In his parables, he distinguishes this new ethic from the prevailing political values through the Nature metaphors of good seed vs. bad seed, edible fish vs. bad fish, fertile soil vs. hard and stony soil, wheat vs. tares, and so

---

16. See Jones, *Jesus and Earth*, 1–68 for the Child of Humanity sayings as they relate to ecology.

on (Matt 13:1–50). Jesus states his purpose—rid government of "all causes of sin" and "all evildoers," so that those who do right may "shine like the sun" (Matt 13:41, 43). But what is so different about his brand of spiritual politics?

The Good Governing is about love in all its facets: caring, kindness, tenderness, generosity, acceptance, friendship, wonder, gratitude, cooperation, fairness, peace, and self-sacrifice directed toward everything in Creation. Undergirding all these qualities is compassion, which Jesus keynotes in line with his central view of God and the subsistence notions. Jesus puts *political compassion* at the heart of lawmaking.[17] He says it clearly: seek the Good Governance with its caring (distributive) justice before anything else and then all needs will be met (Matt 6:33). It's like finding a pearl of great value or discovering a large treasure in a field we would give everything to keep (Matt 13:44–46). Love is also the power that brings political change—that wins people over, even enemies. Jesus underscores these points by invoking a family metaphor that conveys loving intimacy, calling God "Abba," the true Patron/Matron of us all and everything in Creation.

4. *Renewing dignity for the lowly, the destitute, and the abused.* In a world with strict honor codes, loss of Land brought shame and dishonor. Jesus' compassionate ecospiritual politics points the way back to dignity and respect. In two back-to-back parables, Jesus depicts the prevailing political ethic in frank terms. In the first, he describes a judge who lacks any "respect for persons"—who grants a widow justice only because she "keeps bothering me." In the following parable, he portrays a religious leader as "regarding others with contempt" (Luke 18:2, 4, 9). For Jesus, the coming Good Governing sees as God sees—others created after God's likeness. His ecospiritual politics will initiate a complete reversal of the social and economic order; the first and exalted will become last, and those last and humbled will end up on top—his way of talking about turning society around (Matt 19:30, 20:16). Like the prophets of old, Jesus declares that the Good Government belongs to the landless, the destitute,[18] the "no-bodies,"[19] the untouchables, and the expendables—those whose causes he takes as his own. In extending his hand to those crushed by imperial designs, Jesus undermines

---

17. Pannenberg, *Theology and the Kingdom*, 113.

18. "*Ptochos*," the term for "poor," actually means "destitute." See Crossan, *Historical Jesus*, 273.

19. A phrase used by Crossan, ibid., 266–75.

all patron driven hierarchies and their honor politics of disdain and exploitation.[20]

5. *Renewing empowerment and health.* Jesus' new ecospiritual politics points to a specific *realm* or community of those exiled by Rome's daily terrors. When asked about the coming Kingdom, Jesus answers that it is "among you;" i.e., the Good Governing occurs at the grassroots in your farming and fishing villages (Luke 17:21).[21] This rendering spotlights the sociopolitical and ecological dimension of Jesus' slogan over against the King James Version that states the Kingdom is "within you" (although Jesus expects that his renewed politics must reside within a person's spiritual consciousness, as Jeremiah foretold[22]). Furthermore, Jesus begins building his renewal movement in the towns through "community organizing" and a "politics of itinerancy" that refuses to establish a "brokered" power base in any one city dominated by urban corporate elites.[23] The Basileia's redistribution of power must be diffused, as in the ancient Israelite proto-democratic model and our modern notion that "all politics is local."

You might say, "All this talk about subsistence doesn't really matter if God will soon bring Earth to a violent cataclysmic end as the apocalyptic writers meant." Yet, Jesus doesn't act that way. Rather, the radical action of God speaks more of replacing Rome's ruinous economic, religious, Land, and sociopolitical structures than of bringing history to an immediate close.[24] Oppressed people savor graphic and chilling, often violent, apocalyptic, Nature metaphors directed against domineering regimes. Yet, if we humans, in imperial fashion, continue to degrade Earth, an ecological apocalypse is certainly a frightening and very real prospect. We must heed its chilling portend for the future. Jesus, though, looks for the dismantling of imperialism and its supportive ethic by bringing God's past moral and paradise-like sovereignty to present village life and continuing it into the distant future. Jesus was neither a resigned hermit nor a sword-wielding end-of-the-world fanatic.

The imminent Good Governing will start out virtually unnoticed, like leaven in bread; or like the Earth that produces itself by sending out small shoots . . . then stalks . . . then heads of grain

20. Perrin, *Kingdom of God*, 184.
21. See The New Revised Version and The New English Bible.
22. See Jer 31:31–34.
23. Crossan, "Jesus and the Kingdom," 38–51.
24. Wright, *Jesus*, 208–9.

(Matt 13:33; Mark 4:26–29). Jesus understands that through his own teachings and activities the coming Good Government has *already dawned*.[25] He visits villages crushed by extortionary taxation and loan sharking to introduce ecospiritual and community-building elements like health care, sufficient food supplies, legal renderings, and human dignity (honor) as immediate safety nets, in line with the peasant moral universe that assumed a life of shalom. His message of sweet dreams also comes with the power and authority to exorcise the nightmarish imperial order.

6. *Renewing humble, spirit-filled leaders.* Jesus understands that any good government rests on good leadership. Hearkening back to pre-monarch times when God ruled through Spirit-inspired men and women called judges, Jesus charges his twelve, chosen from the lowest ranks, to sit on thrones to judge the twelve tribes of Israel (further confirming his *political* mission [Matt 19:28]). The title of judge was first given to Moses who arbitrated "the statutes and instructions of God" (Exod 18:13, 16). Judges like Moses, however, not only taught and adjudicated the law, but also delivered the people from their overlords.[26] In the meantime, Jesus' volunteers, as the true remnant of Israel, trek around Palestine and, filled with God's Spirit like their leader, bring new laws and perform mighty deeds and wonders of deliverance for the disheartened people, echoing the old Credo that God delivers with "signs and wonders" (Mark 6:12–13; Matt 10:7–8).

What leadership title might Jesus adopt? The signature political term, "Messiah" (Anointed One), would seem most natural, yet dangerous to flaunt, since it unambiguously referenced a king. Jesus secretly embraces it, but on his own terms, since nearly every political player claimed the title. He would also be called the "Child (Son) of God," underscoring the nation-as-family metaphor that served as a common political designation for ancient kings (2 Sam 7:14; Ps 2:7). These titles, along with "Child of Humanity" (which he prefers), serve an important political purpose, including a subtle affirmation of his deity, placing him in competition with the "divine" Caesar.

In and of themselves, however, titles are less important than behavior. Jesus believes that good leaders will govern by a rebirthed ecospiritual politics, modeled after Isaiah's messianic Suffering Servant who is "crushed with the pain of the people," and Ezekiel's vigilant shepherd who feeds the sheep and never fouls their water or tramples

25. Ibid., 243.
26. Horsley, *Spiral of Violence*, 201–6.

their fields.[27] Included is the ideal king of Proverbs and Psalms who defends the needy and rejuvenates the soil (Prov 31:8–9; Ps 72:16). Jesus and his chosen twelve "delegates" will ultimately mirror this same humble self-giving leadership for all the "tribes of the earth," and for us today (Matt 24:30; Luke 22:24–27). A new leadership ethic is unfolding. It will come with authority, so all must be ready for it (Mark13:35–37; Luke 12:46; Matt 24:50).

7. *Renewing civic repentance and forgiveness.* All successful communities need enforceable laws. Jesus wants law grounded in voluntary compliance, but he is aware that we lapse; misdeeds sent Israel into exile. Before Israel can return and enter into the Good Government, its greedy rulers must turn from their evil ways and follow their Constitution.[28] Repentance as a spiritual and political act points to a different way of being a person *and* a nation; it means forsaking a bankrupt spiritual politics for a compassion-filled one. For instance, it rights economic wrongs as illustrated by Zacchaeus, the toll collector (Luke 19:8).

But the God who saves nations also judges them accordingly when they refuse to change (Matt 25:31–46). Highlighting the political nature of this judgment and following in the line of the prophets who condemned both the conquering nations and Israel's bad governing, Jesus castigates whole cities, even an "evil generation" (Matt 12:39–42). Those towns that reject the coming Good Governance and its subsistence standards remain subject to continuing socioeconomic and ecological disintegration. They will end up as ghost towns, like Sodom and Gomorrah (Luke 10:12). Right now, Roman occupation represents God's judgment on the nation. Yet, Rome too will be judged, but Jesus does not see streets becoming "blood-soaked."[29] Judgment, repentance, and return from exile (salvation) occur whenever Jesus tells his parables, exorcises menacing spirits, and reconstructs the political life of Galileans around shalom.

A transformed community, one returned from exile and built on the new ecospiritual politics, understands *forgiveness*. For Jesus, forgiveness reigns when the nation repents from its exploitative political economy. Forgiving debts, as reflected in the Lord's Prayer, reveals the special consideration for those who lost their parcels of Land. However, given fractured village relationships, forgiveness/amnesty must

---

27. See Isa 53 and Ezek 34.
28. Horsley, *Jesus and Empire*, 98–104.
29. See Aslan, *Zealot*, 122, who claims that for zealots God's sovereignty is only established by force.

8. *Renewing immortality and joyfulness.* When people ask Jesus about inheriting eternal life, they thrust him into a universal, sociopolitical struggle over how humans deal with death (Luke 10:25, 18:18). The quest for immortality, however, was often played out over human survival through the distribution of Earth's most important subsistence resource—food.[30] The god/kings and their priests controlled food's upward flow by requiring the peasants to bring meat and grain offerings. In return, the (fertility) gods, they were told, would grant them both material abundance *and* eternal life. The political ethic and military machinery compelling this seizure (under religious cover) reinforced the extreme inequality, Land abuse, and human misery in the ancient world. Close to home, the Canaanite Baal myths perpetuated elite domination and the reason Israel's powerful were easily seduced by them, causing the prophets to rail against such idolatry.[31]

Jesus puts the issue of our mortality on a different table, tying it to the moral question of *how* food is distributed. By giving special consideration to the hungry masses, we gain the treasure of eternal life that moths and rust can never destroy (Matt 6:19–21). Thus, we become "immortalized" through deeds of civic compassion, yielding that for which we all strive—a healthy Planet and flourishing communities, modeled after the life-to-come paradise (heaven). Although we do not live by bread alone, but by the words or commandments of God (Matt 4:4 with Deut 8:3), God decrees an enduring (eternal) *quality* of living and governing that assures bread and fish for all. Inheriting eternal life is another way of speaking about entering the coming Good Governing.

The new ecospiritual politics celebrates the emerging "consolation" of Israel when its long exile will cease, when the common good (shalom) prevails, when its "fortunes" are restored, and the violence ended. That initiates the wonder and joy of a festive messianic banquet (Luke 13:29, 14:15–24). The "eating and drinking at my table in my kingdom" signals the rejoicing of an all-inclusive "banquet of equals" who are in awe of human dignity and of Creation's fruits (Luke 22:29–30). Good governing mirrors a continuous, jubilant wedding

---

30. Becker, *Escape from Evil*, 34. I rely heavily upon Becker's work.
31. Walsh, *The Mighty*, 15–28.

celebration, while the lavish eat-drink-and-be-merry debaucheries of Rome and its surrogate rulers, made possible by the sweat of the farmers and fishers, will soon come to naught (Mark 2:20; Luke 12:20).

These eight touchstones comprise the major ecospiritual, but practical, building blocks of the coming Good Governance—a governing based upon radical change, but not revolution. They mandate moral and legal communities of sustainability, equality, and helping the neighbor in need, all ingredients of subsistence ideals. Their underlying values are: guidance, empathy, dignity, well-being, peace, humility, sharing, change, and joy—nurturing family values, crucial for both the private and public realms. These loftier instincts weave their way throughout contemporary moral documents, especially the Earth Charter. Jesus aimed to re-signify the ancient Constitution and God's rule in a new and imaginative way—restructuring deteriorating Galilean villages around a loving common compact and spirit-filled leadership. The old governing that led to exile cannot be repaired, since sewing new patches on old garments or putting new wine into old wineskins remains futile (Mark 2:22).

Jesus' slogan "Basileia of God," coupled with the details of his far-reaching platform, underscore nearly everything he says and does. His sayings, his re-imagining of the traditions, and his symbolic actions shape his retelling of Creation's, humanity's, and Israel's basic story line—that of disobedience, exile (judgment), renewal, and return. These root elements of his ecospiritual politics will forge the subject matter of the remaining chapters. But how do the values embedded in Jesus' platform resonate with an ecospiritual politics and its ethic in our day?

JESUS AND LIBERAL POLITICS

One of the earlier pioneers of the "Jesus of history" movement, Ernst Kasemann, wrote a best-seller in Germany with a chapter entitled, "Was Jesus a Liberal?" He insisted, "Whatever else Jesus may have been, he was 'liberal.' No qualification whatever of this statement is possible, even though churches and devoted people should declare it blasphemous."[32] (Indeed, one contemporary writer on Jesus' politics asserts that labeling Jesus a Liberal is "untrue, if not blasphemous."[33]) For Kasemann, the Liberal Jesus stands as the "irreplaceable Jesus," and his Liberalism was an uncontested historical

---

32. Kasemann, *Jesus Means Freedom*, 27.
33. Hendricks Jr., *Politics of Jesus*, 318.

fact that "sent him to the cross."³⁴ When we reject this truth, we "endanger" and render "unintelligible" everything else about the historical Jesus. In fact, we fracture faith and even topple his divinity.³⁵

Kasemann unearthed a vital buried truth about Jesus—to deny his Liberalism and its "explosive . . . political effects" distorts his mission in Galilee, and his meaning for us today. Though Kasemann limits Jesus' Liberalism to challenging the status quo with his flexible interpretations of Scripture and his emphasis on universal love ("co-humanity"), might Jesus not also echo other modern Liberal or Progressive ideas? But first, what is Liberalism?

Like the term "Conservative," "Liberal" (with a capital "L") is shorthand for a *particular political morality*, which describes the values and principles upon which the good society and its governance rest.³⁶ The general word "liberal" conveys notions like "tolerant," "open-minded," "generous," "progressive," and "reformist"—values normally associated with political Liberalism. The simplest definition of "Liberalism" is: "Having, expressing, or following political views or policies that favor *civil liberties, democratic reforms*, and the use of *governmental power* to promote *social progress*."³⁷ These major components capture the thrust of Liberalism and unfold its moral dimensions.

Classical Liberalism, as a political ethic, promoted the freedom of the individual to live a fully human life, which historically meant the enhancement of our individual rights, but mostly limited to our basic political, religious, and property rights. Later these rights were expanded in *New Deal* Liberalism with its safety net entitlements. Many believe that Liberalism must evolve to a new "third-stage" to meet our contemporary challenges of cultural superiority, corporate irresponsibility, runaway wealth, the rights of women and minorities, persistent poverty, the culture of war, and especially ecological degradation and its impact on all these challenges.³⁸ Some prefer the term "Progressive" to describe the new Liberalism.

Third-stage Liberalism still holds to the traditional political rights, but expands their scope to admit the flourishing of all our human capabilities, including inner spiritual and ethical factors like empathy, love, and generosity—all nuances of compassion.³⁹ Political philosopher Martha Nussbaum lists the other values as: the length and quality of life, physical and emotional

---

34. Kasemann, *New Testament Questions*, 48.
35. Kasemann, *Jesus Means Freedom*, 18–20.
36. Rawls, *Political Liberalism*, 3–4.
37. *American Heritage Dictionary*, 2nd college ed., s.v. "liberal." Italics mine.
38. Raskin, *Liberalism*, 53–54.
39. Ibid., xiii.

health, the integrity of one's body, free movement without fear of violence, the utilizing of the physical senses and reason, a sense of self-respect, the ability to play and celebrate, the freedom to make political choices, the equal and fair opportunities to flourish, and the concern for Nature.[40] Many of these core goods find residence within the ancient subsistence ethic.

This more expansive Liberalism sees the above values as constituting *the common good*. They are considered as universal—transcending cultures and centuries, allowing us to bridge human differences and spotlight our basic similarities (see appendix 2).[41] They inform our shared aspirations and struggles and point to those dimensions of human experience that good governing ought to enhance. Because some third-stage Liberal writers recognize our inner spiritual and ethical sensibilities as a political goal, they call themselves "Spiritual Progressives."[42] Occasionally, we refer to this new approach as Transformational politics to underscore the need for continual reform resulting in a future fourth or fifth-stage Liberalism. The most salient moral feature of Progressive politics in our day is *empowering the downtrodden while caring for Nature*. All other values presuppose it and flow from it.

Progressives underscore a most important political notion: giving *special* consideration to those left out, ignored, and mistreated. It is wrong when the few high-and-mighty in society live luxuriously and wastefully exploit Earth at the expense of others. It is wrong when the wealthy dominate by influencing legislation for their benefit, when society creates a status system in which some think others inferior, and where affectional and cooperative virtues are low priority.[43] This precisely describes the political and economic realities both in Jesus' day and in ours. To right these wrongs, Jesus knew that justice must be overly generous. John Rawls, one of the most renowned political philosophers of the twentieth century, highlights such justice:

> All social primary goods—liberty and (fair) opportunity, income and wealth and the basis of self-respect—are to be distributed equally unless an unequal distribution of any or all of these goods is to the greatest benefit of the least advantaged members of society.[44]

---

40. Nussbaum, *Sex and Social Justice*, 41–42. See also her *Women*, 78–80.

41. Nussbaum, *Women*, 35. Her chapters entitled, "In Defense of Universal Values," and "Women and Cultural Universals," present a detailed critique of cultural relativism and build a compelling case for universal values.

42. See Lerner, *The Left Hand of God*, 1–36 for an introduction to Progressive spiritual politics.

43. Rawls, *Justice as Fairness*, 43–44.

44. Rawls, *Theory of Justice*, 303, 42–43.

Here Liberalism's egalitarian thrust stands out. Note, however, the second part, called the "difference principle," that mandates extra consideration for those at the lower end of the social and economic totem pole in the game of catch-up.

Third-stage Liberals add that Earth, too, should receive special treatment due to its exploitation and vulnerability. For them, the fair distribution of wealth always carries a green tag (not just the green of money). Ecojustice grows in the same justice garden, yielding the precautionary principle (we need to act now before irreversible damage), the polluters pay principle (major polluters bear the cost of clean-up), and the other Cardinal Earth Virtues listed earlier. When spiritual values such as compassion and generosity are present, ravaged people *and* Earth will receive their restorative rights. This notion of special treatment resonates to the very heart of Jesus' divine mission on behalf of the "least of these," and it included the birds and the lilies, and today the wolves, the polar bears, the mountain lions, and others at the brink. In the famous Matthew 25 passage, the least of these take the very form of Jesus and how we treat them is how we treat Jesus, a sobering thought for us Christians in our relationship to our kind and to the other kinds (Matt 25:31–46).

The core principles of third-stage Liberal politics include the following:[45]

1. *Green Consciousness.* We unwaveringly commit to Earth's integrity (diversity, balance, flux, natural patterns, and processes), its intrinsic worth, its interdependencies, its sustainability, its wonderment, its truths, its limits, its protection, and its renewal. These all percolate throughout Progressive principles and policies.

2. *Transcendence.* We sense a higher reality from whence we derive our moral values, define human dignity, and structure our Earthview. For Christians, a nurturing God, most fully embodied in Jesus, provides the model.

3. *Compassion.* We celebrate political empathy for Creation and its creatures. We identify with those suffering, feel their pain, and empower them. We promote the cooperative virtues, including civic and Earth friendship. Compassion shapes public policy for the common good while rejecting laws based simply on disgust and shame.

---

45. Humphrey, "Enduring Principles," 91. He claims these principles reach back to the Hebrew prophets. I rely heavily upon Raskin, *Liberalism*, 246–48. Also the works cited by Rawls and Nussbaum.

4. *Material Restraint.* We reject the unlimited aggrandizing of goods (concentrated wealth) that quenches the human spirit, destroys the environment, sees others as the means to our ends, and reinforces poverty. We promote material sufficiency.

5. *Generous Justice and Freedom.* We believe in special treatment (affirmative action) for egalitarian outcomes of essential human goods, social standings, and Planet rejuvenation. While we affirm the traditional freedoms, we also include the freedom from want and ravage.

6. *Human and Earth Rights.* We commit to moral ideals such as dignity that support universal human and non-targeted species rights and in the state's duty to realize and expand civil rights and liberties along with the corresponding responsibilities.

7. *Inclusion.* We advance an active, reasoned acceptance of marginalized groups (diversity), cultural forms (pluralism), and differing beliefs.

8. *Government Welfare.* We support community based welfare (shalom) to meet core human needs, including spiritual needs. Government also protects, regulates, and uplifts the integrity of institutions and the environment. The issue should never be more or less government, but better serving government.

9. *Nonviolence/Internationalism.* We repudiate narrowly nationalistic approaches and military (police) solutions to solve social, political, and ecological problems. Instead, we advance international cooperation and global justice.

10. *Reform.* We continually support grassroots political, social, economic, and ecological challenges to the status quo. We urge "activist" court interpretations of common legal traditions—all with an eye to transform society in line with the above principles.

These core Liberal truths infuse the sixteen norms of the international Earth Charter summarized as: inherent worth, compassion, sustainability, future generations, protection and restoration, precaution, sustainable production and consumption, population control, education, justice, gender equality, antidiscrimination, democratic participation, lifelong learning, protecting animals, and peacemaking. They also undergird major portions of the Universal Declaration of Human Rights.[46]

After grappling with these basic ideals in later chapters, you will see a side of Jesus not often portrayed—that his Good Governing, grounded

---

46. See Raskin, *Liberalism*, 249–72 for a third-stage Liberal update of the Declaration.

in the subsistence ethic, *clearly aligns with the above Progressive ideals.* He would not allow these ideals to go unnoticed in his world and his story is part of the ongoing narrative of Progressive values that have shaped Western politics and practice. As Martin Luther King Jr. so elegantly expressed in his *Letter from Birmingham City Jail* when referring to the lunch-counter protesters: "They were in reality standing up for the best in the American dream and the most sacred values in our Judeo-Christian heritage . . . ."[47] By naming these ancient values of freedom and equality as "sacred," and living up to them to the point of death, King embodied a spiritual politics that had been exiled for a long time. King's journey began with Jesus, and they both stand as powerful and eloquent advocates of a Progressive ethic. They proclaimed and died for those *sacred enduring values* that still beg to find a political and ecological home in our world today. They find their place in a Christian political stance and the church's mission to create a better humanity and healthier Planet.[48]

In summary, Jesus zealously pursued Progressive aims by announcing and inaugurating this coming post-exilic Good Governing—his shorthand for a transforming ecospiritual politics for the common good. He hoped to awaken *public* faith, hope, and love where little existed. In a dramatic way he challenged broken systems and he renewed governing (the use of power) by grounding it in the empathic Creator God. Jesus summons the ethic of his peasant world and his prophetic calling and rekindles the time when humans were expected to be their brothers and sisters' keepers as well as keepers of the Garden. He finds this morality enshrined in the egalitarian strands of the Mosaic Charter and in the ancient accounts of the patriarchs and matriarchs who God had mandated to bless all Earth's families (Gen 12:3). This recollected ethic enhances the core goods—life, health, Land, prosperity, freedom, respect, and love—designed to make our lives and all other life better. Herein lies the thrust of the earliest Jesus movement and the best in Christianity.[49]

Jesus' Progressive politics flows forward to future generations and, as its welcoming beneficiaries, we drink its refreshing waters while trekking within a valley of dry bones. He set precedent for some of the most pressing issues in the twenty-first century with his subsistence/sustainability social and Land ethic. We are prepared to explore his *political compassion* and *generous justice* toward Earth and its inhabitants, his run-ins with the

---

47. King, "Letter," 14.

48. See Gottlieb, *Greener Faith*, 216 who states, "Religious environmentalism must take place in the broad tradition of progressive political movements."

49. Mack, *Lost Gospel*, 8–9.

rigid *cultural warriors* of his community, his *affirmative action* toward everyone and everything marginalized, his *poverty program* for people disenfranchised from the Land, his flexible *activist interpretations* of his nation's Constitution, his vision for *universal health care* and the *health of the Land*, and his outright *rejection of militarism and nationalism*.

Before we examine his political views in greater detail, let us stay a little longer in Jesus' world—a world ensnared and crushed by an enduring ethic that has continued to stalk Progressive values and victimize the many throughout history. What were the values that he saw as woefully flawed and how does their resonance today blight our political discourse and misshape our policy decisions?

4

Conservative Opposition

When you drink of clear water, must you foul the rest with your feet?

—Ezekiel

IN HIS BOOK *CULTURAL Warrior*, media pundit Bill O'Reilly bares frustration that his priest seldom preaches as if Jesus were alive today. Even more, he wishes the Father to talk about why Jesus was a traditionalist (a "T-warrior").[1] Mr. O'Reilly laments our nation's grandeur silently eroding because secular Progressives are attacking the traditions that made it great—those built mostly on conventional values. He believes that Jesus could help salvage this wreckage.

Mr. O'Reilly should be commended for prodding the clergy to bring Jesus into the twenty-first century. He is also right that Jesus embraced a tradition. Yet, for Jesus many of the prevailing traditions fed injurious cultural creeds. Intent on shaping his nation's Land program, he was inevitably thrust into a spiritual battle over competing traditions and the hearts of the people. In the modern world, the contest is between two political moralities labeled "Conservatism" and "Liberalism" and has become the major *defining reality* of American politics. Back in Jesus' day a similar moral politics was in play.

---

1. O'Reilly, *Cultural Warrior*, 77.

LIFE UNDER THE IMPERIAL STRICT-FATHER SPIRITUALITY

With the rise of the great imperial powers, an emerging spiritual politics would plague the ancient world through the time of Jesus up to the present. Samuel, an early prophet, starkly describes it and warns:

> These will be the ways of the king who will reign over you. He will
> take your sons to fight in his wars; to harvest his fields and to build arms;
> take your daughters to be attendants and cooks;
> take your best fields and vineyards and olive orchards to give to his friends;
> take one-tenth of your grain and wine and give it to his friends and officers;
> take your slaves, best cattle, and donkeys and put them to his work;
> take one-tenth of your flocks, and you shall be his slaves (1 Sam 8:11–17).

"Take," "take," "take"—the litany of the imperial ethic mirrored in Adam's (humanity's) taking of the forbidden fruit and stated so forthrightly by Samuel—has become history's *dominant institutional ethic*. It reigns as a monstrous moral aberration, creating an alliance between past tyrannies and today's "on the take" marauding corporatism. Repackaged, this ethic takes Earth and fences it, takes air and gases it, takes oceans and dumps in them, takes rivers and dams them, takes mountains and strips them, takes species and extincts them, takes houses and forecloses them, takes jobs and outsources them, takes weapons and uses them, takes other countries and wastes them, takes words and twists them, takes human spirits and breaks them.[2] It sows its tares in our hearts and our nation's soul, leaving sad traces of pain and indignity everywhere. The ghosts of this never-ending upward flow of goods, distributed mostly to well-placed "friends and officers," provides the prototype of misgoverning that haunts even our present-day democracies.

Samuel's "prophecy" ripened as Israel aged. Steeped in the values of gain and pain, this ethic wormed its way into Israel's ruling classes. It crushed the poor, the widows, the orphans and other vulnerable groups. It also undercut the Mosaic Charter, flaunted subsistence standards, and made a mockery of God. The chicanery of its rulers and their cronies began with

---

2. Inspired by Larry Markworth's unpublished poem, "Take."

King David "taking" Bathsheba and the life of her husband. In reproaching David, the prophet Nathan assails *the political morality* that informed David's decision-making—one that justified an insatiable despoiling of social goods and exploiting his hapless subjects (2 Sam 12:1–15). Solomon, David's successor, also embraced imperial ways. He introduced a burdensome tax scheme and a forced labor program in order to erect his magnificent palace and temple. In seizing everything of value, he particularly aggrieved the northern tribes (1 Kings 12:1–19). After Solomon's death, the North revolted and crowned its own king, but later yielded to both domestic and foreign imperialism—eight centuries worth.

Another example of imperial Land-grabbing is King Ahab's desire for Naboth's vineyard (1 Kings 21). After Naboth refuses Ahab's request to purchase it (the Constitution's subsistence principles forbade relinquishing ancestral Land), the king complains to his wife Jezebel, a devotee of Baal. Her response is straightforward and calculated: "Do you now govern Israel?" Jezebel's question assumes that power can manipulate the system as it pleases, which is what governing meant then (and often now). She delivers the vineyard to Ahab through trickery, deceit, and legalized murder, fulfilling the Genesis storyline of "taking" and its attending violence at humanity's dawn.

A strong anti-monarchical ethos is found in Jotham's poignant Parable of the Trees, perhaps the most stinging attack on kingship and corporate power in all of literature (Jud 9:8–15).[3] The magnificent cedars of Lebanon plead for the olive tree, the fig tree, and the vine to be their king. The latter all refuse because they provide the life-giving needs for humanity and the gods. A worthless bramble bush, however, agrees to reign over the majestic cedars, only to devour them by fire. The Parable decries Abimelech's ruthless rise to power by portraying the king as useless "bramble"—an arrogant good-for-nothing consumer of everything excellent.

Samuel, Nathan, and Jotham's Parable set the stage for disrobing imperial practices and exposing their flaws. The later prophets would connect elite pillage to political pride (Isa 2:11–17, 9:9, 13:11).[4] Nearly all imperial kings claimed divine status, leading Egypt's rulers to treat the Hebrews "arrogantly" (Exod 18:11). The prophet Micah insists that God requires justice, kindness, and a *humble* walk with God, which he defines as the "good" (Mic 6:8). The prophets know that hierarchy, with its bed-partner political pride, gives birth to poverty, bigotry, and militancy. Humble leaders identify with the downtrodden, express compassion toward them, and then serve and

---

3. von Rad, *Old Testament Theology*, vol. 1, 59.
4. Also Jer 48:29; Hab. 2:4–5; Zeph 3:11–12.

empower them. Because of the leadership's hubris, the prophets predict an inescapable reckoning—a "day of darkness" and "gloom with no brightness in it"—that will strike like a snake concealed within one's own house (Amos 5:18–20). The elites, by banishing humility with its justice, would bring Israel into exile, a devastating and bitter experience, especially for a people whose whole faith was rooted in the soil. Exile meant unfruitfulness, fearfulness, marginalization, powerlessness, mental wreckage, hopelessness, and possible spiritual death both for those hauled off to other places as well as those left behind.[5] The prophets, including Jesus, believe that a remnant of the faithful will restore humble servant leadership and end the long exile. But what obstacles will Jesus face?

THE IMPERIAL POLITICS OF ROME

Luke begins his gospel account naming Emperor Tiberius, Governor Pontius Pilate, Ruler Herod Antipas, and High Priests Annas and Caiaphas—political figures who govern the story throughout and compel Jesus to voice a prophetic counter-politics. Roman colonization, soaked in blood and with its hydra-head of woes, defined first-century Palestine, continuing the imperialism of past empires with their joyless tidings. Rome reigned with a daily downpour of ruin on the Land. Its river of misery flowed wide and deep, leaving shattered hopes in its backwash. Through the patronage/client system, the honor/shame dynamic, cultic rituals, and fear, Rome controlled everything—the people, the Land, the politics, the social structure, and the religion. In addition, for most Jews, this foreign oppressor had, like a spreading fungus, contaminated the sacredness of the Land.

Under Rome, Jesus not only witnessed grand scale imperial ravage, he and his family undoubtedly suffered from it and they would have felt the unrelenting gnaw of hunger and woe. Caesar, Herod, and their surrogate leaders levied the produce from small farmers (possibly up to 60 percent) to support their lavish lifestyles and fund magnificent monuments to glorify the Empire's enslavements, humiliations, and cruelties. Rome also encouraged predatory lending to squeeze out the small farmers within its conquered nations—all for the sake of efficient "agri-business," but creating a pool of unemployed laborers. Herod Antipas's commercialization of the Sea of Galilee also impacted fishing as evidenced by the first-century patchwork boat recently discovered.[6] The plight of fishers may account for Jesus' ministry close to this sea and why so many in the trade followed him. Few

---

5. Kaufmann, *Religion of Israel*, 204–5.
6. Crossan, *God and Empire*, 121–22.

could sidestep parasitic Roman wreckage. The downward spiral ruptured the norms of the traditional peasant economy that preserved ancestral Land grants and guaranteed at least subsistence living.

Rome courted want and misery everywhere, leaving the peasants with drained sweat and few morsels of joy. The landless, born for plow and hoe as sacred duty, faced not only shame, but also chronic starvation. Their gloomed future seemed to promise only rib-caged children and raw despair as one day groaned into the next. When life became unbearably desperate, the people begged or joined ragtag bandit/rebel groups. A wisp of their downward spiral finds its whereabouts today in the desperate words of an unemployed person: "It's like falling off a cliff into an abyss and I'm frantically reaching out for something to grab on to, but I see darkness, only darkness."[7] (Hear an echo of the Bible's hellish, bottomless pit metaphor?)

Overlying Palestine's harsh economic realities lurked Rome's Legions that waged butchery and unleashed a further torrent of misery. With little provocation, Roman soldiers might swoop down on a village, kill at will, plunder it, rape its daughters, and carry its sons into slavery or battle. Rome acted quickly against any swirls of unrest or winds of resistance, employing a very visible and effective deterrent—a horrible, shameful, torturous death by crucifixion. Rome routinely crucified rebels along thoroughfares, so that all could witness their mutilated bodies, ripped apart and half devoured by vultures or other wild animals. Only when someone with clout would speak for the corpse (as in the case of Jesus) does it escape this usual desecration. Crucifixion was a media event and a teaching device: "See what happens when you defy Roman power." It stood as a sadistic means by which Rome traumatized its subjugated peoples and preserved its values.

We should not be surprised that nearly all of Jesus' speeches, stories, and actions relate to Rome's onerous Land schemes Galilean villagers endured. Like all past empires, Rome governed under a thin veil of justice where gift giving was transformed into forced taking with names like "tribute," "taxes," and "tithe." The Caesars virtually owned everything, including their subjects, who they considered as chattel and treated paternalistically at best.[8] A universal imperial cult, with its mythologies and emperor worship, held the empire together. Rome's self-interest passed through the following normative filters that were taught to every citizen of all classes:[9]

---

7. Actual statement of an unemployed friend.
8. Frankfort et al., *Before Philosophy*, 89–101.
9. Elliott, *Arrogance of Nations*, 28–40. Also Finley, *Politics in the Ancient World*, 27–28.

1. *Piety and tradition.* The ancient gods created Rome and divinized its emperors, sanctioning them to appropriate the whole Earth and civilize the world. The imperial theology, its cult, and its customs construed all traditional virtues (faith, mercy, justice) to serve imperial power.

2. *Hierarchy.* Patronage, honor, birth, conspicuous wealth, rank, and civic displays all defined social position with its vast inequalities.

3. *Luxury.* Riches, opulence, leisure, and entertainment—spoils rewarded for civilizing the inferior conquered nations—marked the good life.

4. *Government and basic rights.* Because it was assumed that the emperor ruled benevolently, obedience was expected. Roman justice favored the rights of the elites.

5. *Peace and order through militarism.* Rome was ordained by the gods to bring peace to the world. The *Pax Romana*, however, meant attacking, occupying, plundering, and keeping order with strict laws, superior military power, strong discipline, and reward.

6. *Nationalism.* Glorification of and subordination to Rome was expected, while sustaining the interests of the Caesars and the aristocracy.[10]

This ethic that shattered life in the provinces flowed from values named as piety, tradition, custom, authority, tribalism, rules, status, gain, strength, and punishment. Rome assumed them to be natural, ordained by gods, and self-justifying. Imperial norms set their stamp on everything: coins, statutes, frescos, reliefs, buildings, monuments, texts, everything. The dark shadows of imperial values resulted in burdensome taxes and debt, lack of daily bread, social and economic gaps, shame, deteriorating health, widening neuroses, fanatical nationalism, degrading ethnocentrism, and strict purity boundaries. They provide the pattern from which human wretchedness in every age has been cut. These all-pervasive, non-empathic ideals that fed all empires compelled Jesus to launch a "frontal assault on a whole way of life."[11] As we shall see, their family genes are found in core Conservative principles today.

Rome preserved its values and power in the far reaches of the empire through the *patron/client* system that brought cohesion through reciprocal favors.[12] Menacing patronage battles lingered everywhere, since clients gained much by generous benefactors and vice versa. (A similar dynamic

---

10. Carter, *Roman Empire*, 3–10.
11. Funk, *Five Gospels*, 202. See Luke 22:25.
12. Malina, *New Testament World*, 100–103. Also Hanson and Oakman, *Palestine in the Time of Jesus*, 71, 74.

exists today when people angle their way up corporate ladders.) Through the patronage system, Rome permitted client rulers to govern as long as they possessed wealth, guaranteed the collection of tribute, appropriated Land, kept the peace, and honored the emperor. By declaring God alone the Parent/Patron, Jesus undermines the degrading imperial patronizing, oligarchic, patriarchal political system upon which Rome depended and the ancient domination ethic rested (Matt 23:9).

In Palestine, Rome's patronage rule filtered through the Temple authorities in Jerusalem. To the Jews, the Temple operated as the government—the symbolic heart of Israel's identity as a nation, the center of the universe, and the dwelling place of the holy God. During the Hasmonean dynasty (160–67 BC), the king became the High Priest and the Temple assumed direct political power. From that time on, it could be called a Temple-*state*. The Temple-state's aristocratic rulers and many of its bureaucratic "retainers"—priests, scribes (the guardians of the Israelite way of life), and Levites—became victimized by Rome's imperial ethic and its schemes. They were forced to hold daily sacrifices for Caesar to prove loyalty. Not only because of its Roman architecture (Herod the Great's nod to Caesar), but also because Rome chose the High Priest, held the priestly vestments, and approved its police force, the Temple-state operated, for all intents, as a *Roman* Temple-state during the time of Jesus.

It disturbs Jesus to see the Temple leaders collaborating with Rome to bully the Galileans, appropriate their Lands, and hinder Israel's return from exile. Every judgment Jesus delivers against the Temple-state leaders and their supporters is, in reality, *a blast against Rome's* invasive imperial ideals. Ignoring this truth blurs our picture of Jesus and unjustly impugns Judaism. His rebuke of the Temple authorities is like someone denouncing the "White House," but means the Bush or Obama administration and not the institution.

THE OPPOSITION PARTIES

An indisputable fact about the historical Jesus is that he engaged in open conflicts with other groups—especially those aligned with the prevailing power structures. These factions, often bundled in religious garb, are best described as *political parties*, not in the modern sense of competing for votes, but in that they all intensely jockeyed for moral/political authority, as did the Jesus movement. They held certain beliefs in common: (1) that God chose Israel to bless the nations, (2) that God gave Israel a governing Constitution, (3) that God promised Israel a bountiful Land and protection if it obeyed their Charter, (4) that God led Israel into exile because of disobedience (by its leaders), and (5) that God will restore the Land to fulfill Israel's mission when it repents. These core beliefs, however, attracted wide ranging interpretations, each party claiming to hold the true answer to Israel's identity, failure, return, and survival. (Much like our battles today over what constitutes America's identity, moral failure, and restoration.) With the rise of imperialism, conflict mushroomed as groups arose to defend their own vision, which Jesus too would address. *Political factionalism,* then, provides a crucial backdrop for understanding Jesus.

When speaking of Jesus' opponents, we enter dangerous waters. Too often Christians have seen Jesus countering a supposedly "normative Judaism" and felt justified in slandering the Jews. Jesus, however, *was a Jew.* It's wrong, then, to label his adversaries as "Jewish" opponents or that he opposed the "Jewish" traditions. Jesus' politics was one of several rival brands of Judaism springing up in response to onerous historical imperialisms (and now Roman) affecting Jewish traditions and culture. Indeed, the feuds between Jesus and the other parties were *intra-family*, Jewish infighting over how best to deliver Israel from exile. Ultimately, the little people were pitted against imperial interests, a conflict woven throughout the Gospels. Like all the factions, Jesus would look deep into Israelite social memory for the nation's true understanding of God, its proper connection to the Land, and its defined destiny. Jesus will always remain, not only as a treasure from God, but also a remarkable gift from Judaism.

The established parties included the *Essenes*, who opposed the Temple and set up an alternative one out in the desert. The *Sadducees* were the wealthy rulers in Jerusalem who believed in deliverance by accommodating Rome. The *Herodian* party, of course, supported the imperial interests of Herod's dynasty. Certain *proto-Zealot* groups believed that God would save Israel through rebellion. They would later figure significantly in the Great War of (66–70 AD), one of many holocausts suffered by the Jewish people. Despite their differences on the legitimacy of the present Temple administration, these parties generally shared common imperial-like political values, supported by traditionalism, hierarchy, privilege, exclusivism, and holy war.

Jesus' most immediate and formidable opposition came from a hardline subgroup of the *Pharisee* party, the custodian of traditions. Although their power had diminished the years preceding Jesus, a few Pharisees sat on the Sanhedrin, the council in Jerusalem. Their strong political aspirations are confirmed when, during Jesus' childhood, a Pharisee named Saddok and Judas the Galilean launched a rebellion against Rome.[13] It's unfair, however, to lump the Pharisees together and stereotype them as "hypocrites," although the charge of elitist hypocrisy (not living up to professed ethical standards) was always a weapon in the downtrodden's arsenal of resistance, and Jesus used it often. The Pharisees were split into lenient (Hillel) and strict (Shammai) schools and Jesus befriended some and dined with them. A group once warned him that Antipas wanted to kill him (Luke 13:31).

For many Pharisees, ending the exile came down to one national command: "You shall be holy, for I the Lord our God am holy" and its corollary, "You shall be for me a priestly kingdom and a holy nation" (Lev 19:3; Exod 19:6). Because holiness defines the essence of God's character, it stood as the main ingredient of spirituality. Here, however, the mandate calls for *national* holiness. Jesus and his rivals clash over what constitutes a "holy" nation. Some hardline Pharisees, campaigning in Galilee to regain clout, seize upon the culture of priest-like purity and its impact on dining etiquette, honor/shame codes, and various rituals as the path to holiness. Jesus considers this, for the most part, spiritual and political folly, and disputes, even discredits, their views at many turns.

Though a few overzealous "cultural warriors"(in our terminology), insist that everyone practice the strict purity rules for Israel's rebirth, some ancient cleanliness rules appeared quite practical—beneficial to the health and well-being of the community. Jesus, as a Jew, embraces many of them. They also represented the awareness of God's presence in daily life and sustained Jewish identity amidst the encroaching Greek and Roman culture. In this sense, purity rules were subversive. Furthermore, purity rules retain a contemporary relevance when we think about the impurity of junk food, cigarette smoke, and the pollution choking our Planet.

Yet, purity became co-opted by the imperial ethic, yielding ill-fated results. The Hebrew term "holiness" implies separation between the sacred (God) and the profane (everyday contaminates).[14] However, severing pure from defiled objects, with its division between clean and unclean, reinforced elitist superiority and erected formidable social walls that shut out a wide range of misfits—the glaring "sinners." Sinners were those with dishonorable vocations or who disregarded the Torah and the oral traditions; they jeopardized the future of the nation.[15] Feeding on superiority and separation, the priestly kingdom expanded cultural negativism into a fabric of life yielding a divided, bigoted, and fearful society. A dark historical truth

---

13. Meier, *Marginal Jew*, vol. 3, 313.
14. Jacob, *Theology*, 87–88.
15. Rengstorf, "*hamartolos*," 327.

emerged: narrow cultural purity poisons the deep springs of compassion that flow within.

Purity's ugly side oozes forth when societies began denigrating different *human physical features* or projecting negative characteristics onto groups they think inferior, they don't understand, or they fear. These outgroups are then considered the bearers of "contagion," which effectively reinforces in-group snobbishness and social disgust. The in-crowd is then provided with moral justification to persecute.[16] Throughout history, *'apiru* (dispossessed), people with skin diseases, prostitutes, women, untouchables, Jews, homosexuals, people of color, the differently-abled, the elderly, immigrants, people at the lower levels of the social pyramid, the houseless, the mentally challenged, and most ethnic minorities have become objects of disgust and shame—the subjects of social exile.[17] Because of society's fences, these groups have suffered horrible atrocities. The Holocaust, slavery, and Rwanda's genocide stand out as ghastly examples.

Strict boundaries and power arrangements were also fortified by *eating etiquette*. Given the priority of food for survival, violations jeopardize the well-being of the community. The choice and preparation of food, how sumptuously one ate, seating arrangements, and washing rituals symbolized social standing and reinforced the honor/shame, clean/dirty, and good/evil taboos. The Gospels often portray Jesus indiscriminately eating with outcasts to highlight his program of sharing food to stave off peasant starvation, while at the same time cutting through traditional honor hierarchies with their exclusionary mores. More positively, Jesus' inclusive dining policy served to *restore equality and dignity*, essential ingredients of the coming Good Governing and its food programs.[18]

One time Jesus' followers, after mingling with "defiled" people, fail to wash their hands before eating, creating "moral panic" among his zealous rivals. For his opponents, Jesus fosters the spread of immorality and stands as a threat to the nation's cherished values, jeopardizing both the community's life-source and its hope for the future.[19] He foments "cultural decline" (sound familiar?). Jesus responds with a pithy parable that illustrates why food entering the body does not pollute. Privately, Jesus explains that contact with an object (in this case food) does not create dirty people, "since it

---

16. Nussbaum, *Hiding from Humanity*, 98.

17. Ibid., 347–49. See her excellent analysis of the destructive elements of disgust when applied to women, Jews, and homosexuals. Also her *Sex and Social Justice*, 184–210.

18. Bartchy, "Table Fellowship," 796–800.

19. Nussbaum, *Hiding from Humanity*, 255–56.

enters, not the heart, but the stomach, and goes out into the sewer.... It is what comes out of a person that pollutes" (Mark 7:15–22).

Why would that teaching offend these cultural warriors? Because if human excrement finds its place—the sewer—it can no longer be the object of concern or fear, and if fear disappears, then so does the political power of the fear-mongers. Most importantly, Jesus dethrones the prevailing "body politic" by relocating defilement away from natural biological processes, and instead, refers them to the human heart, the true vessel of good or evil and the headwaters for a viable ecospiritual politics.

He pinpoints the real "defiling" vices as staked out in Israel's Constitution: "fornication, theft, murder, adultery, avarice, wickedness, deceit, licentiousness, envy, slander, pride, folly." They describe the community-destroying/ Land-exploiting behaviors of those sitting at the top. Jesus washes the starch out of the elite who use cultural purity for political and economic control (as Conservative moralists now do in America).[20] Furthermore, the "You shall be holy" exhortation in Leviticus 19 had already headlined a whole series of "how to be holy" directives. These dealt, not with ritual purity, but with issues surrounding *political* purity: gleaning, stealing, fraud, slander, impartial judgments, and the loving treatment of neighbors and immigrants (Lev 19:1–37). This expansive view of holiness points to *social justice and ecojustice* concerns and because these directives fall at the exact center of the Torah scroll, they are the *holiest* of holies, more holy than other Torah texts, including the purity references.

Jesus' most biting criticism of cultural superiority shines through his parable about a religious leader and a toll collector who come to pray at the Temple (Luke 18:9–14). The sanctimonious cultural warrior displays hierarchical pride as he accordingly treats others with "contempt." Boastfully reminding his strict-father God of his selective commandment keeping (his prayers, fasts, and tithes) only heightens the contrast between himself and the shameful, unclean tax man. However, he remains oblivious to the fact that he, too, is one of the "robbers" and "rogues" he condemns, caught in a pattern of exploitation and appropriation. Fundamentally, he is no different from the toll collector.[21] Indeed, we should feel sympathy for him as we do for the tax collector who prays only for "compassion"—a virtue the cultural warrior's principles muzzle. Jesus concludes the parable with his core spiritual truth that the exalted will be humbled and the humble exalted. Political

---

20. As has been the case since the rise of hierarchical political power. Becker, *Escape from Evil*, 54–55.

21. Herzog, *Parables as Subversive Speech*, 191.

humility, a prerequisite of compassion, dethrones a false holier than others attitude and brings about a great social reversal.[22]

This parable also subtly critiques flowery *prayers* recited in the Temple, the synagogue (the community assembly or *knesset* in Aramaic), and on the street corners for the purpose of political posturing (Matt 6:5). (Some today do the same in our schools and local governments.) Jesus also spotlights *fasting*, a symbol of preserving Earth's resources, which the tradition warrior exploits as a spectacle to bear political fruit. But because the coming Good Government is *here now*, it's a time for joyful, wedding-like dining together as equals and not grim fasting (Mark 2:18–20). Following Isaiah, Jesus would see true fasting as the ecospiritual politics of supporting the marginalized and respecting subsistence principles (Isa 58:6–7).

Jesus also chastises his rivals for headlining *tithing* while soft-pedaling social justice, compassion, love of God, and even faith itself. The aristocrats, blithely inoculated against any guilt for their Land policies, even further coerce the already overtaxed farmers into nickel and diming their tiny herb plots. This outrage prompts Jesus' exaggerated hyperbole of one meticulously straining out a gnat from a cup of tea, but then blindly gulping down a whole camel (Matt 23:23–24). They remain oblivious to the weightier legal matters.

Jesus does not spare critiquing the most sacred of traditions and the one most tied to the Land—the *Sabbath*. The Sabbath rest flowed out of the Creation story and provided a break from constant human labor. Marvelously, out of deep respect, it demanded rest for the Land and animals as well. Nevertheless, a strict interpretation of the seventh day, forbidding this and that, causes Jesus' irked opponents to publicly censure his followers who, out of hunger, pluck heads of grain on the Sabbath in serious violation of tradition (Mark 2:23–28). In response, Jesus cites the story of a hungry David and his armies who entered forbidden (i.e., sacred) space and ate "holy" food reserved only for priests (1 Sam 21:1–6). By choosing this story and likening himself to David on a political mission, Jesus defines this confrontation as a clash of spiritual politics. In line with subsistence rights, he points out that David was justified in disregarding the tradition because his men were "hungry and in need of food," just as the man with a withered hand he healed on the Sabbath needed a functioning limb. Thus for Jesus, keeping the Sabbath holy means fulfilling human need, saving life, and not perpetuating fear, ranking, and unlimited gain (Mark 2:27—3:6). In the incident at hand, Sabbath holiness means food for starving Galilean

---

22. Batey, *Jesus and the Poor*, 18–22. He calls this the great "apocalyptic reversal."

families—a Sabbath surely welcomed and a breathtaking truth for us now where hunger torments billions daily.

With some exceptions, the spiritual politics of the political parties mirrored the imperial ethic by (1) its selective interpretations of traditions and conventions that reinforce and legitimize imperial notions; (2) its strict defining of status and honor boundaries that discourage diversity, encourage the marginalization of those with differences, and enhance male power; (3) its formal and restrictive view of justice that permits economic inequality; and (4) its strong nationalism and reliance on military might to restore Israel (or perpetuate the status quo) and bring about conformity to the above principles.

Jesus believes in Israel's ordained destiny, but his *reform* aims to undercut the spiritual politics pursued by the prevailing rulers (Antipas, Pilate, and Caiaphas) and the wannabe leaders (the Essenes, some Pharisees, and the rebels). He dips into Israel's past and deep within his own heart to challenge the harsh conditions of imperial pillage that takes the figs, the grapes, the grain, the oxen, the money, and even the children of the weak. Jesus, the Jew, wrangles with other Jews over the political meaning and importance of common cultural symbols to uphold the true meaning of national holiness that will finally end Israel's long exile. Whereas Jesus performs in the same theatre, he changes the script with its cultural badges and, for some, steals the show. For this, the overzealous cultural warriors believe he is challenging holiness itself. He looms as a triple threat: a shameful sinner, an encourager of others to sin, and a blasphemer (traitor) who stakes out ground in a conflict that finds its counterpart in the spiritual and political trenches today—the battle between Liberal and Conservative values.

A CONSERVATIVE POLITICAL ETHIC

Conservatism, like Liberalism, is a political ethic.[23] Both claim that their own values are universal and see them as "abiding truths"[24] and "enduring principles."[25] Actually, these political moralities do reach back to the earliest civilizations and address a persistent reality—the clash between the "haves" and the "have-nots"—that proved as acute in the world Jesus roamed as it is today. The battle of moralities reduces to a showdown over the following notions: (1) the priority and application of social compassion; (2) the meaning of common ideals such as justice, freedom, and well-being; (3) the

23. See Kekes, *Case for Conservatism*, 1.
24. Kirk, "Essence of Conservatism," 2.
25. Humphrey, "Enduring Principles," 91.

legitimacy of hierarchy and privilege; (4) the extent of social entitlements; (5) the nature of social order; (6) how traditions are prioritized and laws interpreted; and (7) the meaning of nationalism and the purposes of military power. The terms "Liberal" and "Conservative" evoke strong emotions with advocates of each often distorting the others' ideals. Their difference, however, is not between good and evil, but rather which one adequately defines and applies our common values. Mutual demonizing is a dead end. Both have a conscience; both act from principle.

Casting aside caricatures, the "abiding truths" of a Conservative political ethic—culled and summarized from various Conservative writers—include the following:

1. *Tradition.* A high value is placed on enduring institutions, cultural norms, and religious authorities, especially those that enhance traditional social, political, economic, and family structures and that reflect the ideals listed below.[26]

2. *Difference.* A conception of justice that accepts equal opportunity but rejects egalitarian ideals (imposed equal social and economic results). As a nod to individualism and self-reliance, socioeconomic disparities and hierarchies are permitted, even encouraged.[27]

3. *Basic Legal Rights.* Fundamental rights are embraced, while remaining uneasy with an ever-expanding list of civil rights.[28] More traditional social roles (e.g., gender roles) are elevated, with diversity considered a tentative value. Conservatives oppose governmental affirmative action programs for the poor and minorities, often labeling them "reverse discrimination."[29]

4. *Property Rights.* Individuals remain sovereign over Earth and its resources and possess nearly unlimited rights to own property and to accumulate, consume, and dispose of earned goods as one sees fit, usually within a more strict market economy.[30]

5. *Minimal Government.* Government's role is limited to (a) restraining assaults on those primary values that promote basic rights, human survival, and order,[31] and (b) censoring what many consider to

---

26. Kirk, *Politics of Prudence*, 18–19.
27. Nisbet, *Conservatism*, 50–54.
28. Ibid., 98.
29. Bork, *Slouching towards Gomorrah*, 231–43.
30. Nisbet, *Conservatism*, 56.
31. Wolfson, "Conservatives and Neoconservatives," 224.

be socially objectionable, disgusting, or "incitements to vice."[32] Conservatives dislike social welfare programs and, in their book of rules, the government must never become a meddling (overregulating and over-taxing) parent.

6. *Originalism.* The Constitution is interpreted in a relatively narrow and strict "originalist" way (as in the minds of the framers). Conservatives decry "activist" judges who legislate social change along Liberal lines.[33]

7. *Nationalism/Strong Military.* National sovereignty is strongly endorsed with little faith placed in international bodies like the United Nations. National security receives high priority and superior military strength is crucial for keeping the peace and enforcing national interests.[34]

The underlying priority values of Conservatism—authority, rules, individualism, difference, order, self-reliance, gain, and strength—are shaped by what has been called a "strict-father" family metaphor such as keeping household rules, maintaining hierarchies of authority, enforcing rigid boundaries, and assigning rewards and punishments.[35] From a Progressive perspective, each one of the above principles contains an essential truth, though fragmentary. Thus, Liberal and Conservative world views overlap in seemingly endless variety. Even within Conservatism explosive differences prevail—hence the common designations "ultra-Conservative," "neo-Conservative," "Old Guard Conservative," "the Religious Right," "Tea Partiers," and so on, depending on how its principles are understood and ranked.[36] But the ideals listed above generally describe the core features of the Conservative political ethic.

The issues that divide Conservatives and Progressives today resonate with those Jesus tackled in his time: social status, the family, predatory lending, wealth and poverty, dashed hopes, cultural elitism (racism, sexism), conflicting legal interpretations, access to health care, stewardship of the Land, nationalism, and trust in military might. What immediately catch the eye are the close analogies between the political values of the first-century imperial ethic and present Conservative ideals. Conservatism is a god-child of an ancient, but abiding, ethic; it immortalizes imperial values, buttressing their nearly unconquerable power throughout the ages.

---

32. Bork, *Slouching*, 142. Kirk, *Politics of Prudence*, 23.
33. Bork, *Slouching*, 98–119.
34. Rice, "President's National Security," 82. Also Will, "Slow Undoing," 136–37.
35. Lakoff, *Moral Politics*, 65–140.
36. See Dean, *Conservatives without Conscience*, 20–22, where he lists ten different varieties.

CONSERVATIVE WRECKAGE NOW

In fairness, modern Conservatism would rightly object to political tyrannies that embrace imperial principles *without restraint,* just as Progressives denounce imperialisms such as Stalinism. Yet, Conservative notions are qualitatively similar to imperial values; they share the same DNA. They have changed their names and shapes through the march of history, but come dressed in stylish self-interest versions: the profit motive, equal opportunity, tax relief, border security, self-reliance, gun rights, patriotism, creative destruction, and traditional family values. These breathe life into vices like avarice, pride of position, and retaliatory anger. Conservatism no longer relies on brute force, but rather on the highhanded sway of irrational fear, frayed traditions, outmoded creeds, and archaic customs. They all subsidize someone's misery. Moral analogies to the past are seen in the large nations still pillaging Third World economies, in unregulated corporate expansion, and in vulture capitalism. With worker influence waning and government weakening, corporate giants have ascended to nearly king-like status. They impose their imperial shaped values through campaign donations, lobbying, and media control; and thereby, are hard to buck. The dictatorship of an ever imposing industrial/marketing/consuming complex shapes every sector of American life, compelling a material feeding-frenzy that leaves the poor and the Planet languishing.[37]

Society must also guard against the daily "tyrannies" that out-grouped people experience: such as women kept in traditional roles, employees facing pay cuts and firings while CEO's wallow in luxury, non-believers seeing religious-specific beliefs legally imposed, or detainees tortured. Whereas literal crucifixion is non-existent today, the cross remains a poignant symbol of what undocumented workers bear when "boundary-crossings" are described as "invasions" by an inferior culture, contaminating America's way of life—the "greatest civilization and culture the world ever produced," as some arrogantly claim.[38] Although packaged differently, the cultural battles waged by Conservatives often spring from the same boundary making, the same disgust, the same fears, the same need to expel "contaminants" as of old. The Progressive Jesus rejects the logic of "holier than thou" barrier-building with its imperial consequences both then and now. His serious followers must do the same.

Let's return to Mr. O'Reilly, the self-proclaimed cultural warrior, who believes in preserving American traditions with religious fervor. If Mr.

---

37. Elliott, *Arrogance of Nations,* 9–16.
38. Buchanan, *State of Emergency,* 5, 28.

O'Reilly's priest met his challenge that Jesus should address today's issues, the sermon title might more accurately read, to his surprise, "Jesus Squares Off *Against* the Cultural Warriors." Jesus made important distinctions between traditions typified by worn-out wineskins and those with the strong fiber of Progressive principles. Cultural skirmishes come down to what traditions enhance a nation's governing and what ones need scrapping or reforming. Jesus never questions the view that Israel harbored a manifest destiny embodied in the founding traditions. But he stood strong for those ecospiritual ideals from his traditions that define true political holiness. The remainder of this book is dedicated to exploring his grand truths and their significance for governing today.

5

Holiness as Political Compassion

And he had compassion for them.
—MATTHEW

JESUS AND HIS OPPONENTS wrangled over what spiritual values inspire a nation's holiness, i.e., its highest moral goals derived from the essence of God's character. Of all the political parties in Palestine stressing purity or accommodation, rebellion or spiritual retreat as Israel's way out of exile, only the Jesus party spoke loudly in the voice of political compassion. Jesus found compassion at the very beginning of Israel's story—one that began with the subsistence inspired question, "Am I my brother's (and sister's) keeper?" In defiance of the prevailing political moralities of status, wealth, and might, this story told about an empathic God who creates nurturing communities based on service. Out of this story, Jesus imaginatively changes the "You shall be holy as God is holy" command in the Constitution to read, "Be compassionate just as your Father is compassionate" (Lev 19:2 with Luke 6:36). By substituting "compassion" for "holy," he unearths the "I am Compassionate" nature of Yahweh and assigns empathy as the definitive meaning of holiness and the preeminent national virtue. In so doing, he reclaims from his Jewish tradition the greatest spiritual revolution in politics we could ever imagine.

That compassion forms the basis of morality endures today in the major religions and as a key principle of the Earth Charter. Compassion assumes that human beings are meant to flourish, but along the way something agonizing (or a disproportionate loss from a little misstep) has torpedoed their dreams. When we walk in their shoes and imagine their affliction, something stirs within us common to our humanity—namely, our suffering (hence, *com + passio,* meaning "suffering with"). Compassion binds us to one another and is vital in spurring and shaping our affections. But compassion remains theoretical unless we sense our own vulnerability—our brush with failure, sickness, accidents, misfortune. None of us escapes tragedy and it plays a large part in our spiritual quest. We find ourselves cut off from our inborn well of compassion when disgust or our judgmental eye looks at others and sees moral specks rather than their agony. Other forces also work to suppress it: concern for social status, lingering prejudices, and social rigidities.[1] For example, the rich and well-placed may be tempted to measure their own worth in dollars, and therefore, arrogantly devalue those beneath them, finding it difficult to feel their pain. In fact, the high-and-mighty often believe that the less fortunate *deserve* their adversity—rejecting the notion that their bitter waters might be caused by poisoned social opportunities.

Today's Spiritual Progressives affirm that compassion represents one of our core ecospiritual goods and is an essential pillar in the design of *political structures and policies.*[2] It flows from and contributes to respect and dignity for humans and Planet. Political compassion supports citizens exiled by: life-threatening situations, degrading health, loss of jobs and homes, violence or its threat, lack of fair economic opportunity, fear and anxiety, isolation, prejudice and stigmatizing, human trafficking, toxic environments, and the eroding of basic equality and civil liberties.[3] Progressives also express compassion toward Earth and its creatures and feel their woe. By advancing compassion as a political virtue and an indispensable component of good governing, Jesus becomes a worthy contributor to the glorious Liberal tradition.[4]

Conservatives implicitly acknowledge that civic compassion belongs to Liberalism when they pejoratively refer to Liberals as "bleeding hearts."[5] This besmirch intends to ridicule government welfare programs that Conservatives decry as "compassionate welfare policies" and "giveaways."[6] Sensitive to charges of callousness, Conservatives advance the catch phrase

1. Hoffman, "Empathy," 126–36.
2. Nussbaum, *Upheavals of Thought*, 405.
3. Nussbaum's list of basic human capacities, *Women*, 78–80.
4. Nussbaum, *Upheavals of Thought*, 297–454. I rely heavily upon her analysis.
5. Safire, *Political Dictionary*, 61.
6. Bork, *Slouching towards Gomorrah*, 230.

"compassionate Conservatism." They insist, however, that real compassion must be locked to "moral accountability" and "character building" that (with some truth) they accuse Liberals of ignoring.[7] Conservatism deflects responsibility for the misery it creates by faulting the victim.

In Progressive politics, compassion reaches more broadly and deeply than the Conservative version. While pushing for a personal touch, Progressives believe in exposing the underlying inequities within social and economic structures that lead to suffering and then in devising compassionate laws and policies to eliminate these ingrained wrongs.[8] They embrace a capability approach and, like Conservatives, recognize the spiritual dimension in our human experience—especially when tragedy strikes. Progressives do not ignore personal sin and moral accountability, but apply them in broader social and economic ways—refusing to place all the blame on the victim. Institutions and powerful people that permit dehumanizing hierarchies, social boundaries, sordid gain, and extensive poverty, should not be exempt from moral censure. Accordingly, Progressives are also more likely to be "merciful" rather than accusatory toward those who suffer due to bad choices. From compassion's perspective, the "sins" of the desperate are symptoms; the real sins are those actions and policies that create desperate people and keep them that way.

How does Jesus weigh in on these differences? His ecospiritual politics of compassion delves deep to heal everything broken, reignites responsibility, and gives special consideration to those crushed by structural blights. In Matthew's account this compassion is described as being "perfect"—the highest level of spiritual attainment (Matt 5:8). The Hebrew Scriptures link compassion to the term *rahim* meaning: "from the same womb," a beautiful metaphor for love and its strong family-like tie. God is likened to a mother nurturing "the child of her womb" and celebrated as one who "will have compassion on his suffering ones" (Isa 49:13, 15). (Given the pain of childbirth, the womb also signifies the steadfast family link to those who suffer due to imperial programs.) This "kinship of misery" (as well as joy) comprises the bio-political community and gave birth to Israel. Jesus would highlight this family-like compassion in some of his most famous stories and model it everywhere he went.

---

7. Ibid., 11, 18.
8. Nussbaum, *Upheavals of Thought*, 397–400.

COMPASSIONATE POLITICS AND A SON RETURNED FROM EXILE

Jesus would use a powerful tool to get his message across—the parable. Joachim Jeremias, in his classical work, contends that the parables give voice to the real Jesus.[9] With brilliant imagination they speak to the issue of power, unlocking hidden ecospiritual truths about the coming Good Governing and its subsistence values ("The kingdom of God is like . . . ."). Structured around common realities to open up new vistas for village life, they tell in novel ways the story of Israel's (and all nation's) captivity and return from exile.[10] Their goal, at the most general level, is to grow an "honest and good heart" and bear its fruit (Luke 8:15). Like many peasant folktales, they empower weak and oppressed people, giving voice to their daily indignities, while feeding their hope that life will turn around. Their "moral(s)," however, are only receptive to those attuned.[11] The greatest spiritual and political secret they reveal for us is that good governing must be grounded in Progressive values, especially compassionate justice.

Jesus' Good Government parables also articulate long held grievances and subtly and artfully critique the prevailing spiritual politics, often surrounding issues of Land abuse.[12] Jesus echoes the prophets who told parables to cut through the imperial ethic's never-ending gain and pain by dishing out a subtle political bite. For example, Nathan, in the face of David's adultery and murder, employs a parable to cleverly blind-side the king's legitimizing moral matrix of take, take, take (2 Sam 12:1–15). He entraps the king within his own professed sense of Constitutional fair play. Jesus uses parables in the same way—as subtle commentaries on how our darker side and national sins lead to exile. They indirectly sneak the 'hidden" subsistence principles of the oppressed onto the public stage and provide a safer tool to unfold their "discourse of indignation."[13] The parables have been correctly tagged as "weapons of warfare,"[14] but a form of peasant *nonviolent* resistance. In Jesus' campaign to reform the nation they emerge as forceful instruments in his battle over primal spiritual myths (i.e., political moralities).[15]

---

9. Jeremias, *Parables of Jesus*, 12.
10. Wright, *Jesus*, 126–31.
11. Ibid., 181. Mark 4:3, 9, 12–13; Dan 12:10.
12. Herzog, *Parables as Subversive Speech*, 28.
13. Horsley, "Arts of Resistance," 32.
14. Jeremias, *Parables of Jesus*, 21, 145.
15. Wilder, *Jesus' Parables*, 112–19.

Jesus' well-crafted Parables of the Prodigal Son and the Good Samaritan best give voice to holiness as political compassion. They also provide a fuller picture of his heralded Good Government, while also exposing the shortcomings of a callous Conservatism. The story about a wayward son specifically highlights the nurturing-Parent/God and typifies Israel's exile and return: its rejection of God and the subsistence ethic, its futile embracing of the imperial ethic, its humble repentance, and its final restoration. The parable speaks to the never-ending value conflict between Progressive spiritual politics and the Conservatism of some smug politicians.

A group of Temple-state functionaries, flushed in their virtue and with scowls of scorn, grumble because Jesus "welcomes sinners and eats with them" (Luke 15:1–2). Given the sociology and economics of table fellowship, Jesus' dining with and befriending such people imply more than simply hanging out with them. He effectively honors them, forgives them, and joyfully restores them from social banishment. Most importantly, he models the subsistence ethic by sharing food with the victims of Rome's agricultural policies. In response to his opponents' accusation, Jesus weaves a story to shatter their tightly held boundary-marking, compassion-inhibiting notions:

> A man had two sons. The younger one shocked his father by demanding, "Father, give me my share of the inheritance."
> So a piece of Land was sold off, and the next day the younger son left for a distant country. There he further shamed his family by bad behavior and he soon squandered his money in wasteful living.
> A severe famine spread throughout the Land. When he began to starve, he hired himself out as a day laborer, tending pigs. He tried to snatch some of the pig's food, but was denied.
> That was his wake-up call. He admitted to himself that he'd be better off as a simple hired-hand on his father's farm, than die of hunger. So he resolved to go back, though humiliated, and acknowledge his sin against God and his father.
> He packed up and started the long journey home.
> The father saw his son coming down the road and was filled with compassion. Without hesitation, he ran out and hugged and kissed his filth-ridden son. The son immediately fell to his knees in contrition. "I have shamed both God and you; I no longer deserve to be called . . . your son."
> But the father shouted for his servant, "Come quick! Bring the finest robes for him and place the ring with the family crest on his finger. And go butcher the fattest calf. Let's feast and may

the celebration begin! For this, my son—whom I'd given up for dead—is alive! He was lost—and now he is found."

Meanwhile, the elder son was toiling in the fields. After work he heard the celebration and asked one of the house servants about it who told him, "Your brother has returned safe and sound, so your father has butchered the best calf." The elder son flew into a rage and refused to join the merriment.

His father came out and begged his elder son to show some sign of thanksgiving.

But the elder son disrespectfully grumbled in anger, "See how many years I have faithfully slaved away working for you. I've never disobeyed; I followed your every order. Yet where's my celebration? Not even a young goat to share with my friends. Yet, the minute this morally bankrupt, dirtied son of yours comes crawling back, you slaughter our prize calf for a grand feast. Where's the fairness?"

The father replied, "My son, you have always been with me and everything I have is yours. On this day, we are banqueting for your brother who was dead to us and now is alive; he was lost and now is found" (Luke 15:11–32; paraphrase mine).

By shamefully demanding to sell his small share of the property while his father still lives, the younger of two sons embraces the prevailing aggrandizing imperial ethic where Land is but a commodity, thereby undermining the village subsistence ethic. By leaving his homeland for a far off country (an added insult), the son (Israel) further dishonors himself, his father, and the village by "squandering the property" in wasteful living. Having flaunted the peasant values, he is left destitute. When a devastating famine swoops down, he ends up in the most desperate and degrading circumstances. He resorts to attending pigs, animals taboo to eat and even to the touch, further violating the created order according to Jewish custom. His wake-up call, or the spiritual turning point, comes when he is denied even to subsist on pig slop. He then remembers the Land ethic he abandoned and his father's steadfast love—his, Israel's, and our created destiny. In humbly repenting (humility being the prerequisite of good governing), he renounces the Conservative principles that led him to defile the Land and to revel in elite-like arrogance and wastefulness. His return home to be reborn into the family and its subsistence ideals sets in motion stunning events that run counter to the expectations of stern Conservative values.

The father's reaction to the son's homecoming leaves Jesus' rivals dumbfounded, even repulsed, especially if Jesus intends the father to represent God (the true Creator/Patron). First, he "sees" his son coming down the road and is "filled with compassion," which connects the parable to the Exodus story line of an empathic God who sees suffering and brings political deliverance (Exod 3:7). Second, think of the implications when the father ran to, hugged, and kissed his son, all acts of parental nurturing (as well as protection from angry villagers). Remember, the son ended up tending pigs, which rendered him, and anyone touching him, unclean. Can you imagine how Jesus has scandalized his Conservative listeners? Hugging and kissing the contaminated son (the children of Israel labeled "sinners") marks God—unthinkably—as an "unclean" God. At this point, the dramatic ecospiritual politics of God-like parenting unfolds as purely compassion-filled—the criterion of genuine holiness and good governing.[16] Furthermore, the father, without hesitation and without blaming, acknowledges the son's humble confession of violating the Land morality. He grants him the symbols of honor and power within the family or the Good Governing: the royal robe, the royal ring, the royal sandals, and the royal feast. Here ecospiritual politics with its nurturing-parent morality leaps out. Good governing means *restoration of the compassionate subsistence/sustainability ethic.*

By now Jesus' rivals must have turned livid. The returning unclean sinner usurps political power and authority from the obedient son. How will Conservatism respond? By crafting the remainder of the parable through the eyes of the elder son, Jesus again exposes the imperial morality. The joyless son's grievance mirrors the grumbling cultural warriors who occasioned the parable. He has slaved away for the Temple-state, strictly obeying its commands, always a faithful, clean (and thus, superior), son/supporter. Yet the father (God) rewards the prodigal son with the Land's produce and seats him at the honored head table of the Kingdom feast. However, the obedient son, too, has violated the subsistence ethic—the duty to be his brother's keeper. Like Cain of old, he resents his brother. He rants in shame that he has never received even a young goat—much less the grain-fed calf. The elder son has also been impacted by imperial hierarchy and the treatment of Land as commodity. Yet, the father—though rejecting his elder son's imperial values—reaches out with compassion to him as well.

From Conservatism's ethical/legal perspective, the father's action seems blatantly unfair. However, the elder son's narrow view of justice does not allow him to see with the soft look of compassion, and thus, he refuses to join in Israel's Good Government celebration, despite the pleading of his father (God). Unmoved, his morality finds little home in nurturing. Unlike his brother, he would not change heart and repent. Unlike his father,

---

16. See Jeremias, *Parables of Jesus*, 128 where he proposes the apt title: "The Parable of the Father's Love."

his heart is granite hard. He, too, is exiled from the presence of God and his spiritual destiny. The father's compassion has stretched morality into a much broader panorama, celebrating the subsistence ethic and the special consideration given those seduced and victimized by Conservatism. In the end, the Progressive ecospiritual politics of compassion triumphs over the flawed Conservative spiritual politics of convention, exploitation, and narrow justice. Those deemed "dead," lost, unclean, dishonored, alienated, and landless will, through embracing the Good Government, be the Land's true heirs, leaving an offended and sulky Conservatism to grumble.

The two prodigal sons speak volumes regarding our global crisis. By disdaining subsistence values, by cutting his kinship to the Land, by wasting resources, and by disregarding Creation's order, the younger son confronts each of us and our nation as waste-makers, as polluters, and as lacking kinship to and compassion for our Earth. Fortunately, near the point of no return he finally awoke and humbly returned to the Land ethic. Unfortunately, we too are approaching those ecological tipping points, but it remains an open question whether we will come to our senses in time. The elder son confronts each of us and our nation with the prospect that we refuse to repent and find kinship with our brothers and sisters facing extreme poverty. Could we, like the elder son, become so entrenched that even our heavenly Parent is powerless to move us and that our plagues will persist far into the future? Or will we, like the younger brother, heed the wake-up call?

PROGRESSIVE POLITICS AND THE COMPASSIONATE SAMARITAN

Political compassion is pushed further in Jesus' Parable of the Good Samaritan—another story he tells to help people grasp a fresh spiritual paradigm of national policy, while de-mystifying the political ethic of his adversaries. The Temple-state lawyer's question about what he must do to inherit eternal life intends to shame Jesus (Luke 10:25–29). "Eternal life" speaks to the eco-origins of politics and holiness and is an alternative way of referencing the enduring, life-giving values of the Good Governing. The point of the lawyer's question, however, rests in the word "do." Jesus' own accusatory questions—"Haven't your read the law?" and "What have you learned there?"—neutralize the honor challenge. The lawyer's response combines two separate texts from the Constitution, "You shall love the Lord your God with every part of your being; and you shall love your neighbor as yourself." They summarize the heart of Judaism and the subsistence claim of mutual rights and assistance.

The other Gospels call these obligations to love "the greatest" commandments (Mark 12:31; Matt 22:38). In Mark's account, Jesus prefaces them with the *Shema*: "Hear, O Israel: the Lord our God, the Lord is one." The address to Israel confirms that these statutes originally served as *political* edicts—as *national* standards. They acknowledge the reign of compassion in Israel's legal/civic life and demand heart-and-soul dedication to it. Luke combines the love-God/ love-neighbor commands into *one* command with two parts. Since, as we have shown, God implies good, every other New Testament writer sees the redundancy and thus drops the love-God stipulation altogether, leaving only: "love you neighbor as yourself" (Rom 13:9; Gal 5:14; Jas 2:8).[17] For the biblical faith and for Jesus' ecospiritual politics, devotion to the Creator God (God's in-principled will) and true holiness assume acting with civic, life-sustaining compassion toward the neighbor/citizen/Land—a bow to the mission of serving the common good.

Since quotations from the Hebrew Bible were always linked to their broader literary context, the Levitical command to love one's neighbor included: honoring parents, laws against stealing and defrauding, laws regarding just judgments in court, laws dealing with immigrants, and especially the gleaning laws—all statutes that created and sustained the biocommunity (Lev 19:9–37). Thus, the love directive especially resonates with Jesus' own prophetic purposes since Rome and its puppets with their imposed Land schemes systematically stole and defrauded, leaving subsistence rights in shambles as he will illustrate in his story about a good Samaritan.

Jesus likes the legal expert's answer, but by affirming its correctness, he asserts his authority over him much like a teacher commending a student's good answer. To save face, the lawyer presses the confrontation by insisting that Jesus define "neighbor." Compelled by the political realities of the lawyer's challenge and the prominence of this great commandment to love, Jesus thinks of a story:

> A man was traveling from Jerusalem to Jericho when he was set upon by bandits. They robbed him, beat him, and went away leaving him unconscious in a ditch.
>
> By good fortune, a priest came by and saw him, paused, but kept his distance and went away.
>
> The same thing happened when another state bureaucrat caught sight of him. He went around him and went on this way.
>
> Now a Samaritan came near him. And when he saw the victim, he was moved with compassion. He knelt by him, poured some oil on his wounds, and bandaged them.

17. For a discussion of conflating the two love commands into one see Furnish, *Love Command*, 37.

Holiness as Political Compassion 83

When he finished, he lifted him on his donkey, brought him to an inn, and nursed his wounds.

The next morning he gave the innkeeper some money and said, "Care for him until I return. I'll reimburse you any added expense."

Jesus again cross-examined the legal expert: "So, which of the three do you think was a neighbor to the victim of the bandits?"

"The one who demonstrated compassion," he admitted.

Jesus ended with, "You go and do the same" (Luke 10:25–37; paraphrase mine).

This story about a half-bred, apostate Samaritan who helps an enemy, illustrates what the neighborly Good Governing's subsistence ethic will "do" for those who suffer. When two Temple-state bureaucrats happen upon a man bloodied and unconscious, victimized by bandits (banditry being a result of Rome's Land seizures) they face a dilemma. In response to the lawyer's original question, what will these officials "do?" Their flawed spirituality compels them to keep their distance and pass by. Possibly the priest does not wish to stain his garments with blood shed by violence. Or maybe both are just exercising wisdom's caution. The parable itself provides no excuse because *all evasions* to basic subsistence rights are bogus. By portraying these functionaries as not only refusing to become involved, but also as actively turning their backs on a brother in need, Jesus exposes their Conservative principles as cold and flawed. He places these officials in the same moral bag as the robbers who beat the man and "went away," leaving him unconscious in the ditch. We later learn that Jesus, in fact, considers the Roman Temple-state a den of robbers (Luke 19:46). Thus, already within the parable, Jesus delivers a subtle critique of the Temple leadership's faulty policies and its aloof spirituality.

However, an ennobling spiritual politics is about to appear in the story. Unlike the officials who cast a blind eye and represent indifference, the enemy Samaritan "sees" the beaten man, stirring his innate compassion. This unexpected twist—the apostate Samaritan fulfilling the story line of the compassionate Creator God who sees suffering—will disgust the lawyer. For Jesus, however, the Samaritan epitomizes the ecospiritual politics of openhearted/open-handed subsistence ideals as evidenced by the action verbs that overtake the story, leading to his main and final point: "Go and do the same." He *comes* near the suffering man, *kneels* by him, *pours* wine and oil on his wounds, *bandages* him, *lifts* him on his donkey, *brings* him to an inn, *nurses* him, *gives* the innkeeper money, and *promises* to reimburse him later for any added expense. The Samaritan acts like a brother or sister's keeper, reflecting the new family (nation as family) created by the Basileia. Jesus' message is clear: the coming Good Government is empathic and provides for its hapless citizens until their subsistence needs are *fully met*. For Jesus, the love command summarizes his renewal laws and policies for Galilean households, villages, and the nation.

In this and the Prodigal Son parables, Jesus' brand of Judaism teaches that government should treat its citizens in ways a loving parent or brother/sister would respond to a family member in distress, meeting sustainability needs. The Samaritan's actions never smack of showy public charity or almsgiving. His simple selflessness represents everyday good governance—a true political fulfillment of the love stipulations of the Torah for the nation. In the parable, good governing meets the short and long-range needs of one victimized by Conservatism. It models good welfare policy for all governance henceforth. For Jesus, neighborly compassion is definitive public policy—a mark of national holiness. In fact, it signals the holiest of holies. Also note the partnership with an NGO (non-governmental organization), in the care of the victim. Furthermore, by introducing the detested Samaritan into the parable, Jesus universalizes the Progressive ecospiritual politics of love by extending it to the borderless family of all.

From another perspective, the Samaritan story holds the promise of ending the vicious cycle of violence—violence instigated by the legalized "robbery" of the Roman taxation and Land-grabbing system that forced villagers into social banditry. Now, because of political compassion, the victim in the parable need not himself be reduced to robbing others because of his misfortune. The subsistence ethic is restored. The beaten down and abandoned one now embraces a renewed hope and a recovered dignity. The lesson here is that although Progressives prod governments to compassionately respond to immediate needs, they also push them to alleviate the root causes of catastrophic social conditions like those specific to this parable: structurally induced poverty, the exploitation of the Land, and lack of universal health care. Jesus' parable depicts third-stage Liberal morality at its very best, both in understanding the causes of human miseries and in providing contextual solutions to overcome them.

In his famous "Judgment of the Nations" speech, Jesus reinforces his plea that the compassionate path to sustainability must occupy national policy (Matt 25:31–45 with Ezek 34:17–22). The good (sheep) nations will be separated from the bad (goat) nations based solely on their political actions—a truth often missed by Christians who apply this powerful passage in only personal ways. The good nations, like the compassionate Samaritan-father-God, see the pains, hear the cries. Thus, they feed the hungry, give drink to the thirsty, welcome the strangers, clothe the naked, care for the sick, and treat prisoners with dignity. These nations fully embrace Liberal compassion that proves essential to their political and ecospiritual purpose—meeting the subsistence/sustainability needs as "members of my family." In such service to its citizens, these governments serve the Child of Humanity. However, nations governed by the neglectful, hard-hearted Conservative ethic that has left so many woe-worn will come to a shameful fate. In this speech, Jesus leaves no doubt as to what separates good governing from flawed governing—Liberal policies from Conservative ones.

Today, Jesus' list of programs in his speech translates directly into governments guaranteeing: adequate food, clean water, hospitality for immigrants, clothing and housing subsidies, universal health care, and prison reform. When we support such programs by expressing our views and casting our votes, we do so as unto Jesus and he is magnified. Governance that adds to the hardships of those going through difficult times (like cutting entitlements) belittles Jesus' platform and ought to be a spiritual and political motivation for all Christians to stand strong in opposition.

Jesus did not just tell stories about compassion, but, like the Good Samaritan, acted compassionately toward the marginalized and landless, marking him an awesome example of holiness (Matt 14:14, 20:34; Luke 7:13). One time, he "saw the crowds, and he felt compassion for them, because they seemed harassed and helpless, like sheep without a shepherd" (Matt 9:36). What would be the political fallout of this reference to shepherding? While good leaders will be the "shepherd of my people Israel" (2 Sam 5:2), prophets like Ezekiel bluntly impugn sinister rulers who shepherd "with force and harshness." They do not "strengthen the weak," "heal the sick," or "bind up the injured; they just feed themselves." Ezekiel further berates the rulers for ruining the environment by trampling down the fields and fouling the clear waters (Ezek 34: 1–21; Zech 11:15–17). Defying the subsistence/keeper ethic, the watchdogs have become the ravaging, devouring wolves. The hapless people are devoid of a divinely inspired empathic leader—a caring shepherd—who "seeks out," "rescues," and "feeds" the flock on the mountains of Israel (Ezek 34:22–31). Jesus' mention of shepherd-less sheep subtly indicts defective Conservative leadership that exploits the peasants.

The form of shepherding Jesus brings will be uplifting. The crowd follows him to a "deserted place" (symbolizing exile) where they become desperate for food. And why is food scarce? Ask the ruling authorities whose Land policies have left the people "harassed and helpless." Jesus, like God, sees the needs of the crowd and is moved to cure the people's *malakia* (diseases), a term that implies malaise—a demoralization resulting in powerless passivity, much like bewildered, lost sheep (Matt 9:35). Unable to distribute back the Land, his political love moves him to quell their hunger by distributing its *fruit* and applying the subsistence notion that people share their scarce resources in a programmed way (Mark 6:39–44). Jesus embodies the leadership of Transformational politics—self-giving, practical, and effective. If we Americans hope to regain our moral bearings, we must vote for this kind of caring leadership. But why is this type of governing in little evidence today?

Rollo May, the noted psychologist, observes that the classic psychological disease of our age is apathy, the inability to feel compassion.[18] Sociologist Lewis Yablonsky broadens the scope of this "disease" to include society as a whole. He labels the lack of compassion "robopathology"—the social malady of a robot-like lack of empathy.[19] That this illness resides in so-called "good people"— average everyday Americans—makes it ever so dangerous, even more so than psychopathology or sociopathology. Tragically, this disease, when politicized, contributes to the world's great "macro-problems:" racism, sexism, war, poverty, extreme inequalities, hunger, environmental degradation, and corporate marauding.

In Jesus' time, this compassion dulling pathology allowed already overfed elites to steal the Land and its bounty while most starved. As Yablonsky observes, in our time it permitted Lt. William Calley, the "all-American boy," to shoot babies in a ditch in Vietnam and, by his own admission, not feel even a twinge of conscience. Robopathology means knowing and not caring about millions of children dying worldwide every year due to preventable causes. It feels superior to the many undocumented immigrants that fill our service industries. It callously looks away while billions of tons of pollutants spew into the air and the oceans fill with refuse. It wages costly and deadly "preventive" wars and then cares little about the thousands (millions) of civilian casualties and the massive ecodestruction. It is spiritual blindness, spiritual death. Given the gravity of these and other mega-issues for our future, this moral affliction must be healed. A new ecospirituality of compassion must come to life within each of us and in America's political leadership.

Compassion, the heart of Judaism and a moral/spiritual equivalent to contemporary Progressive empathy, continually faces exile. As the keystone of his platform, Jesus urged compassion's return forcing him into political and cultural battles with burning dedication, deep insight, and grand originality. Jesus engaged in the same residual struggles that present-day Progressives still wage. The victims may have different faces—the look of outsiders,

18. May, *Love and Will*, 27–33.
19. Yablonsky, *Robopaths*, 6–56.

the feature of dark skins, the uncertainty of empty pocketbooks, or the anguish of a targeted creature—but they stumble over the same imperialist obstacles: hardness of heart, self-aggrandizement, blame, institutionalized inequality, and neglect—all waxing when compassion wanes. Compassion compels us all, through political action, to eliminate the causes of human and ecological woe and deliver the biocommunity from harsh and crushing blows. It does so by forging an alliance with the principle of justice and its special consideration for those victimized.

6

Welcoming and Affirmative Action

The exalted will be humbled, and the humbled will be exalted.

—Jesus

From the beginning when property was a prerequisite to vote, Land policy in America has been used against minorities. For instance, my wife and I once resided in an affluent suburb of Philadelphia called the Main Line. A clause in our property deed read:

> That the said premises or any part thereof shall not at any time hereafter, forever, be granted, conveyed, mortgaged or leased to or used or occupied as tenants by, any persons who are not of the Caucasian Race, with the exception, however, of domestic servants.

We considered this an anomaly and felt ashamed that our deed conveyed this blatant racism. When we moved across the country to Santa Barbara, California in 1984, we thought we had left behind such travesties. However, we nearly purchased a view property in which the deed stipulated:

> Article 3.08. The property described . . . shall always be owned and occupied by the Caucasian race. No person of African descent shall be allowed to purchase, own, lease, use or occupy said real property or any part thereof, but this shall not be construed

as prohibiting persons of African descent from residing upon said property while in the employ as servants . . . .

We were dumbfounded. Was this just a coincidence . . . or a pattern?

Even though the courts struck down these restrictive covenants in the late 1940s, the historical results have devastated African-Americans. They virtually imprisoned many within the inner cities by denying them upward mobility through equity in suburban home ownership—a proven engine of wealth for the white middle class. These contracts also tore apart the assorted fabric of human dignity and community. Today's Liberals still confront a quandary arising from the darkest hours of our history: how might we rectify disadvantages that have resulted from past discrimination and bring its victims into the mainstream? Even with the election of an African-American president, social and political inclusion remains a fundamental ecospiritual and moral quest for our nation.

One of the Bible's profound ecospiritual legacies and the heart of the Judeo-Christian political ethic is hospitality to strangers, which includes treating them with dignity (Exod 22:21, 23:29).[1] When compassion attends to the needs of society's "strange ones," those who are different, it relentlessly pursues respect in the form of justice—to right any wrongs against them through law.[2] In turn, justice, in its most spiritual form, sees and hears those society shuts out and unfolds compassion's generosity with its rectifying impulse.[3] Compassion wedded to justice generates policies that are neither punitive nor puny.

Justice, a mostly political term, simply means giving to people what they deserve. Its usual components include (1) *retributive* justice—giving a deserving punishment because of wrong doing; (2) *distributive* justice—giving valued goods (material or non-material) owed; and (3) *compensatory* justice—restoring something unfairly taken away. The most important ingredient of justice is its impartiality—its *equality or fairness*. However, the meaning of justice is highly debated. Take distributive justice. How do we determine deserving people? Is it those belonging to the aristocracy (the predominant view in Jesus' day), or those possessing special merits or abilities, or those who are productive? Or should it be in response to those in need?[4]

---

1. Also Deut 10:18–19; Lev 19:33–34; Num 15:15–16; Gen 19:1–13 with Judg 19:1–30; Rom 12:13; Heb 13:2.
2. Arendt, *On Revolution*, 66.
3. Nussbaum, *Upheavals of Thought*, 388.
4. See Rescher, "Canons of Distributive Justice," 33–40.

Likewise, the extent of equality's reach is hotly contested. Is equality before the law limited to a few basic civil rights or is it open-ended and ever expanding? What about equality in the economic sense? Does it stop at equal opportunity or should it also encompass equality of outcomes (e. g., the right not to be poor in a society of plenty)? An even more divisive question is: What is the relevance of compensatory or restorative justice? How far back should justice go to rectify past social and economic injuries, and should compensation be offered only to individuals actually harmed or may it include whole (minority) groups? What about restorative ecojustice or the claims of a harmed environment?

The first principle of the Earth Charter affirms the inherent worth and dignity of people and Planet. Progressives consider it an affront to dignity when arrangements permit overabundance for a few while the many wallow in want, or when people and Planet are relegated to a lower status—fostering attitudes of superiority and neglect. To remedy lingering prejudices and artificial disparities, Transformational politics insists on special treatment for the downtrodden and exploited, naming it *affirmative action*. Aristotle spoke of rectifying justice when a judge acts to "equalize" the losses of an injured party by taking away the unfair gains of the wrongdoer.[5] Christianity saw Jesus making amends for our awful deeds and called it "atonement." In the broadest sense, affirmative action applies this idea to *groups* of people and Earth unjustly treated, guaranteeing a fair redress.

Conservatives find affirmative action nauseous and label it "reverse discrimination."[6] They show little interest in rectifying past injustices, arguing that "history must be accepted for what it is, history."[7] When necessary, compensation must come case by case, to individuals only. In addition, the gaze of justice stops at equality before the law, or in the eyes of God, or in proven merit, or in production (measured in dollars), or equality of opportunity. In their terms, social and economic differences and its hierarchies, which affirmative action attempts to rectify, are vital to individual freedom and initiative.[8]

In America, affirmative action refers to the preferential treatment of stigmatized minorities in job hiring and education (as the means to procure good jobs). It assumes that in the competition for social benefits some groups (mainly white males) have gained unfair and self-perpetuating advantages over others, grounded in morally irrelevant characteristics (like

---

5. Aristotle, *Nicomachean Ethics* 5.2.1131b4–6.
6. Bork, *Slouching toward Gomorrah*, 231.
7. Ibid., 238.
8. Nisbet, *Conservatism*, 51.

skin color or gender). Because of the historical scars of racist, sexist, and impoverishing structures, affirmative action helps restore equality because it counts skin color, gender, and economic standing as measureable compensation. Because of serious environmental injuries, Earth is also subject to affirmative action or restorative justice, giving rise to the principles of renewal and polluters pay for the cleanup. The higher spiritual purpose of affirmative action, however, rests not only in ending discrimination, vast economic differences, and ecological havoc, but in attempts to create the bonds of civic friendship—a beloved community that welcomes and cherishes the whole of humankind and other kinds as family. For Progressives, hospitality means conferring the respect and dignity that equalizing and restoring policies bring—an ambitious goal, but one that drove the ecospiritual politics of Jesus.

AFFIRMATIVE ACTION AND JESUS

Jesus inherited a lofty affirmative action tradition from which to draw his politics of equality and inclusion. The Law of Moses and its Deuteronomic revision with their gleaning laws and debt-forgiveness Land policies display a neighborly love and ecojustice that provides special treatment for victims of calamity or circumstance. Even the "wild animals" are given gleaning rights, a gesture of neighbor love to all creatures. On the fiftieth year, called "Jubilee," the law mandates restoring ancestral Lands lost through misfortune, along with a proclamation of liberty and Land rest. "Jubilee justice" means "there will . . . be no one in need among you . . . ." a nod to the subsistence ethic (Exod 23:10–12; Deut 15:1–4; Lev. 25:8–17).[9] The idea of showing special political and economic favor toward those falling through the safety net is most fully expressed in Deuteronomy 15. The community must never become "hard-hearted" or "tightfisted," but "you should rather open your hand, willingly lending enough to meet the need, whatever it may be." Because the needy always exist (especially in a high and mighty world), the nation is commanded to give "liberally" and be "ungrudging" in its generosity. Restorative justice stands as a centerpiece of Israel's Constitution. It undergirds Jesus' first/last and exalted/humbled reversal principles—designed as equalizing and compensating mechanisms.

Over time, however, the rulers ignored these affirmative action precepts (or "debt codes") and squeezed out the poor by foreclosing on their Land and houses (Isa 5:8). With egalitarian fervor, the prophets bristle in condemning such abuses. Isaiah forcefully expresses it in a text that later

---

9. Also Lev 19 9–10, 23:22; Deut 24:19–21; Exod 22:25–27.

defined Jesus' political mission: "He has sent me to bring good news to the poor . . . ." (Isa 61:1–2; Luke 4:18–19). What is this good news? Along with other political outcomes, he includes the proclamation of *Jubilee's restorative Land justice*. Around 445 BC (and under similar conditions as America's mortgage crisis in 2008), Nehemiah would appeal to Jubilee's justice when a severe famine prevented the people from paying the king's tax (Neh 5:1–13). Opportunistic nobles and officials offered loans at ruinous rates, causing farmers to languish in a crimping economic vice. They lost their fields, orchards, and homes—everything. Starvation reigned. An indignant Nehemiah demands that the nobles "restore to them, this very day, their fields . . . , their houses, and the interest on money . . . that you are exacting from them." During his Galilean campaigns, this same Jubilee restoration of Lands serves as an important plank in Jesus' call for good governance, reflecting the forgiveness of debts petition within his famous prayer.

At the very beginning of his Gospel, Luke sets the stage for Jesus' affirmative action thrust with Mary's song of praise known as the "Magnificat." (Luke 1:46–55). The hymn describes social inversion by contrasting the normal subservient status of women with God's exaltation of Mary so that "all generations will called me blessed" or honored (the mostly male value). She receives the same special treatment of restorative justice that "brings down" the proud and powerful from their thrones and "lifts up" the lowly, presumably to take their rightful place. This political about-face reflects the peasant dreams of serious regime change, social reversal, . . . and value transformation. The Magnificat also sings of subsistence justice as God "has filled the hungry with good things (assuming Land reform), and sent the rich away empty."[10] This reversal principle that Luke introduces early will govern his story throughout. Mark also begins his book with the same notion by quoting from Isaiah that the "gospel" of Jesus the Messiah shall make level the pathway. Mark's readers would catch Isaiah's egalitarian imagery of the valleys lifted up and the mountains made low and the uneven ground leveled and the rough places made into a plain (Mark 1:1–3; Isa 40:3–4).

Jesus summarizes these celebrations of affirmative action in the two sayings: "all who exalt themselves will be humbled, but all who humble themselves will be exalted" and "the first will be last, and the last will be first" (Luke 14:11; Mark 10:31).[11] Mirroring peasant dreams, these visions reveal the great social and economic reversals Jesus hopes to inaugurate. They are not reversals in an absolute sense, but hyperboles for affirming equality and undoing a Conservative ethic of status and concentrated

---

10. See Hannah's song, 1 Sam 2:1–10 for the same reversal motif.
11. Also Luke 13:30, 18:14; Matt 19:30, 20:16, 23:12.

wealth. Jesus shows us that because affirmative action enhances the morality of inclusion, it stands as a profound ecospiritual truth. Those opposing it do so from a faulty spirituality. We shall explore Jesus' ecospiritual politics of *social* reversal in the remainder of this chapter and of his *economic* affirmative action in the following two chapters. Both are grounded in reversing onerous Land policy.

BRINGING DIGNITY TO THE LOWLY

The cultural warriors seized upon the *honor/shame* dynamic to bolster their contemptuous spiritual politics. Communities existed as "honor" societies, like in many Middle Eastern countries today where possessing honor means worth and power. Losing it brings disgrace and social disaster and makes life bitter.[12] Nearly all social interactions became contests for honor, with adult males fighting constant battles to boost or defend it.[13] Because the honor culture feeds social, political, and ecological arrogance, Jesus introduces his humble/exalted principle to turn that culture upside down by giving *special consideration* for the lowly (Luke 7:28). He intends to restore the dignity of divine likeness within all God's children, irrespective of lineage, wealth, health, gender, social rank, or any other artificial barrier. And with dignity come legal rights.

Perhaps Jesus nourishes a deep sensitivity for the outcasts because he suffered shame from Nazareth villagers who considered him an "illegitimate" child and labeled him a *mamzer*—a crushing, ostracizing blow for a young boy.[14] This deep personal hurt may have been lurking behind his speech about prophets receiving no honor in their own hometown (Luke 4:24). Regardless, Jesus' ecospiritual politics demands equality *on principle*; so much so that even his rivals say of him, "you are sincere, and show deference to no one; for you do not regard people with partiality, but teach the way of God in accordance with truth" (Mark 12:14).

Jesus graphically portrays his new vision of a rebirthed welcoming nation in a series of short "Good Government is like" stories sprinkled with Nature images, beginning with the Mustard Seed Parable (Matt 13:31–32). When seen through peasant eyes, this parable unfolds a political slant, in contrast to the common church growth interpretation today. The Galilean farmer, like many farmers now, faced noxious plants. One of the hardiest was the wild mustard—a fact that sheds new light on the parable. The

12. Pelevnik, "Honor/Shame," 107.
13. Malina, *New Testament World*, 37, 40.
14. Chilton, *Rabbi Jesus*, 12–16.

mustard seed symbolizes the socially small "obnoxious" people, whom God "sows" to eventually overshadow the seemingly good plants (the Roman collaborators and supporters) in the coming Good Government. It echoes Ezekiel's reversal principle that God will "bring low the high tree, and make high the low tree" (Ezek 17:22–24).[15]

Normally a farmer would never hunt for wild mustard seeds to plant in the garden—unless, as in the parable, the farmer represents God in search of the unwelcomed. The small and poor receive the Good Government's protection, a mighty ecospiritual and political truth, but a swipe at the high-powered exploiters. The image also conveys a subtle ecological message: God welcomes "weeds" and lowly creatures most at risk through human profiteering like the spotted owl. The Parable of the Yeast teaches the same affirmative action truth (Matt 13:33). The yeast represents the "contaminated" people who will gradually permeate the Good Governing. The "pure" dough of the imperial ethic of separation, marginalization, Earth exploitation, and class consciousness will be overcome by an equalizing justice that restores the cast-offs as essential ingredients for a viable community.

Jesus' symbolics of *eating* also reinforces his affirmative action slant. At a dinner party hosted by a leader of the Pharisees, Jesus speaks about humility, the anti-hierarchical virtue (Luke 14:7–14). He warns that when invited to a banquet you should not hurry to sit at the "place of honor" (like politicians and "rich neighbors"), since the host might take action and "disgrace" you by giving your place to another. Jesus then cites his famous humble/exalted principle of restorative justice. In defiance of the imperial ethic, honor or dignity comes to all, not just a few. Furthermore, just as God (the Basileia host) honors the lowly and shames the high-and-mighty, so also "anyone who would eat bread in the kingdom of God" must welcome the "poor, the crippled, the lame, and the blind"—a nod to subsistence ideals. One of the guests at the dinner gets the point and says to Jesus, "Honored is anyone who dines in the coming Good Government." To reinforce this ecospiritual truth, Jesus ends his talk with a parable:

> Once a man planned a huge banquet and invited his friends. When the day came, and the food was being set, he sent out his servants to announce, "Come on over, it's time to feast."
> But every one of them backed out with all kinds of excuses.
> The first said, "I have just bought some Land and I must check it out."
> Another claimed, "I bought five teams of oxen and I must test them. I need to be excused."

---

15. See Crossan, *Historical Jesus*, 278.

Yet another said, "I was just married and I can't come."

So the servant went back and told his master about it.

The disgraced host was very upset and instructed his servant, "Quickly, run out in the streets and back alleys of the town and gather the destitute, the disabled, the blind, and all those who are shunned and bring them here."

The servant reported, "I have obeyed your order, yet some seats are left."

The master commanded, "Go out to the main roads and behind the bushes and persuade the landless to come. I want my house full. Let me say, not one of those I invited in the first place shall get even a scrap of my dinner" (Luke 14:15–24; paraphrase mine).

In Jesus' day, an extravagant banquet signified joy in anticipation of the Messianic Kingdom. Yet, it also stiffened the social rankings of the invitees. Because of the current hierarchy, the Temple-state leaders and their retainers would sit in the most honored seats (next to the Messiah), while less important folks would sit near the back of the room. But many were deliberately excluded from the banquet hall altogether: the blind, the lame, the poor, the sinners, and other "unclean" groups. In the parable, however, an unexpected reversal occurs.

The excuses of the host's friends (his equals) not to attend the feast depict the Conservative value of unending acquisition: checking out a piece of property, testing some new oxen, and throwing a luxurious wedding—all actions of the upwardly mobile. Having been rebuffed, the undeterred host searches out and welcomes landless undesirables to sit at his table, illustrating affirmative action in full operation. Here, disenfranchised people are vigorously pursued and included for special honor and respect—to eat as equals in the coming Government. Then the host aims his harshest words toward the original invited guests, denying them even one scrap of food. He intends to starve the Conservative notions of status and unquenchable gain. For the socially marginalized, the parable offers hope: eventually Progressive politics will prevail and all human beings will be invited to the table of dignity, spread generously with liberty, inclusion, and Land justice.

Jesus' Progressive affirmative action especially benefits *women and children*. The persisting constraints placed on the freedom and equality of these two vulnerable groups provides a sound moral link between the first and the twenty-first centuries. Throughout history, fathers have been regarded as divine kings, confirming the saying that "a man's home is his castle."[16] Women and children, like Earth, were treated as property—to

---

16. Becker, *Escape from Evil*, 67.

be exploited. Their status paralleled that of a servant. This imbalance has changed somewhat in democratic societies, although gender bias still persists, often reinforced by outworn Christian teachings.

Most interpreters of the Bible have been male and their renderings (consciously or not) have skewed the Bible to perpetuate male domination. Women and children have suffered under the male "chain of command" (ironically, an apt metaphor that speaks to the bondage it creates). Biblical texts, however, should be interpreted in light of the egalitarian matrix that shaped the Jewish ethic. As a matter of historical fact, women played a decisive role in the life and leadership of Israel, especially in the political movement of Jesus and the early church (Luke 8:1–4).[17] The Jewish faith embraced a variety of beliefs with contrasting and bitterly contested positions on many subjects, including the status of women. Jesus is part of a reform movement *within* Judaism against its more Conservative elements. The dignity that Jesus accords women emerged *because* of his Israelite heritage, not despite it.

The equality of women, like the equality of other out-grouped people, finds its most poignant expression in Jesus' disdain for the Conservative politics of food. Jesus eats on par with "sinners," including prostitutes (Mark 2:15–16; Luke 5:30). These women did not choose to walk the streets, but were victims of collapsing Galilean life due to Rome's Land schemes.[18] Understanding this, Jesus shocks the cultural warriors by declaring that prostitutes are entering the Kingdom of God ahead of them (Matt 21:31). He decrees a great political reversal of shamed women's misfortunes by providing redress against the well-positioned, "holier," male victimizers.

Jesus' ecospiritual politics of affirmative action stands out most movingly when a woman (labeled a "sinner" by Luke) anoints him with expensive perfume (Mark 14:3–9; Luke 7:36–50). Jesus has already ruptured the strict social hierarchy by dining at the house of someone with a taboo skin disease. Suddenly, this woman, who would never have been invited to eat with men, crashes the party. She rushes through a gauntlet of male frowns and attends Jesus' needs by washing his feet and pouring ointment over his head (a common practice in order to smell good before eating). Missing the point of her action, the men spew outrage because she violates their all-male space, purity rules, and prerogatives. Under pretext, they accuse her of wasting valuable oil that could have been sold to help the poor. Poised to beat

---

17. Also Luke 10:38–42 for women's role reversal. See Fiorenza, *In Memory of Her*, 218–36.

18. Ibid., 128.

her, Jesus sees through their cover-up for chauvinism and counters their honor protocols with a vehement: "Leave her alone."

He reveals that this shamed woman anoints his body for death, mirroring the traditional belief that bodies need cleansing to enter the afterworld. Ordinarily, strangers do not anoint a dead body—except for the destitute who depend on a stranger's generosity, which Jesus (as the poor one) graciously welcomes. But more importantly, since anointing also signaled political leadership, he announces that her good work represents a *political* anointing of his "kingship" of humility—anticipating his willingness to suffer and die in solidarity with the marginalized. The woman's act of compassion echoes the ecospiritual politics of the coming Good Governance—sacrificially being a brother or sister's keeper/advocate. Paralleling the Magnificat's honoring of Mary for all generations, Jesus declares her political act as an enduring memorial wherever the gospel is preached. No male in that room (or anywhere) would ever be bathed in such lavish praise. At this dinner table, Jesus welcomes and honors a shameful woman's daring political compassion, immortalizes her Progressive spiritual politics, and calls her into the "community of equals"—opening up to her a thick catalogue of rights.[19] Jesus provides the model for affirmative action in action and inspires all Spiritual Progressives to shout "leave her alone" when women face the wars waged against them.

Jesus also welcomes, elevates, and bestows dignity on children (Mark 10:13–16, 9:33–37; Matt 18:1–14). We tend to picture the children Jesus wanders by as happily playing innocent games in their front yards—a Norman Rockwell-like world. On the contrary, because of exploitive Land policies, juveniles in Jesus' day lived miserable lives (similar to those in some Third and Fourth World countries today). Typically, a day laborer had difficulty feeding himself, much less his family. In times of severe poverty and family disintegration, children, who usually bring hope and joy, were often abandoned or orphaned and left to roam the streets begging. They joined bandit gangs, become enslaved, and the girls were often forced into prostitution. Except the ones that desperate mothers brought to him who were sick and dying, many of the youngsters Jesus encountered were "expendables," without family and living in virtual exile.

Jesus' affirmation of children is two-pronged. First, an unwelcomed child, ironically, represents true greatness. Jesus' followers, still seduced by the imperial ethic, argue about who would be the greatest in the Basileia of God, which raises the question of political leadership. After citing his reversal principle regarding the first becoming last of all and the servant

19. Ibid., 140–51.

of all, Jesus points to a throwaway child as a model for governing. Political leaders must mirror a vulnerable child's humble position—a quality utterly incompatible with social hierarchy and its elitism. Pride that creates and sustains social stratification begets harm or "stumbling blocks," a truth that erects Jesus' second pillar of affirmative action toward children.

Like a good family, good government places highest priority on childhood nurturing. When Jesus' followers (still impacted by strict pecking orders) try to inhibit his honoring of children, Jesus, somewhat miffed, replies, "Let the little children come to me; do not stop them; for it is to such as these that the kingdom of God belongs." Reversing the common view, Jesus insists that these "little ones" (referring also to all lowly people) must not be despised, but rather respected. The inclusion of children into the community of equals proves so important that Jesus claims it is equivalent to welcoming him; even *welcoming God*—a comment that locates the treatment of children at the heart of both morality and spirituality.

Children now, like then, are extremely vulnerable to the indignities of violence and death. A United Nations report in 2005 noted that 50,000 children die every month in Africa—a catastrophe economist Jeffrey Sachs calls a "silent tsunami."[20] We also know that God's little ones, our younger brothers and sisters, face molestation and abuse everywhere. Each year over a million boys and girls worldwide are sold into forced labor, slavery, and prostitution.[21] Jesus brought dignity to all children, especially those compelled to fight regional wars, scavenge garbage dumps, roam streets in gangs, spend their lives in refugee camps, walk around with bloated starving bellies or tropical diseases, and suffer from neglect, poor diets, and lack of education. He emphasized the importance of nurturing-parent values for raising children—values that focus on empathy, fairness, independence, proper education, community, openness, and respect. For Jesus, imperial values harm children—as they do all people and creatures.

Jesus' Progressive justice, that elevates women and children, also enhances *the family*. Seeing firsthand the deterioration of Galilean village life, where displaced male rage fell hard upon household members, Jesus offers new family values to govern the home. Then as now, Conservative family values—built on inequality, subordination, and humiliation—perpetuate male control and are often reinforced by overstretched biblical passages and sometimes by violence. When Jesus exhorts his followers to "call no one your father on earth, for you have one Father—the one in heaven" (Matt 23:9), he challenges the emperor's divine claims and Rome's self-serving

---

20. See Dugger, "Big Reduction in Extreme Poverty," n.p.
21. LaFraniere, "Africa's World," B1, B4.

patron/client hierarchy. Yet, in the same breath, he also aims to divest patriarchs of their dominion over families and over everything else in creation.

His Progressive summons for equality leads Jesus' honor-conscious mother and brothers to believe he has "gone out of his mind" (Mark 3: 21, 33; Matt 12:46–50). After catching wind that his family seeks him, he responds, "Who are my mother and my brothers?" Pointing to those around him, he shockingly proclaims, "Whoever does the will of God, my Father in heaven, is my brother and sister and mother." With this one striking platform in his new Beloved Community, he redefines "family" in the Palestinian world . . . and for us as well. The new family, he says, is not based on lineage, but on a people united around doing the heavenly Parent's bidding, i.e., actualizing God's nurturing and sustaining values everywhere on Earth. Jesus reinforces this change in family values when he demands that one must give up traditional familial duties to follow him (Matt 8:21–22; Luke 9:59–62). For Jesus, then, a true family includes all the villagers who care for and sustain one another during harsh times. This resonates with contemporary notions, as voiced in the phrases "global village" or "it takes a village to raise a child." A true family will reconstitute village life so that no one holds special privilege and everyone treats others like a brother or sister, just as the compassionate Samaritan did in the famous parable. At another time, Jesus declares that those who see the Basileia community as one large sharing family will receive back a hundredfold. What a startling message for starving Galileans as well as for our own ever shrinking and hungry world—further compelling us to care for one another as family (Mark 10:28–31).

Jesus also transforms family values by placing marriage on firmer ground (Mark 10:2–12). Some cultural warriors challenge him (to dishonor him) with the loaded question, "Is it lawful for a man to divorce his wife?" They follow up by pointing out that Moses gave his approval to divorce. In response, Jesus first notes that Moses' concession to divorce results from "your hardness of heart"—a serious spiritual defect. This direct insult shames the male defenders of the present laws, where divorce is so easy that, for all intents, it simply legitimizes male domination, serial sex, and the exploitation of women. Divorce and remarriage also prove a popular move to enhance one's political advancement, as in the marriage of Herod and Herodias (over which John lost his head). Also, divorce is the cultural warrior's means for preserving social purity, especially for those Israelites who had married foreign wives. Thus, by rejecting divorce, Jesus undermines the foundational Conservative values of aggrandizing, boundary building, and exploitation. Furthermore, Jesus knew that the deteriorating lives of these throw-away women would force many onto the streets.

Second, Jesus appeals to the Creation story to highlight the original intents of marriage—spiritual unity and equality: "A man leaves his father and mother and clings to his wife, and the two become one flesh." Ignoring the male/female part of the verse, he comments only on the second phrase—the moral component: "So they are no longer two, but one flesh. Therefore, what God has joined together, let no one separate" (Gen 2:24, 2:8–9). Not only is Jesus affirming the integrity of Creation, he subtly repudiates the purity dynamics that "separates" people because of ethnic (and gender) differences. Most importantly, Jesus implies that men and women exist on the *same moral plane*. Marriage means two intimate, "one-flesh," equals. In the Good Governance, males will lose their usurped power over women—a power permitting them to discard women like unclean meat.

Third, Jesus continues his challenge to the Conservative marriage ethic by stipulating that "whoever divorces his wife and remarries commits adultery against her . . . ." In the way Jesus structures his response, he speaks to the man who divorces his wife *so that* he marries another ("and" here implies result). This ethic licensed serial divorces and the destruction of family life and village solidarity. Also, pure Liberal equality stands out as Jesus asserts that women, too, possesses honor (dignity and rights) that can be violated ("against her") by a male, and that she, like him, is *fully* protected under the law. Because Jesus applies the same legal stipulation to both men and women, one could insert the term "equally" when he concludes, ". . . and (equally) if she divorces her husband and (as a result) marries another, she commits adultery."[22] Jesus ends any hierarchical rule where one submits to the other, where one uses the other for their own selfish ends (such as inappropriate sexual desires), or when the law favors one over the other. Women commend just as much honor and the same rights as men, a stellar belief in that day.

His views will incur the wrath of Conservatives who focus on the family and claim exclusive jurisdiction over its values. Jesus presses for the higher nurturing family values of equality, freedom, and well-being that flow from compassion and follow the path of sustaining the male/female human community. Today's Progressives have Jesus on their side and can unabashedly claim the moral high ground in the family values debate.

As we have seen, Jesus believed his Good Government would also restore *the Land* (to sustain family and village life). So our Planet, deteriorating at an alarming rate, also deserves affirmative action or restorative justice. Some think we have already reached the irreversible tipping point of climate change. Overpopulation, water and air pollution, depletion of scarce

---

22. See Paul's same pairing of male and female obligations in 1 Cor 7:2–4.

resources, species extinction, and lack of arable Land add to our largely unaddressed issues.[23] Our Planet possesses the right that its destruction not only be stopped, but also reversed. A prime example: when wolves were eliminated from Yellowstone Park, the elk proliferated and overgrazed the willows next to the streams. This caused extensive erosion and the rise in water temperature that killed the fish and left the waterways barren. By restoring the wolves, the elk no longer forage on streamside plants, halting the erosion and allowing the birds to nest and bugs to fall into the water, feeding the fish. Beavers use the small trees to build dams that regulate water flow, also benefiting the fish and small mammals. Once again, the streams have come alive. Giving special treatment or taking affirmative action toward wolves has not only saved the species, but has created a dramatic "rebalancing effect" throughout the whole Yellowstone ecosystem, down to the very microbes in the soil.[24] Thanks to foresight and the wolves, some part of Earth is being restored to its proper destiny.

Jesus' affirmative action to counter Conservatism's ravaging of the Land is fittingly expressed in two highly symbolic metaphors found in the Hebrew Scriptures—the vineyard and the fig tree. In the Bible, Nature metaphors capture our imagination to aid us in understanding social/ ecological realities, while providing the emotional power to reshape those realities. For instance, God is called a "rock" in Scripture, underscoring God's strength, stableness, and dependability and plays a part in Jesus' vineyard parable (Ps 62:1–12). Yet, it also prompts an ecospiritual truth—that rocks and minerals bear the sacred and to misuse them is to demean God.

The *vineyard* image is the setting of Jesus' Parable of the Bad Tenants, which he tells shortly after causing a ruckus in the Temple. Although the vineyard originally referred to Israel, its moral dynamic looked further— where *all* Earth's inhabitants are seen as God's people. The social and ecological dimensions of this parable are more fully understood by evoking its biblical antecedent—its musical accompaniment entitled, "Love-Song of the Unfruitful Vineyard" found in Isaiah (Isa 5:1–2, 5–7; also Ps 80:8–19). The song intones the degradation of a vineyard that yields only useless wild grapes. The watchtowers, walls, and hedges are destroyed. Chaos results: the vines shrivel; the vineyard is trampled down and devoured; climate change occurs as the clouds fail to produce rain. Isaiah bespoke devastation as judgment on Israel's leaders because "God expected justice, but saw bloodshed; righteousness, but heard a cry!" One verse later, the prophet condemns those who take the Land and "add field to field." Disaster inevitably follows

23. Meadows et al., *Limits to Growth*, 190–95.
24. Chadwick, "Wolf Wars," 34–55.

from the lack of compassion and widespread political and ecological injustice. This theme is echoed in Jesus' parable:

> A man planted a vineyard and put a fence around it, dug a pit for a wine-press, built a watchtower, and leased it out to tenant farmers because he was going away for a long time.
>
> At harvest time, he sent his servant to collect his share of the produce; but the tenants assaulted the servant and drove him away with nothing. He then sent another servant and they shamefully roughed him up as well. He sent a third servant, who they murdered. So they did with many others: some they beat up and others they killed.
>
> Then the owner of the vineyard figured he would send his favorite son. Certainly, they will honor him, he thought. But when the tenants saw him, they conspired, saying, "This is our opportunity! Here's the heir. Let's kill him and claim the property." So they murdered him and threw out his body.
>
> What now will the owner do to these tenants? He will return to prosecute them and give the vineyard to others. What do you think these words mean?
>
> "The stone the masons threw away will become the most important.
>
> Anyone tripping on that stone will shatter their bones;
>
> On whomever it falls, will be flattened" (Mark 12:1–12; paraphrase mine).

An aftertaste of Genesis resides within Isaiah's song and Jesus' parable. The vineyard with its protective fences, watchtowers, and wine press, represents the ordered life-support systems within God's Creation. Its bad tenants, like Adam, embrace the imperial spirituality and appropriate Earth's resources without limit. They behave no better than Cain of old, refusing to be one another's keeper, selfishly resorting to violence, and hastening ruin. The meaning within Jesus' political context is clear: out of arrogant greed, the Conservative Roman leaders and their collaborators repudiate the ethic of the vineyard's owner and become parasitic Land-grabbers and despoilers (following their ethics of corporate entitlement). Moreover, like lions crouched for blood, they destroy those calling for the restoration of the Constitution's Land policy.

The evil tenants' heinous acts, however, prove futile; their ethic does not prevail. In a great reversal, the owner drives them out of their pollution-filled paradise and "gives the vineyard to others." The owner saves the vineyard and vindicates the beaten, insulted, and murdered servant/peasants—farmers who are Earth's savoring salt; its true tenants and destined to inherit it (Matt 5:5). By the owner's affirmative action, the Land will be stewarded, its crops harvested, and its produce shared in non-exploitative, non-accumulative, and ecologically balanced ways.

Isaiah and Jesus' meaning must be read as a rejection of a Conservative ethic that leaves all in peril. Jesus' parable extends hope to the vineyard/ Earth that it will be restored by the policies of a government committed to the common sustainable good. The pun on the son/stone at the end of the parable, echoing the stone that crushes empires in Daniel, refers to Jesus' Good Governance that will, like a huge rock, "crush" the false spiritual foundation (political ethic) of governments that defile the Land.[25] Earth, too, takes recourse on us eco-sinners.

Like the metaphor of the vineyard, the nonbearing *fig tree* also signals special treatment toward Earth because of neglect. The fig tree not only symbolizes the future blessing of Israel, but also references the ecological well-being of the Land. Yet, in Jeremiah, the barren fig tree speaks to injustices that both abuse the people and alter the processes of Creation (Jer 8:8–13). In this same vein, Jesus' parable points to ominous disaster—we will all perish if we do not repent from our ways (Luke 13:1–9). Like our Earth and its people, the fig tree has been grossly neglected. The owner wants it cut down since it is "wasting the soil." A compassionate worker acts affirmatively and begs the owner for time to dig around it and fertilize it; to take loving care of it. The worker's apocalyptic choice—that if the tree does not bear by the next year then chop it down—brings its viability to the forefront. Today the parable speaks to ecological time constraints. Catastrophe is close at hand and demands not just affirmative action for rejuvenating deteriorating ecosystems, but also *immediate* action. The barren fig tree stands as a powerful ecospiritual symbol; it warns us against dishonoring Creation through heedlessness and compels us to restore it without delay.

Jesus' vineyard and fig tree symbolism point to the same pathological values of domination and neglect pursued by Roman imperialism that leads us into our sustainability crisis today. Now *corporations*, seduced by the Conservative ethic, pose the greatest threat. Jesus' message strikes at the heart of all predatory forces of greed that shape consumer habits, build in obsolescence, create superficial needs, worship increased profits, protect corporate self-interest against community well-being, determine disproportionate distribution of goods, appropriate natural resources at will, spew carbon into the atmosphere, and refuse to clean up one's waste. The bad tenants became locked into a vicious ecocidal/homicidal circle, in which corporate greed plunders people and Earth with always greater

---

25. Wright, *Jesus*, 500–501.

relentlessness—"get while the getting is good" and do not let anything get in your way.[26] Jesus told these stories about a vineyard and a fig tree to ridicule the Conservative ethic with its downward social and ecological spiral and to call for a hasty turnaround.

Clearly, Jesus believed that the ecospiritual politics in the coming Good Governance would do everything in its power to remedy existing inequalities. He advanced the modern Spiritual Progressive's dream that all people and creatures be recognized as created by God, be treated with dignity and possess rights, and be welcomed as part of one biotic family.[27] Jesus stands as a significant link in the *moral history of Liberal egalitarianism and its affirmative action* to restore the fortunes of people and Planet. As spiritual people and a nation, we must repent of the Conservative hierarchical values that have fostered unwelcoming attitudes and bad policy. We need to reaffirm affirmative action as essential to faith, and urge the mending of past injustices. Never straying from his Jewish roots, Jesus campaigned for a return from exile that only comes when first seeking the coming Good Government and its restorative social justice and ecojustice. Yet, the Good Governing we are asked to seek includes justice's *affirmative economic action* as well.

---

26. For example, the slaughter of buffalo and now the depletion of ocean fish and reserves of oil.

27. Miller, "Civil Rights," 250–52.

7

Prayer and a Living Wage

> Give us this day our sustaining bread.
> —The Lord's Prayer

Jesus' clash with the Temple-state leaders raged when he denounced their sacral economics. The Temple was corporate Judea, serving as the central bank and the major employer in Jerusalem. Back then, like now, money talks. Rome always turned to wealthy aristocrats for its surrogate leadership, figuring that these elites would have a vested interest in maintaining the status quo and guaranteeing its onerous Land and tax schemes. The ruling class embraced a harsh conception of economic justice, as the imperial ethic left only a few to prosper and most to languish, even though Moses' Charter had been designed to eliminate disparities. In all the great empires—Egypt, Israel, Babylon, Assyria, Persia, Greece, and Rome—the same gaps loomed. Like today, Conservative principles permitted—sometimes encouraged—large economic gulfs between the "haves" and the "have-nots." This remains one of Conservatism's abiding truths, but a moral, spiritual, and economic calamity. Since these gaps exist mostly due to misusing the Land, ending poverty links with redistributing its resources more equitably, as noted in the Earth Charter. Jesus pushed this truth centuries ago.

Jesus' economic plan for the Good Government followed the peasant moral notions and the ancient Constitution with its rectifying justice.

For him (1) accumulating Land, wealth, and material goods in the midst of the poverty this creates is inherently unjust and a sin against God; (2) disparities of wealth are corrected by restoring a sustainable livelihood through cooperative generosity and affirmative economic action; and (3) economic empowerment is a deeply spiritual and prayerful exercise. These notions, the major thrust of his teaching, would surely stir corporate waters. Let's look at each.

LAND GENERATED WEALTH AND EXILE

Under the Roman political economy, wealth defined life, especially political life—its honor and its power. Furthermore, a moneyed economy meant that Rome and its surrogates could, in an impersonal and seemingly impartial way, collect extortionary taxes and shape Land policy in their favor. In addition, money in the ancient world was considered sacred—tied to the gods and their fertility myths, myths designed to perpetuate disparities. Jesus believes that money masquerades as a false god (Mammon), vying, like all gods do, for absolute devotion. Those possessing wealth bow their knees to it and inevitably contaminate their hearts (Luke 16:13; Matt 6:21, 24). Jesus stands with the prophets in railing against this idolatry and its exploitive deviltry. One's relationship to riches was a deeply spiritual/ethical matter.

Furthermore, the peasant economy assumed that wealth, like honor and authority, remained in short supply. The rich accumulated their hoard at the *expense of others*—a "zero-sum" game, as we call it today. Many peasants, of whom Jesus was one, believe that the hearts of the wealthy are filled with greed. One early Jewish scribe graphically portrayed it: like lions preying on helpless animals, so the poor are the feeding grounds for the rich (Sir 13:19). Wealth, the birth parent of poverty, represented evil; and therefore, it would be dishonorable for a family to possess riches beyond the village's economic norm.[1]

Jesus' scorching denunciation of money and rebuke of the wealthy become obvious when he directs a rich ruler to sell all his Lands and goods and re-distribute the proceeds back to the poor (Mark 10:17–31; Luke 18:18–30). After the man predictably walks away in shock, Jesus turns to his volunteers and warns, "How hard it will be for those with wealth to play a part in the Good Governing!" His followers, somewhat seduced by the prevailing ethic that Land wealth brings honor, look perplexed and urge Jesus to explain "how hard" it is. He doesn't disappoint them: "It is easier for a camel to go through the eye of a needle than for someone who is rich

---

1. Malina, *Social Gospel*, 103–11.

to enter the kingdom of God." Basically, it's impossible . . . with one exception—when God steps in and miraculously changes a rich person's heart from pride of wealth to its embarrassment, and he or she returns the ill-gotten goods to the poor. According to Jesus, those who "do not store up treasures for themselves, but are rich toward God" reflect the true bent of the coming Good Governance.

At another time, Jesus reproaches the love of money as "an abomination in the sight of God" (Luke 16:14–15). The one percent who indulge at the expense of peasant subsistence brings divine outrage. With this plank, Jesus, along with the prophets, repudiates any concocted Conservative assumption that safeguards wealth in the midst of poverty, and then flaunts it as a blessing from God. This denunciation of wealth troubles many Christians today. Some ignore it, while others numb their consciences by assuming that Jesus condemns the *love* of money and not its accumulation—a subtle but convenient distinction to legitimate excessive wealth. However, Jesus has no use for such rationalizations, undercutting all the prosperity preaching that we see on TV. With his alternative governance, Jesus opposes the basis of the whole religio-political economy that leaves a few rich while most grovel. Persistent poverty was and always will be a moral and spiritual scandal . . . and so is concentrated wealth.

Jesus plainly shows how money corrupts both our spirituality and the political community with his Parable of the Rich Fool:

> The Land of a rich man yielded a bumper crop, so he said to himself, "What am I to do? I have run out of room for all my goods."
>
> Then he said, "I know what I'll do. I'll tear down my barns and build bigger ones to store the crop. Then I'll tell myself, 'Soul, you have plenty of goods to last the rest of your life, sit back and indulge yourself.'"
>
> But God said to him, "Fool! Tonight your soul is taken; and those full barns, what becomes of them now?"
>
> So that's what happens when you hoard things for yourselves and you are not rich to what God requires (Luke 12:16–21; paraphrase mine).

The wealthy landowner represents an ethic that encourages people to hoard so much they don't know what to do with it all (like the two year old child dwarfed amidst a mountain of opened Christmas gifts who pleads, "More!"). His flawed spirituality becomes evident in his inner dialogue: "Soul, you have plenty of goods to last the rest of your life." His conclusion, "sit back and indulge yourself," parallels that of other wealthy nobles—a fixation on their own quenchless hoarding of goods *and* their heartless disregard of causing others to have so little (even though the well-off were expected to be generous patrons). By addressing his soul, the rich man betrays his worship of ill-begotten possessions. When he dies, what good comes of his stockpile? He never asks himself that question. Instead, his values leave him labeled a "fool," which the Bible defines as one who scorns God—a grave spiritual and moral failing (Ps 14:1–3).

Before he told this parable, Jesus had already telegraphed its ecospiritual meaning and a deep truth: "one's life does not consist in the abundance of possessions." The folly of amassing more and more that defines success in the Conservative economic ethic brings only destruction—to self, to others, and to the Planet. Jesus labels it "greed," a vice inherent in that ethic (Luke 11:39). Combining material gain with the drive for status, a never-ending American obsession, has been called "conspicuous consumption"—bigger garages for bigger cars and bigger boats for bigger egos. At the corporate level, it's referred to as the "the profit motive" and the "bottom line." Standing as a powerful cultural force, it makes fools of us every day, as in the recent Great Recession. Moreover, it inhibits ecospiritual growth and compassion for downtrodden groups, leading us and them into deeper exile, while placing an enormous strain on the environment and it very limited resources.

Jesus' compelling Parable of the Rich Man and Lazarus, like that of the Rich Fool, further illustrates his rejection of the prevailing political economy that banishes the subsistence ethic and blinds one to human misery:

> Once a very wealthy aristocrat, dressed in purple and the finest clothes, gorged himself daily.
>
> At his gate lay a destitute man, covered with weeping sores, named Lazarus. Out of gnawing hunger, he craved the crumbs that fell from the rich man's table. The dogs would come along and lick his sores.
>
> Lazarus died and was transported by angels to be with Abraham.
>
> The wealthy aristocrat also died and was buried. From his torment in hell, he looked up in the far distance and saw Abraham holding Lazarus.
>
> "Father Abraham," he yelled, "Have compassion on me. Send Lazarus to dip the tip of his finger in water and cool my tongue, for I am in such anguish."
>
> But Abraham replied, "Child, remember that during your lifetime you received good things while Lazarus received evil

things; but now he is at ease and you are in agony. Besides, a great gulf separates us from you that no one can cross."

"Then, father," he pleaded, "I beg you to send Lazarus to my father's house; to my five brothers—to warn them, so they will not end up in this horrible place."

Abraham answered, "They have Moses and the prophets; they must listen to them."

The aristocrat countered, "No, father Abraham, if someone returns from the dead, they will turn from their ways."

Abraham replied, "If they are hardened to Moses and the prophets, they will never be moved by one who rises from the dead" (Luke 16:19–31; paraphrase mine).

This folktale aptly displays the unconscionable lifestyle of the wealthy Roman collaborators and Herod's court. First, it describes a rich man dressed in purple and the most expensive clothes who gluts himself daily. These emblems of corporate pride and wanton waste suggest that he represents power and cares little that his affluence is wrenched off peasant Lands; that he snatches the pauper's daily bread to overfill his belly—gross violations of subsistence principles embedded in the Mosaic Charter.

Second, the story contrasts the rich man's palatial way of life with the destitute Lazarus who, starving and blanketed with sores, shamefully lies exiled outside the aristocrat's gated community (possibly referencing the mansions close to the Temple gates). Undoubtedly, he suffers as a victim of hierarchy, Land aggrandizing, and shame, resonating with the many Galilean villagers who had tumbled down the economic ladder. The Conservative ethic provides this desperate man no shelter, no food, no medical care—nothing. The depth of Lazarus's indignity is pictured by scavenger dogs publically licking his gaping sores. These creatures (symbolizing dishonor) live significantly better than Lazarus, and ironically, show more humaneness than the aristocrat.

Third, that the crumbs a starving Lazarus craves elusively "fall" from the rich man's overfilled table heightens the imperial ethic's callous indifference and Lazarus's vista of dogged gloom. Pitifully, he receives ne'er a crumb. The aristocrat treats Lazarus like just another fly hovering over his opulent feast. He lacks the slightest compassion; he could never see or hear Lazarus because he refuses to "listen to Moses and the prophets" and remains far from God. He is spiritually dead—blind to groveling, deaf to cries—not a hint of shame to redden his double chin face.

In the end, the ecospiritual politics of reversal comes into play when angels transport Lazarus (meaning "God helps") to be with Abraham. Meanwhile, the rich man becomes a victim of his own economic ethic, experiencing hellish torments parallel to those Lazarus himself endured—the lack of subsistence necessities (his cry for one drop of water that never comes). The reference to Abraham, the father of the nation, points further to the parable's impeachment of *political* callousness. Appealing to his family lineage for deliverance, the rich man cries out for Abraham's compassion—a spirituality that he himself lacks. Abraham responds with the restorative justice principle: "Child (with its nation-as-family meaning), remember that during your lifetime you received good things and Lazarus received evil things; but now he is at ease, and you are in agony." The glamour of wealth and standing has now lost all its power to dazzle. But more remains at stake here. The real judgment points to the "great gulf" between heartless, failed economic principles and a caring sustainability morality.

The tenacity of the prevailing political economy shouts loud in this tale. Because of his lack of compassion, the rich man, even now, is more concerned about his five wealthy brothers than the many poor in Israel. His brothers, too, are so entrenched in their ethic that even Lazarus's return from the grave could never convince them to repent and shed tears for the crying thousands who daily scrimp for bread and barter for dignity. Furthermore, the parable unveils Conservatism's myth that all goods must flow upward for society's well-being, including what's good for the poor (through patronage and almsgiving). Jesus exposes the spiritual bankruptcy of a "trickle-down" economy for what it truly offers—the unlikely possibility of even "crumbs off the table" or "drops in a bucket." It never beckons for an equal stake *at* the table—a table of empowerment and sustainability that flows with milk and honey for all.

For Jesus, economic and ecological neglect are destined to the garbage heap they create. The imperial values ignore the conditions of the many houseless and poorly paid workers lying at the gates of compassionless governments, foraging only scraps, while the few bath in luxury. Lazarus's story—the saga of billions around the world today and the millions in America who crouch with scrawled cardboard, gleaning slim charity for scanty food—underwrites a major plank of good governing: treat all people with dignity and affirmatively act to provide them their deserved daily bread as originally promised in the earliest Israelite creed. Translated into the context of sustainability, it calls for a *living wage* and not just the "crumbs" of a minimum wage. In the story, Liberal-like preferential (affirmative action) justice continues into the afterlife, pointing to its universal validity. Jesus speaks to governments about human wretchedness, Land misuse, and the conditions of restoration with the voice of eternity.

GENEROUS JUSTICE AS AFFIRMATIVE ECONOMIC ACTION

Jesus' affirmative action economics further unfolds with his Parable of the Day Laborers, one of his "Good Governing is like . . . ." folktales. This preface determines its explicitly *political* meaning and Jesus' intent to address the immediate life and death economic and Land issues facing Galileans. This counters the traditional interpretation that the parable speaks to lifelong Christians being resentful over deathbed conversions (something no Christian would ever begrudge). This story upholds the Progressive truth about generous justice and the government guaranteeing a decent living for everyone as a prelude to dignity, civic affection, and the sense of community. Furthermore, it graphically portrays the actual miserable condition of Galileans cheated out of their Land and competing for scarce day labor jobs. He prefaces the parable with his reversal maxim:

> But many who are first will be last, and those last will be first.
> For the Good Governing is like a landowner who started out early hiring day laborers to tend his vineyard. They contracted for the usual living wage and went to the vineyard.
> At 9 a. m. the owner noticed other unemployed laborers milling about. He hired them and promised, "I will pay you a fair wage." At noon and at three o'clock, he did the same.
> Around 5 p. m. he saw others standing around and asked, "Why are you standing here unemployed all day?"
> They answered, "No one will hire us." He told them to go to the vineyard.
> At the end of the day, the owner instructed his manager, "Assemble the labors and give them their pay, beginning with the last hired and ending with the first."
> So those that were hired at 5 p. m. came and received a full day's wage. When the first hired came, they expected more money, but they received exactly the same as the last hired.
> They looked at their pay and grumbled at the owner and complained, "These last laborers worked only one hour and you have treated them as equal to us who have sweated all day under the blistering sun."
> The owner replied to their leader, "Friend, I have not treated you unfairly. Did you not agree to the regular living wage? Take what you are entitled to and leave. I see fit to give to the last an equal amount as I give you. May I not do what is right with my own funds? Are you envious because I am liberal?" Let

me repeat, the last will be first and the first will be last (Matt 19:30—20:16; paraphrase mine).

When the spiritually attuned landowner questions some men why they were not working, he hears their despairing "no one will hire us." He feels the shame and overarching gloom of their perilous situation—one more foodless day for their families. Thus, he hires all those men flogged by desperation and promises them a fair wage. They consider themselves fortunate to obtain work, even part-time, even for an hour.

At the end of the toilsome, sun-scorching day, the owner, contrary to expectations, pays the part-time field hands the *same* wage promised to those "privileged" workers hired in the early morning: the amount needed for their families to survive one more day—a sustainable or *living wage*. It's not surprising that the full-time laborers, having borne the whole day's sweltering burden, grumble at the apparent unfairness of receiving the identical pay as the one-hour workers. Their complaint of "making them equal to us" is the parable's ecospiritual and moral key. It points to the last/first restorative justice principle that begins and ends the parable, vindicating the subsistence principle that everyone has a right to a piece of general prosperity. Here, Jesus highlights beneficial reciprocity or corrective justice, i.e., affirmative action.

Another key to the parable rests in the clear "us" vs. "them" distinction within the grumblers' objection, exposing a deeply fractured community. Here Jesus instills another ecospiritual truth—the value of civic friendship. He exiles envy, whining, and stinginess, all markers of an underlying group selfishness that saps affectional politics. Ending the class warfare that sets "us" against "them," created by large economic gaps, remains one of humanity's greatest challenges.

The first-hired laborers symbolize the Conservative ethic of strict and limited justice. Like the elder brother in the Parable of the Prodigal Son, the complainers believe they deserve much more. They reject the landowner's "liberal" or generous justice in lieu of their bottom-line/us-them thinking. The owner calls them friends but rebukes their envy—a vice that chips away at compassion. Many of us might agree with these angry laborers. Is the employer unfair? But he represents God—and how can God be unjust? Rather than undermining justice, he reaffirms the Good Government subsistence ethic with its ancient equalizing Jubilee and gleaning laws that guarantee survival.[2] Joachim Jeremias captures the parable's truth: "God is depicted as

---

2. Lebacqz, "Uncomfortable Kingdom," 40–43.

acting like an employer who has compassion for the unemployed and their families."³

With the backdrop of institutionalized restorative justice, the landowner promises all the workers a fair wage—a living wage—enough for daily bread on the family table, averting a sustainability crisis. Jesus' belief in the full cup of justice means that the coming Good Government will never allow Galilean families to starve or go without basic necessities in the midst of plenty, no matter how little or much they produce or merit. Compassion, with its last/first rendering, provides a much fuller account of economic justice, leading to families fed and dignity bestowed. The parable represents the stark contrast between Conservative and Progressive justice; between a strict earn-your-own meritocratic justice and a compassionate rectifying justice, while also urging civic friendship. Its Progressive bent unfolds as probably the strongest testimony to affirmative action in all of Western literature.

Contemporary Liberal philosophy, with its difference principle, or preferential treatment notion, endorses Jesus' ecospiritual politics by making affirmative economic action the community norm. Jesus' parable teaches that every person deserves a "sustainable livelihood" (the Earth Charter), while reaching further to include the spiritual dignity of social belonging that complements it. These ideas counter onslaughts by Conservative forces that: resist wealth redistribution, curtail programs for the poor, provide tax breaks favoring the well-off, hoard Land, and inhibit civic empathy. The parable speaks to an ongoing obscenity in our time—that the top five per cent of Americans control more wealth (59 percent) than all the remaining 285,000,000+ people and that, in 2009, fifteen percent of American households were "food insecure."⁴ Jesus would call these realities moral atrocities, spiritual bankruptcies. So should we.

Yet, does not the affirmative action of the landowner seem to wreak havoc with America's ingrained meritocratic culture? Would we, too, not grumble if a fellow worker were paid the same for one hour's work when we slaved for twelve? We wonder about the phrase, "the first shall be last and the last shall be first." Once, during my presentation of this parable, a person retorted brusquely: "That's Socialism!" But is egalitarianism always socialistic?

Looking at it through the lens of professional team sports connects the first/last notion with contemporary American realities and helps make modern sense of Jesus' Progressive economic views. Most people see as

---

3. Jeremias, *Parables of Jesus*, 139.
4. See Domhoff, "Power in America," n.p.

self-evident and fair the general rule that the last-place teams procure the next year's first picks of the new player draft, while the better finishing teams obtain the last picks. The NBA also practices "revenue sharing" (a euphemism for wealth redistribution), where teams in larger markets distribute to those in smaller ones. Yet few would maintain that these practices are socialistic; they guarantee the survival of professional team sports and underscores, in a clear way, the need to rectify glaring inequalities.

Progressives believe that these simple compensatory principles, applied successfully to team sports, should govern the political economy to balance massive disparities of wealth, restore a ravaged environment, and prevent the consequent marginalization of the runner-ups. In the short run, rectifying mechanisms will inconvenience the well-positioned and anger Conservatives, but will bring millions at the lower levels on board. This is not only a wise choice, but the right one. Jesus helps us shift our economic and political discourse from selfish profit-driven beliefs to those grounded in loving generosity. All people of good conscience and spiritual depth should, matching Jesus, welcome affirmative economic action and promote it as an essential quality of good governing, human dignity, and environmental respect.

Yet what ecospiritual practices embolden people to embrace hope and begin the long march to achieve fair governance and a sustainable life? Jesus provided for that as well.

THE PROGRESSIVE POLITICS OF THE LORD'S PRAYER

Destitute people need *empowerment* to realize, and then act upon, their dignity and worth. The ancient world universally believed that power resided in the hands of the gods. Invoking a god's name meant tapping into that god's strength. Prayer is primarily petitioning God for help, but also a vital spiritual discipline that includes praise, gratitude, confession, etc. Because the Hebrew term for "word" (*dabar*) also means "act," to pray a word means to perform a spiritual/moral action both on the part of God and the one praying. Someone once said that prayer not only changes things, but it also changes people who change things. Prayer provides a way to call forth divine power and its attending political power to reverse onerous policies. A good example is America's Civil Rights movement, in which prayer played a mighty tune, empowering the struggle. Jesus' political and economic Land reform movement relied on people praying for it, functioning as a *ritual of resistance*. His most famous prayer, the one he taught his followers to take to the villages and many of us today know by heart, is the Lord's Prayer (Matt 6:9–13; Luke 11:1–4).

The Lord's Prayer profoundly affects the worship and devotion of all Christians. Millions pray it daily and thousands recite it weekly in churches. The prayer is simple, short, and eloquent—the epitome of religious devotion . . . and subversion. Not everyone, however, recognizes the *political and economic* riptides within its deep ecospiritual message and Jesus' real-world intent. The prayer's theme echoes the slogan of Jesus' whole mission: "Your kingdom come." It epitomizes Jesus' platform—his challenge to Rome's presence and polices and his easing of the everyday struggles of destitute people. In pleading for the coming of Good Governance, people will begin realizing it. Let's see, phrase by phrase, how the prayer accomplishes this.

Our Father. "Our," "we," and "us" sprinkled throughout the prayer confirm its focus on broader community concerns, rather than on exclusively private issues. Strict Israelite practice held God's name so holy that it remains unspeakable. But in Jesus' world, power resides in the name and the voicing of it. Addressing God as Father (Parent) spotlights the "nation-as-family" metaphor and challenges the moral adequacy of the strict-father God of the male-dominated patron/client system including the godfather of all, Caesar himself (See Matt 23:9). God's Kingdom is, then, the "kingdom of their father" (Matt 13:43). This new designation for God eliminates all hierarchies and is an act of political, cultural, religious, and economic defiance—the taking of sides in a bitter political war. On the other hand, praying to *Abba* (a Hebrew equivalent to our words "daddy" or "mommy") emphasizes God's intimate and nurturing side, which impels the community to be caring members of a household who unreservedly share equally Earth's necessary goods.

In heaven. By locating the Father's dwelling place in heaven, Jesus trivializes any belief that God might reside on Caesar's throne in Rome or reign in the Temple at Jerusalem, which highlights three truths. First, any claim by these rulers to proprietary access to divine power is undercut (Ps 93:1–5). God transcends the imperial spirituality and its ethic, usurps its authority, and exposes its religious fraud. Power resides in the Father/Matron alone, and so the people no longer need fear the alien, distant power of Rome or its surrogates. Second, the heavenly Parent can never be limited to narrow political boundaries or parochial interests, but universally cares for all tribes under heaven. Third, as later articulated by Isaiah, God's sacred dwelling place (or "house") is one built by God not humans. Furthermore, it is furnished with the heavens as God's throne and Earth as God's footstool (Isa 66:1–2). In God's house all of creation is essential decor.

Hallowed be your name. Jesus is not through imploring God to deal with the established order. The prophet Ezekiel declared that God's holy name, which had been profaned among the nations because of Israel's imperial sins, would once again be hallowed when Israel repented and its exile ended (Ezek 36:16–36). By honoring the Father's name while under the domain of Rome, Jesus denies honor to Caesar and his puppets. He also declares the defeat of their exploitative ethic, the inauguration of a new ecospiritual politics, and the restoration of Israel. In God's hallowed name, not in Caesar's, will compassionate justice be guaranteed.

Your kingdom come, your will be done. Jesus has scored another direct hit, yet he is relentless. The first phrase of this petition explicitly reveals the political direction of the prayer. The call for the impending Good Governing implies that the current politics is ruinous—a moral coup against imperial values. It invites frank and perilous political discourse. As evidenced by the two phrases "your kingdom come" and "your will be done" standing in synonymous parallelism, the Prayer describes the shape of the coming Good Governance—God's will (the renewed Constitution) put into practice for the common good. More specifically, Jesus' new order (God's will) equates to practicing generous justice, which he voices in the Sermon on the Mount (see chapter 9).

On earth as it is in heaven. Lest any doubts linger, this phrase clearly signals that the ecospiritual fruits of the coming Good Government will occur within the depths of Earth, precisely where ecospirituality reaches its profoundest heights. The people must cry out to their Matron that the surge of eternity, heaven's Good Governance, comes right here, right now, to clean up a messy world. Because "Earth" also implies "Land," the phrase alludes to the jeopardized farmland and lake shore of Galilean families to whom Jesus' followers will bring the prayer.

This second mention of heaven calls attention to the traditional "as above, so below" view in which the celestial battles between God and the "evil one" mirror the conflict between their spiritual politics on Earth. God's victory in the heavenly realm will be seen in the defeat of Rome's hierarchical values, as especially evidenced in Jesus' exorcisms. He gifts humanity with a pinch of heaven's values in a world where the recipe calls for greed and violence. That the struggle between nurturing and strict-parent values is cosmic, suggests its contemporary relevance. The prayer beckons God for empowerment to undo specific but enduring Land injustices and to provide for universal needs, which leads us directly into the prayer's very practical petitions.

Give us this day our daily bread. This appeal is the prayer's heart and soul. All its previous elements—Our Father, Good Government come, and

God's will be done on Earth—point toward providing a sustainable (the meaning of "daily") source of food, the heart of the peasant subsistence ethic. Whereas humans do not live by bread alone, the fair distribution of the Land's resources is basic to realizing most other values. For the landless and jobless Galileans, food was no longer a daily given, as parents awoke to their sunken-eyed children groaning with hunger. The mantra of the powerful was "we take your daily bread and your fish." God, as the nurturing-Parent, can be counted on to give the children their immediate needs rather than worthless substitutes, if they only but ask and act (Luke 11:9–13). In reality, this petition is praying for a *sustainable or living wage*—securing enough for the family's daily fare, rendered by Good Governing's generous justice. The Parable of the Laborers is an extended commentary on this living wage request. Also, praying for daily food empowers people to share their meager food supplies with each other as Jesus illustrated in his famous feedings. Then whole families and villages are sustained, thus fulfilling this petition while holding out until Good Governing comes and, as expressed next, debts be cancelled and plots returned.

And forgive us our debts, as we also have forgiven our debtors. The return from exile means repenting from the imperial ethic with its ruthless and crafty ways of using others to satisfy selfish desires (or transgressions) and from an unwillingness to forgive. This petition also stands as a major plank in Jesus' Land reform program, reinforcing his claim that lending and debt forgiveness mirror God's very character (Luke 6:35b–36). Under the Mosaic Charter, relieving debts and returning foreclosed Land provided sufficient means for daily subsistence. This petition confirms Jesus' determination, like Nehemiah's, to reinstate the debt-forgiveness laws and ratify the rectifying Land justice of the Jubilee. It also endorses and empowers beneficent reciprocality through micro lending between Galilean villagers—even if a needy villager is an enemy (Luke 6:35a). Praying this petition turns the Conservative spiritual politics upside down, vindicating human generosity and the village subsistence economy in the face of a soulless, centralized bureaucracy.

And do not bring us to the time of trial. This more accurate translation of the familiar "lead us not into temptation" means Jesus possibly has court trials in mind. However, personal enticements are also implied, especially the lure of imperial values—temptations from the Evil One that Jesus personally faced during his forty day wilderness fast. The trial that Job went through, losing everything, may also lurk in the backwaters of this plea. Nonetheless, pray not to be dragged through the sham legal system, where, like in the time of Amos, the courts heavily favor the rich and powerful (Amos 5:12). Villagers should settle their disputes between themselves, and quickly (Matt 5:25–26). The prophets of old came to trial because they stood up to economic injustices, and Jesus will face the same fate at the hands of Rome. But in the coming Good Government true justice will return.

But rescue us from the evil one. Newer translations of this phrase highlight deliverance from a specific vile being, rather than from evil in general. The "evil one" refers to the great Accuser embodied in the acculturated imperial order. In battling its force, the people struggle against the spiritual power of darkness itself. The prayer assures the petitioners that God is defeating the flawed spiritual politics. Their exile is ending. Their deliverance is near.[5] This plea, like the others, is already coming to pass in the exorcisms of Jesus.

For the kingdom and the power and the glory are yours forever. This traditional ending (absent in the newer versions) stands as the most political and subversive part of the prayer, again referencing an alternative Basileia. It leaves absolutely no doubt that divinity, eternity, power, and honor do not belong to Caesar. By implication, when the existing imperial system comes to its end, the people will be fed, the Land restored, and the courts fair. This conclusion summarizes the ecospiritual politics of the whole prayer and, by praying it, people feel empowered to actualize it.

Every element of the Lord's Prayer drips with a Progressive critique of the prevailing Conservative political economy, while also promising a program of hope. It mirrors piety at its highest—thoroughly immersed in the social, economic, and political realities grounded in subsistence policy. The prayer describes the nature of good governing and serves as the vehicle by which civic compassion breaks into the lives of overwhelmed Galilean families, as illustrated when Jesus insists that only prayer is effective in the difficult exorcism of a convulsing boy (Mark 9:29). This superior ecospiritual power and its new form of governing will drive out the lingering imperial devastation, which renders people speechless and "rigid" and "dashes them down" from childhood on. Knowing how to pray becomes a forceful ecospiritual feature in Jesus' program when he sends his followers out to transform and empower crumbling households and villages. Life will be different because "whatever you ask for in prayer, believe that you will receive it, and it will be done" (Mark 11:24).

Dream what changes could happen today if all the Christians who pray the Lord's Prayer personally and in their places of worship understood its original political and economic significance. For instance, what if they prayed every day, "Give us this day our *living wage*," as the prayer originally implied? We might then solidly embrace its Progressive politics and fight

---

5. Wink, *Powers That Be*, 63–67.

for a kind of wealth redistribution that assumes a family-like community. Think of the impact of praying for debt forgiveness where the majority of Americans are engulfed in red ink. Consider what could happen if, through the help of prayer, good governance did come on Earth to fix all the brokenness. Indeed, we are more likely to create the world we pray to happen.

Prayer empowers people to make needed changes. But what specific policies in Jesus' ecospiritual politics will make life better for the common folks of Galilee and for us and our environment today? Jesus spelled out an economic platform, plank by plank.

8

Sustainability vs. Destitution

Honored are you who are destitute, for the Good Government belongs to you.

—Jesus

THE SINKHOLE OF POVERTY continues as a national scandal in America and a catastrophe worldwide. Christians too often ignore the plight of the poor and, on occasion, wantonly sneer at it. Fueled by self-interest and indifference, poverty's persistence is a spiritual disease—a matter of sin on a breathtaking scale. Moreover, the poor bear the brunt of an environment turning toxic. As true then as today, poverty reaches into politics, affected by competing political moralities. The new form of governing Jesus announced pinpoints the problem. He identifies the spiritual/moral bankruptcy of the Roman economy that buried the people in the quicksand of destitution. Through his affirmative economic action, ecospiritual focus, and community building, Jesus fashions six major economic planks to bring them hope that still resonate today.

CONFERRING DIGNITY ON THE DESTITUTE—THE BEATITUDES

Just as ecospiritual values invade the social realm, so they also storm monetary matters. In the ancient world, economics was sacral and deeply impacted by issues of human dignity. Riches guaranteed honor; destitution brought only shame. With the backdrop of sustainability values, Jesus calls for a reversal of this pattern in his famous Beatitudes ("Blessed are . . . ."). They form a preamble to his new Constitution (the Sermon on the Mount) that Matthew arranges as Jesus' legislative program. Given the Mediterranean honor/shame culture, a better translation of "blessed" would be "honored" or "esteemed," terms with ecospiritual/moral meaning, suggesting a more accurate title for the Beatitudes: "the Declarations of Dignity."[1] Dignity implies that something possesses intrinsic worth and is not to be treated as a means or a commodity; it confers legal rights. In this piece of his campaign platform, Jesus defines his mission—ushering in a great reversal by bestowing spiritual and political majesty on those traditionally treated like flotsam in the backwash of plunder:

> Honored are you who are destitute, for the Good Government belongs to you.
>
> Honored are you who are now hungry, for you will be filled.
>
> Honored are you who weep now, for you will laugh (Luke 6:20–23; translation mine).

The mention of the Basileia of God within the first "article" sets the political tone, as does a later reference that honors prophets persecuted for opposing injustices in their day. These declarations of independence reflect the universally harsh conditions of desperate people forced to live under iron-fisted policies.

Throughout the Gospels, Jesus centers on the "destitute," or the desperately impoverished—those at the brink of disaster, worse off than the "relative poor."[2] By today's standards, they grovel at the lowest end of the economic scale, living in extreme poverty.[3] By honoring the very poor, Jesus understands the spiritual side of ruinous Land schemes that foster personal and communal indignity. Matthew calls it "poor in spirit," recalling when Moses announced deliverance from Egypt, yet the people turned a deaf ear "because of their broken spirit and cruel slavery."[4] Destitution means not only abject material want, but also an impoverished, exiled spirit. Now, through the rectifying (reversal) justice of the new politics, the wretched of Earth gain dignity *and* legal standing. The coming Good Government with its shalom now "belongs" to them; it's an entitlement; they are its

---

1 Neyrey, *Honor and Shame*, 165–68.
2. Crossan, *Historical Jesus*, 272–73.
3. Sachs, *End of Poverty*, 20.
4. Matt 5:3; Exod 6:9.

empowered children. Jesus also honors the groveling people who hunger and mourn, living at life's precipice, unable to shut out the muffled cries of their pale, emaciated children. Jesus promises that with the coming Good Governing they will be filled and their dark despondency will turn to joy.

After the Declarations of Dignity, we find a series of parallel woe sayings. More accurately translating "woe" as "shame," these verses negatively mirror the above reversal sayings:

> Shame on you who are rich, for you have received your consolation.
>
> Shame on you who are now full, for you will go hungry.
>
> Shame on you who are now laughing, for you will mourn and weep (Luke 6:24–26; paraphrase mine).

The Land politics of the rich allows them to live lavishly and believe they are the honored beneficiaries of God will. Jesus, however, shames the upper crust for their excessive wealth in the thick of poverty, their plenty in the midst of hunger, and their revelry when so many mourn. Dishonor will be their "consolation" prize as they lose their "rights" to plundered Land and people-exploited benefits in the expected Good Governance. In reality, Jesus shames their Conservative political ethic.

In Matthew's Gospel (5:1–12), Jesus also honors the meek or the oppressed (as in psalm 37:11) who will soon inherit Earth, promising the time when confiscated Land will eventually be returned to these humbled farmers, regaining their legal rights to it. Jesus also brings spiritual dignity to those who hunger and thirst for compensatory justice—for redress of property taken or exploited. His new politics will satisfy them. He continues by esteeming those who embrace his economic ethic and act compassionately—the key value in his moral politics. He then celebrates those who replace the politics of boundary building with a purity that springs from the heart—the pure values of care and responsibility for people and Land. These spiritual people truly "see" God as God sees—looking through the eyes of justice. The peacemakers are also honored, being called God's children, which was the ancient designation for divinely inspired leadership.

Jesus' Declarations of Dignity highlight the values he considers most important within his spiritual politics: humility, justice, equality, compassion, holiness, peace, courage. Where self-respect had crumbled, they confer spiritual dignity commensurate with a new economic standing and its accorded rights. In all of his reversal speeches—about penniless sons treated royally, part-day workers given full-day wages, or despised Samaritans modeling socioeconomic leadership—Jesus unwaveringly seeks to assure the inherent self-worth of the destitute. He envisions them flourishing and standing up with dignity to cultivate the Land and face the world they are destined to serve. That all humans and all Creation deserve such honor remains the hallmark of an ecospiritual Progressive economics. What are the specific ways Jesus believes this will come about?

SHARING SCARCE RESOURCES AND MICRO LENDING

The shredding of the economic fabric and its safety nets in Galilee (considered a breadbasket province) riles Jesus, and he is dedicated to stop it. But Rome and Antipas would never permit it. How will Jesus respond?

Jesus often sees that the crowds around him are hungry, moving him with compassion toward them, "because they are like sheep without a shepherd" (Mark 6:34; Matt 15:32, 14:14). Like the bad shepherds mentioned by Ezekiel, the present leaders "feed themselves, but do not feed the sheep," an egregious violation of subsistence values (Ezek 34:1–4).[5] Jesus' people-orientated Good Government demonstrates the contrast when he multiplies some loaves and fish to feed many thousands.[6] He aims, not only to re-enact the manna feedings God provided in the wilderness long ago; but also, through great "signs and wonders," to model multiplication by *sharing Earth's bounty*. He conveys the message that many can be fed in village communities, provided people cherish subsistence/sustainability notions and miraculously overcome brokenness to ration their meager resources with others. On another occasion, Jesus mentions that under his new politics these scarce goods will be multiplied up to a hundred times, fulfilling overwhelming needs (Mark 10:30).

Jesus' mass dispersal of food to the hungry subtly protests the Land seizures and the resultant gluttonous living by the wealthy aristocrats. By giving out loaves and fishes, Jesus redistributes the ground and sea's *produce*, symbolizing the coming Good Government's resolve to restore their Land rights. So when his followers start campaigning, Jesus prohibits provisions, but rather instructs them to rely on the people "welcoming" them with food and lodging (Luke 10:1–16; Matt 10:5–15). The villagers' willingness to apportion basic necessities signals that "the kingdom of God has come near" and shalom (general welfare) will flow to their towns. Villages that refuse his new politics will suffer ecodevastation like Sodom and Gomorrah that had "excess of food and prosperous ease but did not aid the poor and the needy" (Matt 10:14–15; with Ezek 16:49). Exploitation and misery—the outcome of

---

5. See Myers, *Binding the Strong Man*, 206–7.
6. Bartchy, "Table Fellowship," 798.

the prevailing imperial economy—will fall hard on unwelcoming Galilean towns. The coming Good Government anticipates the old spiritual ideal of hospitality to the stranger. When devoted to community sharing, families and villages actualize the promised peace and the Land flowing with milk and honey—the end of exile.

For Jesus, this sharing also means that villagers should lend money, even to their enemies, without expecting to be paid back—a policy one biblical scholar has called "stunningly liberal" (Luke 6:34–35).[7] By reviving the ancient debt laws, Jesus is not acting out of some unrealistic pie-in-the-sky idealism as we might think today. His insistence on lending addresses peasant subsistence ideals by undercutting unscrupulous loan sharks hungry for the political privileges that accompany Land confiscation. Today, micro lending is championed to bring economic and ecological viability for the poor who reside in mostly failed states. Even in America the Small Business Administration touts a significantly growing micro loan program for fledgling businesses.

The political economy of hospitality and lending resounds forcefully in Jesus' Parable of the Friend Who was Awakened at Midnight, a story about the economics of prayer:

> Let's suppose you have a good friend and you rouse him at midnight and ask him, "Friend, lend me three loaves of bread. An acquaintance of mine arrived unexpectedly and I don't have anything to feed him."
>
> And his friend called out, "Don't bother me now; the door is locked; my children are with me in bed; I can't possibly get up and give you anything."
>
> But I can assure you of this, even though he shamefully refuses to get up as a friend would, if the neighbor persists, he will finally get up and give him whatever he needs (Luke 11:5–8; paraphrase mine).

This parable expands on the Lord's Prayer and its push for sustainability. It speaks of sharing food with a needy neighbor by faithfully articulating the Conservative me-first ethic—*only to contradict it*. Even though it's midnight, a frantic villager with an unexpected guest relies on his friend to lend him three loaves of bread (the link to the daily bread and debt petitions of the prayer). However, the code of hospitality is seriously breached when the self-serving ethic booms out from within the house, "I can't be bothered."[8] Like other wealthy aristocrats and leaders, the man has exiled

---

7. Kirk, "Love Your Enemies," 681–83.
8. See Herzog, *Parables as Subversive Speech*, 201.

the Torah laws about lending and locks out those in need, considering them a nuisance—including his desperate friend. Shame looms large.

Then the parable takes a dramatic left turn. Because the neighbor persists, the beseeched friend will preserve his honor, the honor of his family, of his friend, of the village, of the nation, and ultimately God's honor by springing out of bed to "give him whatever he needs." The man's dramatic change of heart, from an ethic of stinginess to meeting serious need through sacrificial lending, aptly illustrates an unwavering economic program in Jesus' platform and models true devotion to God, neighbor, and the nation's destiny. Jesus then comments that in God's way of governing, one in dire straits simply asks and knocks with the full expectation to receive, not stones and snakes, but Earth's gifts of sustenance—bread and fish (Luke 11:9–13). In our age of predatory lending, where people live at the brink of liens, judgments, foreclosures, and bankruptcy, the "whatever they need" plank remains an enduring mandate and a priority for contemporary politics . . . and the object of constant prayer.

REDISTRIBUTION OF WEALTH

Besides undercutting the honor/shame hierarchy and prompting the sharing of scarce necessities and micro lending, Jesus adds wealth redistribution to his economic platform to halt the plummeting fortunes of Galileans. His approach plays hard when a rich ruler challenges Jesus about inheriting eternal life (the Kingdom) and then proudly lists his virtues (Luke 18:18–25; Mark 10:17–22). Jesus never disputes the man's devotion to the Constitution, but he "lacks" something basic. The ruler, because of his position and flawed economic ethic, refuses to follow subsistence principles and at least one of the Ten Commandments. He covets the possessions of others, especially their Lands. Like all the rich folks in his day (and many in our own), he believes that he deserves his wealth, having embraced a Conservative principle that sanctions unlimited appropriation as divine favor and a guarantee of Kingdom well-being. Jesus shows what side he takes in the wealth-is-a-sin/wealth-is-a-divine-blessing debate by declaring that if the rich are to enter the coming Good Government, they must *repent* of their flawed economic creed (their accumulation ethic) and re-distribute their ill-gotten gain back to the poor. This spiritual transformation and rectifying justice then accrues "treasure in heaven."

Understandably, his loss of wealth would cause the ruler much grief. It means jettisoning his honor and his power, reducing his family to shameful destitution and begging. Even more, it flaunts the Roman imperial ethic—an act of treason. His governing principles demonstrate his loyalty to Caesar, but betray his nominal devotion to God. Like most rulers, the man lacks a soft heart, humble repentance, and a sense of justice that affirmatively and gladly restores what has so heartlessly been taken. Realizing that this ruler, like all humanity, is exiled by imperialism's spiritual economics, Jesus does not loathe him, but longs for him to repent and restore his ill-begotten gains. Jesus learned from one strand of his Jewish tradition that the true enemy is never a human being, or even an institution, but rather the power of a tainted *economic and political morality* that possesses them.

A positive example of Jesus' program of wealth redistribution unfolds in his encounter with Zacchaeus, the well-to-do toll collector, who is described as "lost" (Luke 19:1–10). Again, Jesus chooses to eat with a "sinner," bestowing on him dignity, after which Zacchaeus gladly restores half his possessions to the poor and returns fourfold to those he defrauded. He models the Progressive politics of *affirmative economic justice* that underscores the coming Good Governance and all good governing henceforth. For this, Jesus declares Zacchaeus a son of Abraham (a political reference) and assures him that "salvation (the salvation of Israel) has come to his house;" his exile has ended. In contrast to the forlorn rich ruler, he publically spurns the Roman economic ethic and shows breathtaking devotion to subsistence values. Jesus explicitly politicizes Zacchaeus's policy of redistribution by then telling his famous Parable of the Talents, a parable Christians often misinterpret to promote the profit motive and entrepreneurialism. In reality, the folktale teaches that Land-extracted wealth should be given back to the productive peasants (as the saved Zacchaeus models) and not sit idly buried within the Temple vaults (Luke 19:11–27).

The stories of the rich ruler and Zacchaeus bring into relief an important question for all Christians: "When I see those with meager goods, what goods of theirs have I?" They also show how a modern Progressive ecospiritual politics will reign—restoring the fortunes of the lower classes through wealth redistribution while chiding our aggrandizing economic morality and its devastating effects. This point has been driven home today by Warren Buffett, one of the world's richest persons, who announced he would turn $35 billion over to the Gates Foundation in the belief that wealth should be used for humanity's good and not all be given to one's children.[9] Christians might consider this when planning their own estates, while at the same time advocating for greater economic redistribution through inheritance and other tax reforms. Speaking of taxes.

---

9. News conference, June 26, 2006.

TAX RELIEF FOR THE POOR

Galilee's economy was quite brisk, but few benefits "trickled down" to the majority.[10] For the peasants, the Roman tax levies and the Temple tax and tithes meant institutionalized thievery, supporting lavish life-styles and magnificent construction projects. Taxation was just another way Rome violated subsistence principles. It is not surprising, then, that Jesus talks about taxes. Everyone wants to hear a politician's view on that subject. His opportunity comes when members of two parties, the Pharisees and the Herodians (normally bitter rivals) attempt to entrap and discredit him over the question of paying produce taxes to Caesar (Mark 12:13–17; Luke 20:20–26). On the one side, if he explicitly rejects payment to Rome, he provides grounds for the Roman authorities to move against him. On the other, if he endorses the much-hated taxes, he repudiates peasant values and sabotages his standing among his constituency. Jesus' opponents seem on the verge of unmasking this popular prophet and shaming him for good.

Jesus presses his adversaries to furnish a Roman coin which, of course, these collaborators can easily provide. He asks, "Whose image is this and whose title?" The answer is obvious—the coin bears Caesar's imprint and the phrase "divine son." By calling on his Conservative critics to produce the coin and to verbalize its contents, Jesus deftly shames them by exposing their false spiritual base and their disregard for the ancient Constitution that forbids graven images and devotion to other gods.[11] But what Jesus says next could change the course of world history.

His response, "Render unto Caesar what is Caesar's, and unto God the things that are God's," though often quoted, is generally misunderstood. Many think Jesus intends to separate politics from religion, something virtually unheard-of in the ancient world. His well-crafted answer confounds his opponents by undermining their fear-driven politics in two ways. First, although Jesus appears to encourage paying taxes to Caesar, his reply actually counters it. Ancient tradition had already proclaimed God as the owner of Earth/Land, its produce, its wealth—everything. "Earth is the Lord's and all that is in it" (Ps 24:1, 89:11). Thus, giving to God what belongs to God implies giving God *everything*. With this, the distribution of Creation's bounty is determined by the moral mandates of justice, freedom, and shalom for all. Giving Caesar all that belongs to Caesar implies, then, rendering him precisely *nothing*, except to rid Palestine of his illegitimate coinage. The coming Good Government means the end of corporate claims on Earth.

---

10. Freyne, *Galilee*, 46, 167.
11. Myers, *Binding the Strong Man*, 311.

Jesus subtly undercuts the legitimacy of Caesar's extractive tribute and all tax systems that benefit only the very few.

Yet, Jesus is not through with the imperial ethic. Giving to God what belongs to God also means giving back to the peasants what God intends them to have—their rightful ancestral Lands and the *full* produce thereof. Jesus' opponents get this seditious message and later accuse him before Pilate (and rightly so) of rejecting the payment of taxes to Caesar (Luke 23:2). Moreover, by separating Caesar from God in his famous response, Jesus also negates the emperor's divine status, undercutting Rome's authority and that of its puppets. Jesus cleverly and subtly dismantles imperial economics and its spiritual basis.

Another event that defines Jesus' attitude toward taxes occurs when the collectors of the Temple tax seek to shame him by publicly asking Peter whether Jesus will pay up (Matt 17:24–27). Safely out of their hearing (because he is about to utter a subversive message about power), Jesus asks Peter a telling question regarding the Temple tax: "From whom do kings of the earth take toll or tribute? From their children or from others?" Peter gives the obvious answer, "from others." Jesus responds, "Then the children are free." By declaring the children free, Jesus announces the end of all exploitative systems. Moreover, as formerly victimized people, they will become the true heirs of right governing—its royal children. Put simply, they no longer need to pay the tax.

Jesus voices his opposition to the Temple tax in a subtle and farfetched way. So as not to offend the authorities even further, but to poke fun at the tax and Rome's takeover of the fishing industry, Jesus tells Peter to go catch a fish, find a coin in its mouth, and pay the tax, his glib way of saying, "Yes, pay the tax, but only when you find a coin in the mouth of a fish." If the Temple rulers tried to stay afloat with revenue from a fish's mouth, their ship of state would soon sink. Jesus' witty stratagem for dealing with tax extortion takes the wind out of imperialism's predatory schemes and sends a clear message: the immediate Good Governance will not extract Earth's bounty and provide nothing in return.

The Progressive message is that good governing does not skew tax policy to benefit the wealthy while the majority suffers. Giving to God what belongs to God means respecting Creation and sharing it for the common good. In this sense, paying taxes is a responsible course for all citizens and, like tithing, an expression of political compassion and a profound *act of spiritual devotion*, strange as that might sound to Conservative ears. But a more fundamental change must be made for government to be more responsive to human need.

CLEANSING THE GOVERNMENT OF CONSERVATIVE ECONOMIC PRINCIPLES

To actualize his program of a reconstructed nation, Jesus must finally enter and challenge the heart of the problem—the capitol, ensnared by the aristocratic political economy (Mark 11:1–20).[12] He approaches Jerusalem for the last time riding a donkey, a pointed symbol of humble leadership and of his solidarity with Israel's earlier proto-democratic judges (Judg 10:3–5). The city is now very hostile territory—the home turf of his political competitors, most of whom are devoted employees, supporters, or beneficiaries of the Temple-state's extractive schemes. Nevertheless, some of his followers shout out a subversive message: "The kingdom of our ancestor David is coming." This is the day that the political and economic tidings he has often disguised by carefully chosen phrases and stories, and sometimes out of earshot of his enemies, now break out into *overt* rebuff and reform.

Any protest against the Temple, the center of the economy, its central bank, and Jerusalem's largest employer, would be perceived not only as blasphemy, but also as rocking the economic boat . . . and as ultimately dishonoring Rome's authority. What a disruption when Jesus, the leader of a group of disgruntled Galileans, enters the Temple, drives out those selling and buying, overturns the tables of the money changers and the sellers of animals, and blocks celebrants from carrying sacred objects. Jesus' disturbance *defines his ecospiritual politics and his mission*. Yet, what was Jesus up to by halting the Temple-state's business? Did his actions, as some think, simply challenge the sacrificial system? Was he angry with some opportunistic vendors? Maybe he intended to incite a rebellion.

The key to interpreting Jesus' disruption fits within the prophetic tradition of political protest. After his ride into Jerusalem on a donkey (also an action parable ridiculing Rome's high horse parade), the crowd shouts: "The prophet Jesus from Nazareth" (Matt 21: 11). Every prophet in the Hebrew Testament renounced corruption within Israel's main institutions: the monarchy, the priesthood, and especially the Temple. Even before he enters the Temple, Jesus performs an action parable by cursing a barren fig tree that "withers away at its root," as the ancient prophets and John the Baptist had predicted about imperial governing (Jer 8:13; Hos 9:10, 16; Luke 3:9). The fig tree, normally a symbol of Israel's security and prosperity, now, in Jesus' eyes, bears no fruit. For him, the Temple-state's political economy must wilt away.[13]

---

12. See John 2:13–22 where the cleansing marks the beginning of Jesus' mission.
13. Myers, *Binding the Strong Man*, 297–98.

Entering the capitol as a reform prophet, Jesus' fiery speech that day shouts with the voice of Isaiah and Jeremiah: "My house shall be called a house of prayer for all nations. But you have made it a den of robbers" (Isa 56: 7; Jer 7:11). When Isaiah called the Temple a "house of prayer," he affirmed its divine mission of beseeching God in prayer for shalom (the common good) and its role to "maintain justice and do what is right" (Isa 56:1). During the days of Isaiah and Jeremiah, however, the leaders had transformed the Lord's Temple into a "den of robbers" and a "safe-house" for injustices (Jer 7:5–10). For Jesus, these injustices still prevail. By calling the Temple a "bandit cave" (bringing to mind banditry, the last resort for peasants victimized by Rome), Jesus dishonors the elite aristocracy. They have legalized theft and are, in reality, themselves bandits, devoted to blemished, self-serving principles and a flawed spirituality. The same robbers (called "banksters" by some) sit in board rooms today, foreclosing on their bad loans, ravaging human lives in every way possible, and destroying life-support systems with virtual immunity, sheltered by the common market euphemism of "creative destruction."

Not ending with words only, Jesus and his followers overturn tables and snarl Temple trafficking, causing its virtual shutdown—a disaster during Passover. By paralyzing this spiritual center, Jesus undercuts its imperial economy, legitimized through its flawed interpretations of purity, ritual, and social convention. His disruption will echo inside the halls of all capitols dominated by hierarchical and mercenary values. Thus, Jesus is not inciting a rebellion or just slapping the wrists of a few opportunistic vendors, but he is "cleansing" the Temple-state of its *ingrained Conservative economics*.

Later, Jesus would reinforce this message. When his volunteers stand admiring the Temple's magnificent architecture, he forewarns that it will all soon tumble down: "Not one stone would be left here upon another . . ." (Mark 13:2). Shortly, his accusers will claim that he wanted to destroy the Temple (Mark 14:58), but in fact Jesus only desires to drive out woeful economic principles—its false and flimsy pillars. So, too, in our day, the values in Washington that support the rich getting richer and the world getting pillaged must topple. We should see this as a compelling ecospiritual summons. The powers-that-be consider this un-American and will muster every force to oppose it, including labeling it "Socialism" and enlisting the "gospel of wealth" evangelists. In Jesus' day, those powers hungered for his death. In a few hours, their appetite would be satisfied. Indeed, Jesus knew that his renewed economic and Land policies would only come with great sacrifice.

THE LORD'S SUPPER, ECONOMICS, AND SACRIFICE

Near the end of his life, Jesus sums up his economic agenda at an event Christians call Communion, the Lord's Supper (Table), or the Eucharist (Matt 26:17–29; Luke 22:7–30). Significantly, it is a Passover meal, memorializing the liberation of the people from Egyptian domination and the creation of a new nation. For Jesus, the meal symbolizes the fulfillment of Israel's destiny by bringing God's rule of compassionate justice, liberation, and peace out of exile. Jesus intends to celebrate the arrival of the Good Governance and the "remembrance" of his new legislative program for the downtrodden long after he leaves. His dramatic interpretation of this meal is so extreme that one of his own followers, Judas (a Judean and, as such, probably more sympathetic to the Temple), feels compelled to betray him.[14] Why did it spark such mutiny?

Today, Christians celebrate the Last Supper as a devotional act commemorating Jesus' body broken (the bread) and his blood shed (the cup) on the cross for our salvation. Yet, we must not miss the Progressive politics and economics embedded within this meal as essential ingredients of Jesus' own aims. They flavor its deeply reverential and salvific meaning. After eating, Jesus explicitly connects the supper to his ecospiritual politics when he vows that he will not drink of the vine again until he drinks it anew when the Good Government comes. He further declares, "I confer on you, just as my Father has conferred on me, a kingdom, so that you may eat and drink at my table in my kingdom, and you will sit on thrones judging the twelve tribes of Israel." For Jesus, this meal celebrates the arriving Good Governance, the fruitfulness and sustainability of the Land it brings, the table of social and economic equality it assures, and the assembly-style governing he has promoted.

Jesus centers the traditional Passover symbols on the ecospiritual economics of compassion. With broken bread representing his body "given for you," and the cup signifying the "blood of the covenant poured out for many," Jesus heralds devotion to sacrificial political service that empowers the countless weak and excluded. Significantly, his mention of the "covenant" specifically references Moses' blood covenant after descending Mount Sinai with the original Constitution and eliciting a promise of obedience from the people (Exod 24:7–8). Jesus' symbolic cup of blood, poured out for "many" (a restored Israel of the nations), means that vulnerable Galileans will, when the Good Governance arrives, sacrificially enfranchise one another in obedience to the "new" Charter Jesus has refashioned from the

---

14. See Chilton, *Pure Kingdom*, 125.

old. They will drain their cup of all malice and drink from the chalice of their common suffering and their common hope, thereby displaying true devotion to God and one another.

But all this talk of blood will take a more ominous turn as good governing may require *extreme* sacrifices. Because Jesus' alternative ceremony testifies to the bankruptcy of the Temple-state's self-serving economy, he falls within the sights of Rome's imperial values. Thus, Jesus knows his own "kingly" atoning martyrdom is coming and so he hands his followers broken bread and wine symbolizing his impending, self-sacrificial death "for you" and "for many." Here he identifies with the story line of Israel—Isaiah's Suffering Servant (Isa 53). Good governance is infused with his Liberal ethic of generous justice for the masses—*at an ultimate cost to himself.* By pouring out his love on the altar of politics, Jesus voids, once for all, the crimson-stained imperial ethic and its covenant of misery.

Later, the Apostle Paul confirms that Jesus' Last Supper memorializes his ecospiritual economics of self-giving justice. He criticizes the wealthy Christians at Corinth for devouring the food before the poorer members ("those not having") arrive (1 Cor 11:17–33). Just as the Lord's Table meant that the have-nots may sit and share equally and responsibly in Earth's bounty, so we today should willingly sacrifice for the *economic and social goal of sustainability*. Hopefully, this "remembrance" of Jesus will so permeate our ecospiritual politics that it renders poverty, hunger, and inequality but bad memories of the past. It anticipates the day when markets will trade not only in goods, but also in *the* good. In this way, practicing the Lord's Supper compels devoted service to God, to Earth, and to humanity through compassionate economic justice—the mark of a deep ecospirituality.

In summary, Jesus affirms the socioeconomic equality of people who possessed little human dignity—those considered scum and the destitute. He models ecospiritual devotion, an earnest attachment to the neighbor in need and to Earth in peril, with a fervor driven by generous love. In so doing, he levels a devastating prophetic reproach against the Conservative spiritual politics of hierarchy and of Land exploiting excesses that reach back to the beginnings of the human story. He confirms John Kenneth Galbraith's famous quote that Conservatism is humanity's "oldest exercise in moral philosophy: i.e., the search for a superior moral justification for selfishness."[15] Jesus strove to overcome this ethic in his day and fulfill the Jewish vision of an egalitarian justice that moves beyond the idea of formal equality to headline restoring community through sustainability. Everyone possesses equal political, legal, social, and economic rights *and outcomes*,

---

15. Galbraith, "Stop the Madness," interview.

grounded in the spiritual side of justice called dignity. This equality affords entrance to a reversal ideal that consigns special considerations to the least well-off—those entitled to "more equality" in order to right social, economic, and ecological wrongs. How remarkably this corresponds to the difference principle of political philosopher John Rawls mentioned earlier.

Even though the realities in Jesus' day differ from our own, the spiritual conflicts and the resulting political moralities remain much the same: the struggle to sustain or dismantle social and economic hierarchies, to assign honor or shame, to encourage or oppose undue gain, to build or tear down walls, and to respect or degrade the Land. With the boot of unfairness pressing hard on the throats of so many, will social and economic fairness ever reign? Jesus has given us hope, for he crafted a comprehensive platform commensurate with his vision. That everyone, including Earth, deserves equal respect and the means to flourish is the Progressive's loftiest ecospiritual/moral dream. For this pinnacle of hope, Jesus willingly suffered an excruciating death at the hands of the prevailing morality.

Christians ought to be proud that their Lord and Savior held out the Progressive ideal of affirmative action. As devoted followers, we must seize it and act on it as an *ecospiritual imperative* and a discipleship duty. This calls for continual repentance, especially for Christians with riches and rank who have shown little devotion to social, economic, and ecological recompense. Yet, the hunger for justice always remains a *spiritual pang* to be felt deeply in our souls and the soul of our nation until fulfilled by good laws and policies.

9

Ecospiritual Insight and Judicial Activism

> You have heard that it was said... but I say unto you.
>
> —JESUS

SPIRITUAL FORMATION, FOR THE Christian, is a matter of oneness with Jesus and following his everyday commands within the whole biocommunity. At the centerpiece of his renewal movement stood reformulated subsistence laws mined from Israel's ancient Charter, designed for his Galilean constituency and beyond. Indeed, Jesus, like all Jews, revered his Constitution as we do our own. Yet, each political party in Jesus' day bent the Law to support its own political and economic interests, believing that Moses stood with their group. Because Jesus deems that most parties exiled the true purpose of the law, he constantly wrangles over legal meaning and authority. In a famous mountain top vision (a reminder of Sinai) known as The Transfiguration, he meets Moses the lawgiver and Elijah the prophet. God once again chooses to voice through Nature (from a cloud) confirmation that Jesus is the beloved son and his followers must "listen to him" (Mark 9:7). Here God transfers Moses' legal authority and Elijah's prophetic prowess to Jesus, who will interpret and re-fashion the Constitution from its own deep moral base. Jesus emerges *as a prophetic lawmaker* or legislator—an authoritative spirit-filled interpreter of the ancient Charter in the tradition of the Hebrew judges. Like them, he challenges imperial orientated legislation by promoting specific Land-related statutes. He represents, as two respected scholars conclude, "a very liberal view of the Torah within Judaism."[1]

Today's Conservatives are rankled by judicial interpretations that favor the poor and the marginalized, especially affirmative action rulings. They rampage against "activist" Liberal judges who continually "inflate" new rights, labeling them "adventures in [corrupt] egalitarianism"[2] Progressives respond that our Constitution should be considered a living document, flexible enough to address and rectify social problems that the original framers could not foresee, such as global warming. Fundamentally, interpretation (whether of Scripture or of law) is a political act with specific ends in view. In reality, then, both Progressives and Conservatives are legal activists since each interprets law in light of their own cherished values and dreams.

How does Jesus weigh in on the question of judicial activism? Remember that law, morality, and religion could never be separated in Jesus' world, so we must be careful in pitting legality against morality and spirituality. Moreover, we should not assume that Jesus teaches grace, love, and mercy while his "Jewish" opponents push only law codes. Judaism also teaches love and mercy and Jesus reveres the Torah as a nation building legal document and vigorously debates its fine points. He renders past texts and laws from his unrelenting commitment to deeply embedded ecospiritual subsistence values, much like Isaiah who, hoping to prick the national consciousness, dramatically reinterpreted the fasting laws to indict a Conservative legality vested in maintaining Land exploitation and it resultant hunger (Isa 58:2–12).

In his initial campaign speech to his Nazarene townsfolk, Jesus gives an early clue that he, too, expounds texts in the spirit of Isaiah. Taking one of Isaiah's prophecies about God benefiting victims, he interprets it, contrary to expectations, as favors showered, not on a suffering Israel but on Israel's *enemies* (Luke 4:16–30). His anti-nationalist interpretation causes such hometown outrage that the people drag him to the brow of a hill, intending to hurl him into a deep ravine (foreshadowing his later death). In Luke's mind, Jesus' is scorned due to his activist interpretation of past texts *in light of Progressive values*. This incident also footnotes the intensity of the conflict over the Liberal and Conservative interpretations of the Constitution and the Bible in Jesus' day, much like now.

---

1. Theissen and Merz, *Historical Jesus*, 370.
2. Bork, *Slouching toward Gomorrah*, 96–99, 105, 107.

In the Sermon on the Mount, Jesus states the basis of his Constitutional renewal: "I have not come to abolish the law . . . but to fulfill" (Matt 5:17–20). The present interpreters of the law (often influenced by imperial values) ignore it, or worse, corrupt it. In claiming to fulfill the law, Jesus does not plan to radicalize it by making it much harder to keep. Rather he strives to recover the inner morality, or the *spirit*, of the law with its empathic, subsistence undertones and then apply it to devastated Galilean communities.³ Thus, in an ironic sense, Jesus' brand of Judaism embraces "originalism"—believing that the nurturing God's primary intention of law is to meet core needs (a Progressive goal). For example, Jesus declares that the Sabbath laws exist not to burden the people, but, rather, to benefit them and the Land—to revive and "free" them (Luke 13:16; Matt 12:12; Mark 3:4; 2:27). In such cases, he claims to "exceed" the strict Conservatism of some overzealous politicians by defying their extra-biblical traditions that benefit only the few. He impugns their justice as limited and flawed, unsuitable for the coming Good Government or, indeed, for any good governing (Matt 5:20).

Jesus illustrates his love-based approach to law by heralding the Constitution's statutes about loving God with your whole being and loving your neighbor as yourself. In Mark's account, a scribe notes that these commands are more important than all the animal sacrifices (Mark 12:33). Given the scribe's connection to the Temple-state, his point is delicate but "wise" because he recognizes that the Progressive ecospiritual politics of empathy transcends a Conservative mark of devotion—traditional ritual offerings. Jesus tells him he is close to understanding the Good Governing. The scribe possesses great spiritual insight, unlike some of his colleagues. They strain out gnats and swallow camels by "neglecting the weightier matters of the law"—justice and compassion—in favor of extracting tithes from everything Earth produces, even tiny herb gardens (Matt 23:23–24).

The statute about loving your neighbor as yourself, addressed to the nation, reflects the ancient peasant ethic that mandated reciprocal sharing of goods to ensure sustainability. Jesus fashions this notion into the Golden Rule: "do to others as you would have them do to you" (Matt 7:12a). The rule is essentially egalitarian—all parties in a transaction count morally the same. It also encourages people to empathically put themselves in another's shoes (sometimes called the "magic shoes" principle), identify with their sufferings, and act accordingly. Given its peasant base, the rule also calls us to treat Earth as we would want to be treated, to walk in its shoes.

---

3. Moo, "Jesus and the Authority," 102.

Significantly, Jesus considers the combined love-God/love-neighbor command and its sister, the Golden Rule, not only as *moral/legal* yardsticks, but also as principles for *interpreting* the law. On these "hang all the law and the prophets," he says (Matt 7:12b, 22:40b). According to Jesus and other Jewish teachers at the time (Hillel), compassionate justice—the inner morality of law—becomes the *hook on which all laws hang*. It is the basis for updating Israel's ancient Charter within the context of tattered village life. It shapes the coming Good Government's legal structure. Empathic justice, as a hermeneutical principle, is the Spiritual Progressive's strongest legal point, determining laws and defining good governing. Ecospirituality makes it presence known by insisting that all laws foster loving justice within the biocommunity.

PROGRESSIVE VALUES INTERPRET THE TEN COMMANDMENTS

The core articles of Israel's Constitution were the Ten Commandments. These statutes defined the nation and governed community life; and because they mirrored the very character of the divine, they were called God's "words" (Exod 20:1). Against the backdrop of failing Galilean villages where friendships have dissolved and traditional responsibilities disappeared, Jesus' in-principled, activist renderings will relieve their hardships. His twelve followers will be the proto-democratic judges, mediating justice in a completely fair way, not tied to any powerful political and economic interests. His legislative principles prove relevant for all people trapped under heavy social and economic pyramids. We have already noted how Jesus reinterprets the Sabbath laws to promote human and Earth's flourishing (shalom). What about some of the other Ten Commandments?

His Progressive politics honors senior citizens. To illustrate the clash of opposing legal interpretations, Jesus criticizes the particularly egregious practice of declaring one's wealth Corban (assets in holy trust to the Temple). For Jesus, the Corban law, though pious in sound, nullifies both the fifth commandment to honor your father and your mother, and another statute in the Constitution that prohibits cursing them (Mark 7:9–13 with Exod 21:17). Neither of these ancient commands explicitly orders children to financially support their elderly parents. So, according to Conservatism's literal interpretation, rich people could selfishly divert financial resources from parental support, justify it under the guise of devotion to God, keep their wealth intact, and remain immune from violating the law. Jesus decries this cold, calculating indifference.

Once again, Jesus exposes the dirty linen of the elite, while he unpacks the essence of the honoring parents command. If sons or daughters refuse to support their elderly parents, they actually pronounce a curse on them—a gross violation of the law and the commandment's inner morality. Jesus' activist interpretation *broadens* the definition of honoring parents to include, in this case, their financial support. This fulfills the Golden Rule's reciprocal justice that parents and children meet each one's subsistence needs when the other is vulnerable. Compassionate justice, as both a moral and an interpretative principle, will enact laws that enhance the well-being of the elderly, further helping to stabilize community life. The onerous use of legislation, with its obvious rationalization of personal greed and self-interest, "makes void the will of God" and only confirms that "their hearts are far from me." By speaking against this weaselly legal manipulation under the semblance of holiness, Jesus undoes imperial rulings that shortchange the powerless everywhere.

Such callousness is hard to imagine until we look at the varieties of elder abuse in our own society, one being the ongoing efforts by Conservative politicians to eliminate or reduce guaranteed government benefits for seniors. At best, this political ethic throws crumbs and tidbits of relief (as in the first Medicare prescription drug plan). Consider also the many elderly who are neglected, rejected, abused, and abandoned without "support"—even by their own children. Progressives promote legislation to protect the aging and provide them sustenance, health care, and dignity to the end. Expecting as much and more is a compelling ecospiritual matter, another mark of national holiness.

Many of Jesus' Progressive interpretations of the Ten Commandments and other laws for rehabilitating village life were later compiled in the Sermon on the Mount (more appropriately renamed "the New Constitution"). Some appear as "antitheses," following the formula, "You have heard that it was said . . . but I say to you . . . ," and are clearly meant as activist rulings (Matt 5:21–48). He seeks not only to internalize the law, but also to *broaden* it to cover those precipitating spiritual attitudes *and* actions that ultimately result in murder, adultery, and other illegal acts. By extending the law, Jesus creates new duties and *expands* the rights these duties create, which leave the Conservative legislators cringing. Their literal interpretation of the Constitution permits them to ignore, for instance, their own complicity in peasant starvation (death/murder). By rejecting these word-for-word interpretations, Jesus gives us ecospiritual insight about the law's real meaning and preserves its relevancy for holding people and governments more accountable.

His Progressive politics and hate crimes (5:21–26). Conservatives interpreted the sixth commandment, "You shall not murder," to mean the unjust taking of human life and nothing more. Certainly, this remains the core meaning of the command—a law directed to prohibit a heinous crime. But given his immediate concerns, Jesus expands the definition to include a broad range of acts and attitudes that precede murder, often driven by the honor culture. For him a "social killing" is as culpable as murder. For the Progressive, whether one fosters quick deaths from guns, bombs, or the unsafe construction of automobiles; or the slow deaths caused by the denial of equal access to life's opportunities, environmental pollution, cigarette smoke, or poor nutrition, the name remains the same—it's a form of killing.

Specifically, Jesus understands the murderous potential of anger among Galilean villagers who are up against a wall. Desperate people become susceptible to self-hate and last-ditch survivalism, where even slight honor provocations could escalate into violent fury (not unlike modern road rage). Uncontrolled anger, itself a form of violence, moves quickly to revenge and often its murderous results, especially between nations.

In like manner, Jesus expands the prosecution of murder to include ethnic slurs (*raca*) and religious name-calling (fool), what we today call hate speech. In our day, he could have substituted "nigger," "chink," "kike," "faggot," "chick," "whore," "spic," "alien," "illegal," "cripple," "vagrant," "drunkard," "ex-con," or a host of other degrading (shaming) terms in place of *raca*. Progressives stand against cultural superiority behind which lurks a bigot's creed with its insults, the germ of many social crimes. Branding undesirable groups could quickly mutate into their *elimination* from our sight and our communities. In the worst case, as George Kelsey, a noted Christian ethicist chillingly argued in his classic work on racism: the political logic of social division is ultimately genocidal.[4] It leads to *extermination*. And the perpetuators consider it morally right.[5]

Our last two centuries bear witness to the results of prejudice, reinforced by denigrating stereotypes and epithets. Look at the unimaginable horrors that rained down on the supposedly "impure" Jews. America is not blameless in its history. Once, we labeled certain women as witches and killed them. Slurs reinforced the genocidal treatment of Native Americans,

---

4. Kelsey, *Racism and the Christian*, 96. "Since in-races consider out-races defective in their humanity, there is no solution to the problem created by their presence in the world short of genocide. Spatial separation and quarantined on Earth are not enough. Defectiveness in the order of being can only be overcome by reversing the creation. Defective human beings must be exterminated."

5. See Goldhagen, *Hitler's Willing Executioners*, 14 who argues that killing Jews sprang out of the German moral conscience.

the lynching of African-Americans, the murder of early union organizers, and the ushering of Japanese-Americans into detention camps.

Denigrating language has help exile our LGBTQ brothers and sisters, who, for decades, have cried out to our legal system for the full rights of citizenship. Some misguided religious people weigh in by misinterpreting isolated biblical verses to deny their rights.[6] What the homosexual community fears most, however, is that hateful language and its attending social logic contributes to a literal rendering of a Leviticus text (referring to male cult prostitutes and mistakenly applied to gays) that calls for the death penalty (Lev 20:13). In fact, a few extremists have interpreted this as an invitation to violently attack homosexuals. The same could be said about the unusually high death rate of our houseless brothers and sisters. They experience the same denigration when people refer to them as "bums," "panhandlers," or "vagrants." Murder, the last scene in a horrible hate drama, begins with the first act of anger or initial contemptuous name-calling. Jesus saw this cultural dynamic at work, and he addressed its seriousness with his interpretation of the law against killing.

Conservatives resist efforts to change language biases such as substituting "humankind" for "mankind," contemptuously labeling these as ventures in "political correctness." For Spiritual Progressives these are exercises in *moral* correctness, in fact, *spiritual* correctness, and in some cases, *legal* correctness. They recognize the power of words to assault human dignity, such as using the "N" word, and work to classify such as hate speech with its sanctions (like shouting "fire" in a crowded theater). When we embrace social attitudes or speak and act in ways that demean other human beings, we affect their life chances. Even if they die a slow death, we still kill them. However, we must always be careful to guard free speech.

Jesus also taught that labeling someone a "fool" is murder. In almost all societies, calling one a fool verbalizes deep contempt, but within Israel's wisdom tradition, this affront also carries a more pointed religious meaning. Whereas the wise person fears and seeks after God, the fool says, "There is no God" (Ps 14:1–2). Here judging someone a fool implies intolerance toward another's religion (or nonreligion). It lies at the heart of religious persecutions and of blasphemy laws. How many murders, wars, and atrocities have been perpetrated in the guise of a crusade for *the* "proper religion?" Reducing the ongoing tensions between Muslims, Hindus, Jews, Christians, and atheists is crucial in today's splintered world. A broadening Progressive approach means discovering the common threads that string together the

---

6. See the award-winning book by Boswell, *Christianity, Social Tolerance and Homosexuality*, 91–117 for a discussion of these passages.

pearls of religious and nonreligious ideals. One moral truth that reaches to the heart of all traditions and teaches mutual respect is the Golden Rule. Tolerance hangs from this sacred thread. In this post 9/11 world, our *common* Progressive values must prevail; our universal human capabilities must be realized. If not, the Fundamentalist elements of these religions will drive history and the world will remain a ticking time bomb.

His Progressive politics and sexual exploitation (5:27–30). By sticking to a strict interpretation of the Commandment against adultery, the Conservative leaders sustained their property interests, fed their power, and perpetuated the ethic of inequality and objectification. Jesus challenges their literalism and strengthens the adultery law by insightfully linking it to the Tenth Commandment that forbids a man from coveting his neighbor's wife. The Lawgiver never intended women to be the objects of male whims—the means to their selfish ends. Jesus states that to (continually) *look* on a woman (or another man's wife) desiring to seduce (exploit, subordinate) her begins the first step toward infidelity. Thus, Jesus includes *philandering* within the definition of adultery. His statute also encompasses sexual abuse between married couples. In one swoop, Jesus condemns mate rape along with *any* misuse of another, whether in the home, on dates, in common work areas, or any place.

Jesus' deciphering of the seventh Commandment especially hits home for Galilean villagers where the imperial ethic is unraveling strong family ties. Because houses are connected around common ovens and threshing floors, women prove especially vulnerable to the prying, preying eyes of their unemployed, shamed, male neighbors. One could recover lost honor by seizing the opportunity to seduce the wife of one who fortunately found work. Jesus' anti-adultery regulation addresses this problem while also reversing the hierarchical male honor culture. Jesus' statute gives women honor and dignity as equal members in the family of humanity. The coming Good Government guarantees women—and men as well—the right that their bodies will not be used in ways they do not freely choose, affirming a long-standing Progressive principle: no one should ever be the means to someone else's ends. Progressives design public policies that advance equality and uphold human grandeur, joy, and community, while discouraging men and women from using one another for economic or sexual exploitation. By ennobling human sexuality, Progressives stand on the high ground of the "family values" debate. For us today, Jesus' illumination of the Seventh Commandment in light of his Progressive moral norms means the right of everyone to non-harassing, non-exploitative, and nonviolent sexual relationships that are grounded in nurturing love.

His Progressive politics and truth-telling (5:33–37). Jesus is very straightforward: when you say yes, mean yes; and when you say no, mean no (Matt 23:16–22). Why does he need to legislate against lying when the ninth Commandment clearly prohibits speaking falsehoods? It's because he faces a world in which truth becomes a casualty when it, too, is treated as a commodity. Cunning leaders devise clever ways to say what they do not mean. For example, they teach that if one establishes a vow by mentioning the *gold* in the Temple sanctuary or a *gift* on the altar, the vow must be kept; but if one swears by the sanctuary or the altar alone, the vow can be broken. This subtle distinction permits the unscrupulous to make promises or enter contracts with no intention of keeping them.

Jesus denounces this practice for two reasons. First, he subtly notes that the Conservative spirituality and its ethic of unlimited gain places more importance on gold and gifts than on truth itself, or even on the God of truth who indwells the sanctuary and sanctifies these objects. Second, this system of deception permits the wealthy to steal the peasants' Land. When they say, "Yes, I swear by the sacred vessels that I will not call in your debt," they veil a hidden "No, it shall not be forgiven and I will foreclose" (a deception we today call "nondisclosure" or "the fine print").

To reverse the community's downward slide, villagers must be honest and trusting in their transactions and all deceptive contracts eliminated. Lying and its variants—half-truths, spins, hypocrisy, cheating, manipulation, pandering, concealment, corruption, and high-sounding phrases to hide crimes—must cease. Unfortunately, garnishing words with falsehood has always plagued humanity and the political process. It has led us into wars and into denying the deadly effects of cigarettes, the causes of climate change, or the harm of assault rifles. Progressives demand truth in all its dimensions, including an insistence on political integrity within campaign financing, advertising, and promises. Yes must mean "yes" and not "well . . . maybe."

When we consider the dreadful effects of imperial/Conservative values on the human race—the billions subjected to poverty, enslavement, torture, violence, oppression—it takes our breath away. Add to these an assaulted Earth. Jesus held out the only solution—a heaven inspired Kingdom or a governing of the common good with strong laws and regulations. Conservatives who voice skepticism whenever "the government" is mentioned have consistently called for voluntary assent in solving social and economic problems. Although Progressives believe NGOs play a significant role in preserving people and Earth, they also posit comprehensive regulations and stronger sanctions for everyone's good. Laws with a strong inner morality must regulate human interactions or as the late Garrett Hardin called it:

"mutual coercion mutually agreed upon."[7] Although he was referring to ecojustice issues, his phrase speaks to social justice as well. His point: we must not permit our world to become a grazing "commons" in which everybody *voluntarily* agrees to curb their appetites (as Conservatives insist), yet no one is sanctioned for harming the public interest. Four decades ago, Hardin exposed the logic of mutual ruin in these voluntary schemes with the analogy of a bank robber who treats banks as grazing grounds to be robbed at will. Society does not protect banks with only stern warnings against theft, hoping people will voluntarily comply. Rather, it restricts the freedom of all would-be bank robbers through strong laws and severe penalties.

Having been a former building inspector, I came to appreciate the hundreds of codes designed to protect the public from shoddy, unsafe construction. Good laws and regulations are essential to protect the general welfare of all the people. Jesus, the perfect legislator, shows us the way to create such laws. In following Jesus, Christians should appreciate government's regulating power.

JESUS AND POLITICAL AUTHORITY

Christians claim that Jesus is the greatest spiritual authority that ever lived. Yet his renderings of the law came not with an authority from the end of a sword, but a higher source with the soft moral power of suasion and loving care, acclaimed by the people (Mark 1:22; Matt 7:28–29). In a world that linked politics and religion, his ecospiritual/moral authority also entailed legal clout. To accept Jesus' authority means rejecting the mastery of the imperial ethic, both then and now. When a Centurion, accustomed to barking out orders, submits to this Galilean and declares, "I am not worthy to have you come under my roof," his humility outflanks his ingrained authority. The message is clear: Jesus, indeed, possesses more political clout than even Herod or Rome, to their chagrin. The same authority extends over Rome's client rulers when they challenge him in the Temple: "By what authority are you doing these things?" Jesus wittingly responds by posing a question about whether the popular prophet John and his baptism carried heavenly, or merely human, authority. The rulers' refusal to answer unmasks their "vulnerability to the social power of prophetic movements" and exposes their political standing as self-serving but shaky.[8] These leaders should be ignored, even defied. On the other hand, Jesus' nurturing

---

7. Hardin, "The Tragedy of the Commons," 1247.
8. Myers, *Binding the Strong Man*, 307.

ecospiritual politics, judgments, laws, and insights for interpreting the Constitution must be accepted as final authority.

A broader issue of legal authority is raised by Jesus' act of defiance in the Temple. What is one's obligation to obey the law, and when is it appropriate to engage in *civil disobedience*? In America, acts of resistance reach back to the origins of the nation—from the Boston Tea Party through the Abolition and Civil Rights movements, the anti-Vietnam War protests, to Cardinal Mahoney's call for the priests in his Los Angeles diocese to disobey a harsh immigration law being considered at the time by the House of Representatives. Martin Luther King Jr., Cesar Chavez, and the Berrigan brothers stand out among the many who have defied unjust laws in the name of higher values. In this same vein, Jesus' violation of Temple law rises above common lawbreaking and exemplifies civil disobedience because (1) it did not arise out of selfish whim, but targeted "robber" laws that clearly violated the fundamental principles of justice; (2) the normal means of redress remained futile; (3) it was a public act; (4) he did not intend violence; and (5) he was willing to suffer the legal consequences of his action.

Progressives firmly believe in everyone's obligation to obey the law, even when not in one's interest to do so. Yet, they also insist that inhumane and exploitative laws may (and sometimes must) be disobeyed for moral reasons. Although disobeying the law should remain rare and never be taken lightly, extreme moral failure might demand it. Some believe that given the looming ecological crises, the time calls for civil disobedience.[9] In a democracy, nonviolent civil disobedience appeals to the noblest nurturing values for effecting change and leading a captive nation and a maltreated Earth out of exile. Jesus stands as a moral authority and example, but it requires a community's prayerful ecospiritual/ethical insight.

In summary, Jesus said that compassionate justice must season, not only the human heart, but also the legal character of community life. He was an activist interpreter of law who applied Israel's ancient Constitution on behalf of villagers faced with Land seizures and all that implied. Like Jesus, modern Spiritual Progressives (whether Christian or not) welcome ecospiritual insight and judicial activism in service to the common good. For Transformational politics, the vision of justice also clearly sees the distinction between gnats and camels, focusing on issues that really matter. Many Conservatives seem preoccupied by judicial battles over hot "cultural war" topics such as the phrase "merry Christmas," embryonic stem-cell research, contraception, and creationism. They tend to downplay core ecospiritual issues such as full equality under the law, the horrors of war, the degrading

---

9. Stephenson, "Thoreau's Radical Moment," 11–15.

of Creation, and concern for those waging a daily battle with economic woe. Another major concern is health care, as battles rage between Progressives and Conservatives on how best to provide it.

10

Sustaining a Healthy World

> Cure the sick . . . and say, "Good Governing has come near to you."
> —Jesus

OUR SPIRITUAL JOURNEY IS littered with casualties when the human body and mind become the battlegrounds of physical, mental, spiritual, and ecological warfare. We hope that this Earth and our stay on it will be hardy and hale, yet how quickly sickness and disease can change the music in life's dance. Moreover, our mental/physical health and the well-being of Earth are interwoven and interdependent. Given these realities, we shall explore what Jesus' Good Government offered in health care for people and its connection to the Land's health, captured in the ancient notion of shalom (general welfare). Because Spiritual Progressives and Conservatives are divided on how best to bring wholeness to human life, conflicts over the meaning of good health, the most efficient health care delivery systems, and the basic economic control of health care often lead to political impasse.

The health of Americans exposes an enigma. We are a rich country with the best technology, yet our overall health levels, as measured by standard indices, compares poorly with that of other industrialized nations.[1] Our major killers—obesity, strokes, heart disease, diabetes, and cancer—are

---

1. See Davis et al., "Mirror, Mirror on the Wall" for an update on America's health care.

strongly linked to lifestyle, and lifestyle connects to social and ecological factors. Many illnesses are labeled "diseases of civilization"—those strongly influenced by living in poor and/or chemically toxic neighborhoods, skin color, or position on the socioeconomic ladder. In some parts of New York, men die from heart disease and cancer at an earlier age than their counterparts in Bangladesh.[2] Scientists estimate that every year 300,000 deaths result from human induced climate change with its extreme weather conditions (flooding and drought) and its impact on chronic hunger, malaria, and diphtheria.[3] The poor, of course, are hit the hardest. Additionally, ecological degradation contributes to the poor health of all living creatures. Good health and decent care are inhibited by flawed political values, with many exiled from even the most basic health information and needs.

Spiritual Progressives believe that health, a core human good, must be protected and enhanced by political structures that are grounded in the principles of compassionate justice, human and Earth well-being (shalom), and freedom from harm. Every person deserves the best physical and mental health care available, regardless of their social standing or their ability to pay. Conservatives also believe in providing good health care, but see it as a matter of personal responsibility and, like a commodity, should be controlled by the private sector and market forces.[4] Ignoring the fact that nearly all other governments in the industrialized world ensure universal access to quality care for their citizens, American Conservatives generally scoff at greater government involvement to set higher health standards, provide better corporate and environmental regulation, control spiraling costs, and furnish health insurance for all its citizens. What might we learn from Jesus about health care as a "Kingdom" (Good Government) entitlement and the ecospiritual politics of wholeness?

Jesus offers health policies that reveal his deep love for humanity and that relate to Land politics. The prophets looked forward to an age when healing would signal a rebirthed Land of Israel. Jeremiah, for instance, longed for a restoring balm in Gilead (Jer 8:22). Matthew interprets Jesus' healing activity as a fulfillment of Isaiah's prophecy: "Surely he has borne our infirmities and carried our diseases" (Matt 8:17 and Isa 53:4). Christians often apply this passage to Jesus' atoning death rather than to his day-to-day healings, as Matthew intended. Yet, for Jesus and the prophets, healing was a matter of national atonement—the result of good governing and the confirmation that a long political and spiritual exile was about to end.

2. Epstein, "Enough to Make You Sick," 19.
3. Schnellnhuber et. al., "Solving the Climate Dilemma," 13.
4. See Fried, "Analysis of 'Equality' and 'Rights,'" 494–95.

After watching Jesus heal a group of ailing people, John the Baptist's followers inquire whether Jesus might be the promised one. Jesus responds, "Go and tell John what you have seen and heard: the blind receive their sight, the lame walk, the lepers are cleansed, the deaf hear, the dead are raised, the poor have good news brought to them" (Luke 7:22; Matt 11:4–5). In these few words, mostly about healing, Jesus virtually lays out his political platform of good government—*restoring physical and economic health* to the common people. The good news to the poor is the news of their Land being restored, a prerequisite for their sustenance and good health. Jesus sends his most committed campaign volunteers into the villages and commands them, "Cure the sick, raise the dead, cleanse the lepers, cast out demons," sure signs that the Good Government has "come near to you" (Matt 10:7–8, 12:28; Luke 10:9). Jesus revels in God's promise that "I am the Lord who heals you," but links his healings to good governing (Exod 15:26).

As Jesus' parables *describe* the Basileia of God, his healings *actualize* it. They play the same sociopolitical role as his reversal of the dining/honor/patronage customs—bridging the social and economic gaps. Confronting a Conservative medical establishment that excluded many and where money meant treatment, Jesus provides medical care without cost, without considering status, and without judging character (Matt 10:8; Mark 5:26). His healings and exorcisms provide the initial episodes to prove that good governance springs from compassion . . . and that it will alleviate the suffering caused, in large part, by imperial policies. Ultimately, Jesus' healings point to a time when *holistic people/Planet health care* will become a political priority of any good governance. For this reason, he heals whole villages and commissions his volunteers to do the same (Mark 6:13; Luke 10:9).

In the first century, healing pointed beyond the surface appearance of a cure. Thus, when Jesus heals, he is "making claims about who regulates social boundaries, who determines cultural norms, who defines religious authority, and who decides political power."[5] More specifically, Jesus' healings are episodes of liberation from longstanding oppression that had undercut the subsistence ethic.[6] Healings, then, point to spiritual, physical, *and* biocommunity wholeness. The common perceptions that sickness is caused by sin and devilish forces opened the door for ancient power brokers to firmly control medicines and cures, as well as the cleansing rituals that accompanied them. Jesus assails this unhealthy spiritual politics as actually the cause of illness. Going out of his way to heal those exiled by the medical establishment, Jesus intentionally engages in a broader political conflict. He counters

---

5. Crossan, *Jesus: A Revolutionary Biography*, 94.
6. Myers, *Binding the Strong Man*, 144.

imperial power and overcomes its devastating effects on the human body and psyche, the primary points at which sin is connected to illness. The sin, however, does not rest with the victims, but stands squarely on Rome, with its unlimited pillage of the Land and crude use of military force. How will Jesus deal with imperialism's casualties and its spirit of domination?

HEALING CONSERVATISM'S CASUALTIES

Jesus' healings had an immediate political focus: (1) to *alleviate human suffering* in a holistic way by confronting the political powers whose schemes cause acute stress, crushing physical/emotional affliction, severe mental illness, and death; (2) to *overcome economic exploitation* by those who wish to control healing; (3) to *neutralize Caesar's divine legitimacy* by locating divinity within himself, with its consequent political authority and healing power; (4) to compassionately *expand health care access* to include everyone equally, especially those medically marginalized; and (5) to *signify the return from exile* and the establishing of a new ecospiritual politics. If we place the healings of Jesus within the struggle between a Progressive and a Conservative ethic, then we see his strategic thinking. His healings aim to protest the politics of the prevailing health care system while relieving suffering and bringing wholeness to all. Jesus' healings demonstrate that the arriving Good Government's restoring of the subsistence ethic establishes *an egalitarian, non-exploitative, and community building quality health care structure* accessible to everyone. Yes, health is cure, but it's so much more.

By defying the health-harming structures of empire, Jesus' healings serve a "socially subversive function" and appear "politically dangerous."[7] Take the case of the Sabbath healing of a man with a withered hand (Matt 12:9–14). Jesus' rivals carefully observe whether he will heal on the sacred day, so they might accuse him. Jesus asks the subtle question whether they would rescue one of their own sheep from a pit on the Sabbath. Given their ethic of animal exploitation and material accumulation, they would certainly not object to this rescue. Jesus then declares, "How much more valuable is a human being than a (commodity) sheep!" With these words, he exposes the Conservative ethic that justifies self-gain (protecting one's investment in livestock), while unveiling its loathsome lack of concern for suffering people. His adversaries then conspire to destroy him, not because he heals, but because his healing implies a rejection of their exploitive ethic and their political power. Most of Jesus' healings are wrapped in such political intrigue.

7. Crossan, *Jesus: A Revolutionary Biography*, 93.

EXORCISING CONSERVATISM'S DOMINATION

Jesus' most devastating critique of the afflicting imperial ethic emerges from his specialty—exorcism. Forbidding and tormenting spiritual forces take possession of the human body, compelling people to act out in antisocial and violent ways. In first-century Palestine, vexing spirits and politics went hand-in-hand with the following assumptions:

- A struggle between God's rule and the Ruler of darkness (or between right and wrong) occurring in the heavenly realm spills over into and shapes the earthly sphere, especially in the clash of nations to dominate one another.
- Tormenting or "unclean spirits" engage in their battle for political control by entering the bodies and psyches of individuals who act out in bizarre ways. This battle finds expression in the spiritual war between the political myths (moralities) that "possess" people.
- The "holy" spirit of God restores people and communities from the personal, social, economic, and ecological devastation caused by forces labeled "demonic."[8]

Essentially, demon possession is another way of describing imperial occupation. Jesus' skirmishes with political opponents come down to disputes over who stands on God's side and who partners with the spirits of domination. Today we put it less harshly: the conflict over good political values and flawed or inadequate ones. Exorcism provides the context for Jesus' response when told that Herod wants to kill him: "Go and tell that fox for me, 'Listen, I am casting out demons and performing cures today and tomorrow and the next day . . .'" (Luke 13:32). Jesus wants Herod to know that his expelling of repressive spirits directly threatens imperial rule.[9]

The classic example of Jesus casting out the alien spirit of Rome happens to an ostracized man considered irredeemably violent and forced to reside in a cemetery (Mark 5:1–20). Because the man howls in the night and bruises himself with rocks, he is restrained with heavy chains, which he continually breaks. This graphic description obliquely refers to the unrestrained and irrational power of Rome, as made clear by the troublesome spirit's name, Legion (referencing Rome's soldiers). The ravaged man symbolizes the woe and devastation that the Roman armies and their retainers mete out on Galilean farmers and fishers. Like other unclean spirits, Legion fears Jesus' political power—the power of a "Son of the Most High God"—an

---

8. Guijarro, "The Politics of Exorcism," 171.
9. Ibid., 166, 171.

alternative divine-king power to that of Rome's. The afflicting forces now plead for mercy: "Do not torment me" (as Rome has tormented the people). Usurping Rome's judicial authority, Jesus compels the spirits to enter a herd (a military force) of unclean pigs. They rush (a military charge) into the sea and drown—a veiled allusion to the fate of Pharaoh's armies at the Exodus, but also a reference to the impure Roman armies and its values being thrown back into the sea (chaos) from whence they came. The legions of imperial miseries, caused by never-ending taking, are defeated; the imperial ethic is routed.

Jesus' most antagonistic encounter with the political authorities happens after the healing of a mute man. He is accused of casting out vexing spirits in the name of Beelzebul (originally Baal), the demon leader (Mark 3:20–30). By "name-calling," they aim to dishonor Jesus and neutralize his political influence.[10] Jesus, however, turns the table and claims that *their* exorcisms are inspired by alien forces, while he performs his by the "finger of God"—an Exodus image and a sign that the longed-for Good Government has come (Exod 8:19). Jesus presses his campaign on two fronts. First, he shames his opponents by pointing out the illogic of darkness casting out darkness: a divided basileia, like a divided house, cannot stand. Second, Jesus' liberating of possessed persons signals the ultimate end to the ongoing vortex of violence that the elites perpetuate.

To these points, Jesus tells a short parable: "No one can enter a strong man's house and plunder his property without first tying up the strong man; then indeed the house can be plundered." The term "house" conveys an explicit political meaning, as in the house of Israel or in referencing the Temple or Rome. By binding the forces of domination, Jesus restrains Rome and its footmen from wreaking havoc on people. The property "plundered" conveys the idea of re-claiming and returning the Land seized by the plundering nobility, as echoed in Isaiah's prophetic words of hope: "Even the captives of the mighty shall be taken, and the prey of the tyrant be rescued" (Isa 49:25). Jesus will smash through the bulwark of imperialism and plunder the present kingdoms (houses). He will plunder the plunderers and bind the "Man," a reference to the exploiters in any society (even our own). The ecological reference to plundering is also explicit and contemporary. Casting out the imperial values rescues both people and Land.

Jesus' exorcisms speak to the tyrannical way of life that lurks within all of us and our institutions. For instance, we are encouraged to overindulge—leaving, on a grand scale, a plundered world: poor, sick, and reeling—while inviting obesity, clogged arteries, diabetes, and cancer. It contributes to the

---

10. Guijarro, "Politics of Exorcism," 162–64.

legions of social pathologies for which millions stuff themselves with antidepressants or self-medicate with alcohol and drugs. On the surface, these appear as individual spiritual matters but are essentially linked to ecospiritual politics. Jesus' healings and exorcisms boil down to political change—to overthrow the power of the occupying imperial ethic and bring recovery to all of Creation that has suffered so long and so deep under its spell.

A VISION OF UNIVERSAL HEALTH CARE

As we have seen, Jesus' cures seem incidental to the political intrigue and the honor challenges that the healings raise. This might explain why his healings occur as single *ad hoc* episodes along the way, as opposed to grand wave-of-the-hand cures that affect large segments of humanity. Through the arriving Good Governance he so loudly proclaims, he envisages *universal health care* (a goal heralded in the Earth Charter and a Progressive's continuing dream).

Within his inaugural campaign speech in his hometown, Jesus touts universal healing (Luke 4:23–30). His neighbors have come to the synagogue service expecting him to heal, as they heard he had done up in Capernaum. Instead, he assumes the larger role of a prophet/healer, likening himself to Elijah who saved a Gentile woman from starvation and Elisha who cured a Syrian general of leprosy, both in lieu of suffering Israelites. Yes, the people heard correctly—in lieu of suffering *Israelites*. Jesus rebuffs the villagers' folk belief that the in-group holds first claim to God's sustaining bounty and healing powers. His opposition to the Conservative restraints on universal healing continues in nearly all of his subsequent cures and exorcisms, especially those of the Centurion's servant, the Syrophoenician woman's daughter, and an enemy Samaritan (Matt 8:5–13; Mark 7:24–30; Luke 17:11–19). Jesus' twist on the notion of who deserves medical coverage reverberates to the marginalized everywhere. Good governing offers compassionate, non-exploitative health care for all people.

Without prejudice and without pay, Jesus heals women, children, untouchables, the blind, the lame, the deaf, and the poor. In so doing, he breaks the wealthy male cartel's monopoly on health care. His curing of Jairus's daughter and a hemorrhaging woman confirm his reach to the most shamed and healing's universal application (Mark 5:21–43; Luke 8:40–56). That the little girl is twelve and that the woman suffered for twelve years also point to an ailing Israel's story (referencing the twelve tribes) and, thus, the political nature of these healings. Because Jairus, a synagogue leader, falls at Jesus' feet, he underscores Jesus' growing political clout in heralding universal health care.

The account of the bleeding woman especially highlights the inadequacy of discriminatory health politics. Mark wryly adds that under official care she endured much, spent all her money, and "she was no better, but rather grew worse." By acknowledging her (contaminating) touch and healing her, Jesus shames the official medical establishment as uncompassionate, exclusive, ineffective, and mercenary, while affirming his commitment to women's health (another fundamental Progressive dictum).[11] Jesus stops the discharge and calls her "daughter," declaring that her exile is over and she now stands, like Jairus's daughter, as an honored and valued member within the family of the nurturing God's Basileia.[12] He commends her faith in that government and grants her its shalom. On another occasion, he heals a woman on the Sabbath and shames the Conservative ethic for denying her health care while allowing its rules to be self-servingly bent for the sake of one's investment in farm animals (Luke 13:10–17).

Universal health care links to ecospiritual politics through *faith*, an indispensable ingredient for a sustainable future. In the Hebrew Scriptures, faith carries the idea of "trust" in God and is "in the first instance . . . concerned with the fate of Israel."[13] Thus, faith relates to politics, trusting in God's destiny for the people (Isa 7:9). In commending a number of his patients for their faith, Jesus recognizes their community loyalty and trust in the Good Government to meet their health needs (Mark 2:5, 5:34, 10:52; Luke 7:9, 17:19; Matt 8:10, 15:28). When Jesus heals all the sick in one region, the people appropriately praise the God of *Israel* (Matt 15:31). His healings nourish the political faith that the nation is returning from exile, the subsistence Land laws are being reestablished, and health is restored to all its citizens. Unfortunately, a "faithless generation" falls victim to the all-pervasive royal ethic that paralyzes the landless like the evil spirit who seizes an epileptic child (another nobody in the eyes of the medical establishment), renders him speechless, dashes him down, and makes him rigid (Mark 9:14–29). However, all those who locate their faith in Jesus' government program will once again be able to "stand," like the boy, in wholeness and dignity.

Jesus further highlights his point about trust when he asserts that destructive worry (dread) results from "little faith" (Matt 6:25–34). The political context of this theme comes out of villages traumatically caught

---

11. Love, "Jesus Heals the Hemorrhaging Woman," 91.
12. Weissenrieder, "Plague of Uncleanness?" 214–19.
13. Michel, "Faith," 597.

in the unrelenting whirlwind of psychological wreckage caused by imperial Land policies. Today, psychologists describe the fading rays of hope as acute social stress, and it lurks within America's deteriorating inner city neighborhoods.[14] In a recent survey of Los Angeles high school students, 67 per cent reported they felt ongoing sadness or hopelessness, sure signs of clinical depression.[15] Jesus, who cares about mental health as well, encourages devastated people to place their trust and hope in the arriving Good Government, since a culture of despair ultimately breeds violence.

Continuing his counsel to keep faith, Jesus reassures exploited people who despair over scarce food and clothing: "Can worry add a single hour to your span of life?" Yet how do these goods come? Using a Nature image to convey an ecospiritual truth, he reminds people of God's steadfast care for the birds and the lilies. He guarantees humans that life's subsistence needs will inevitably be met, but only when seeking the arriving Good Governance and its distributive justice. Possessing this political faith will end their ongoing anguish.

Jesus' politics of faith speaks to America today, where trust in government wanes, causing people to trust in the marketplace. Yet, we know that the stress caused by our faith in a roller-coaster stock market or in accumulated stuff could affect our health, even reduce our life span, similar to those who lack basic necessities.[16] Moreover, all our trappings and trash degrade the Planet's wellness, further jeopardizing human health—a vicious circle. Progressive ecospiritual politics trusts that good government will make life less worrisome by discouraging quenchless fancies and by guaranteeing a decent, sustainable life for everyone, including quality holistic health care that presupposes a healthy Earth. What a welcomed reversal for those victimized by Conservative values. Even though corporate interests often exile the best health care, faith and hope temper political cynicism and transform it into needed change.

ON POLITICAL GRIEVING

In the meantime, life continues with its joys and its sorrows. A dimension of good health includes the handling of *grief*, a universal human capacity and a critical factor in our ecospiritual growth. Most of us have experienced the death of a loved one and have grieved—often bitterly—over that loss. Sorrow, however, is not always private but may also be public, as when a

14. See Clark, *Dark Ghetto*, 81–108. "The dark ghetto is institutionalized pathology."
15. Landsberg, "In Poorest Schools," sec. B.
16. Fanon, *Wretched of the Earth*, 249–310.

person or group grieves over adverse political realities. Grief strikes when one's candidate loses or favorite bill in Congress fails. America's grieving after 9/11 is a prime example of political mourning. Many now lament over a dying Planet and pass through the various stages of grief, including the political anger typically associated with such great calamities. Our political grief compares to Jeremiah agonizing over the loss of his people's Land (Jer 9:1). The entire book of Lamentations mourns over Jerusalem's misfortunes. After their national defeats, the exiled Israelites could no longer sing songs in foreign Lands, but only weep and wail in the dust before God (Ps 137:4, 44:24–25). In first-century Palestine, Galilean peasants grieve over loss because of heartless policies administered by aristocrats who sit in their palaces laughing and snickering.

Like Jeremiah, Jesus laments over Jerusalem because its political ethic has murdered many prophets "between the sanctuary and the altar" (Luke 13:31–35; Matt 23:37–39). This arouses his "righteous anger." He aches for the triumph of his ecospiritual politics within Jerusalem that he likens to a hen gathering her chicks under wing—a Nature image that traditionally alluded to political power and protection.[17] Living under the shadow of God's (feminine) wings means taking shelter from the "destroying storms" (political powers) that "trample" on the peoples' subsistence notions, causing them to mourn (Ps 57:1–3, 91:1–6). Whereas this grim reality now plaguing Jerusalem brings grief to Jesus, it never paralyzes him, but provides him firm resolve to reverse its condition. Hope in the new ecospiritual politics turns deep mourning and its anger into comfort and joy (Matt 5:4; Luke 6:21b). Seeing the humanitarian impulse of many religious and nonreligious people united to alleviate some of the world's most scourging moral plagues is uplifting. Political grief is a necessary prelude to political change.

In America, we collectively grieve over political missteps, and one is the lack of health care benefits for so many. As of this writing, nearly 45 million people remain without any health insurance; 89 million were uncovered at least one month during the years of 2006–7.[18] Scores have insufficient coverage. It should make us angry that, with all our wealth, medical skill, and technology, the U. S. isn't providing better health care here and around the world. Hopefully, the Affordable Health Care Act will reverse this grim reality. Our government could also do better at encouraging preventative measures—bringing health home, so we treat our body as a temple, as sacred, and worth protecting and not abusing. Holistically, it promotes proper exercise and education, while regulating the foods we eat, the air we breathe,

---

17. Mendenhall, *Tenth Generation*, 61–68.
18. Families USA report, "The Clock is Ticking," 1.

the water we drink, and our general safety—all of which assume a healthy toxic free Earth. Yet, the Conservative ethic challenges what little political gains have been made in health care while also leaving our Planet under the weather. For these reasons, we continue to grieve and become indignant. Nevertheless, all Progressive people will direct their righteous anger toward bringing shalom to all of Creation by pushing for local, regional, and national solutions. Most of the problems plaguing us, however, reach around the globe and affect all nations.

11

Sustainability Is International

> People will come from east and west, from north and south,
> and will eat in the Good Government.
>
> —Jesus

A MOST COMPELLING ECOSPIRITUAL mandate of our day is the creation of nurturing communities characterized by compassion, fairness, sharing, tolerance, diversity, awe, but that live in peace with one another. Progressives long for the day when people, religions, and nations exist in unity (not uniformity); where everything and everyone on Earth are considered kin. But in our time, a most dangerous alternative ethic divides countries, resulting in collective grandiosity, extreme nationalism, bitter rivalries, and ecodegradation. When antagonisms prevail, saber rattling often portends the chosen strategy.[1] Former Secretary of State Condoleezza Rice once expressed her ultimate vision of America as maintaining "twenty-first century military forces that are beyond challenge."[2] Many consider this the governing principle of international relations and the heartbeat of patriotism.

---

1. See Kristol and Kagan, "National Interest and Global Responsibility," 68–74.
2. Rice, "President's National Security Strategy," 83.

THE CONCERT OF NATIONS

Patriotism is generally recognized by both Conservatives and Progressives as a positive virtue. Conservative patriotism, however, often breeds nationalism: that one's nation is superior to others and that national sovereignty remains supreme never to be ceded to any other authority. The late Conservative commentator William F. Buckley stated it in stark terms: "No superstition has more effectively bewitched America's Liberal elite than the fashionable concepts of world government, the United Nations, internationalism."[3] These remarks send unifying, peacemaking, and Earth healing values into virtual exile. Progressives believe true patriots serve their country best by cooperating with other nations and negotiating solutions to problems utilizing international organizations like the United Nations. What might Jesus say about the love of country and uncompromising nationalism?

All the parties in Palestine believed in a reconstituted Israel, but Jesus, unlike most others, flatly rejects a strict and militant nationalism. He broadcasts a dressed up old vision: that "Israel" stands as a historical symbol of God-like/Land-based egalitarian governance that serves all peoples and tribes alike and thus, unites them. From its beginning, Israel broke through elitist nationalism to organize around the political values common to all peoples—equality, freedom, and shalom. After Israelite kings arose and ignored these values, a line of prophets, as lone voices, predicted that unyielding nationalism will bring exile. Isaiah, reflecting the essence of faith, saw beyond his borders and, in a remarkable text, declared that God blesses (honors) Egypt and Assyria just like Israel, and all *three* nations are to be "a blessing in the midst of Earth." By calling Egypt "my people," Assyria "the work of my hand," and Israel "my heritage," God confirms international unity (Isa 19:25). Many of the prophets would echo the salient truth that, once they shed their imperial designs, all the tribes and nations are of *equal moral worth* and are destined to realize the same ecospiritual/moral values. In line with the biblical message, the nations' blessings resound further to include the whole Earth, to everything on and within it.

Jesus' cosmopolitan sensibility did not grow out of a vacuum. Roman and Greek cultures greatly influenced Galilee; after all, it was called "Galilee of the Gentiles" (Matt 4:15). Jesus demonstrates his global consciousness at the very beginning of his campaign, when he visits his provincial hometown of Nazareth (Luke 4:14–31). Like all good politicians, Jesus begins the most important speech of his career by making political promises: the release of

---

3. Buckley, "Credenda and Statement of Principles," 205.

prisoners, the blind gaining sight, the oppressed being freed, and the reestablishment of the Jubilee Land laws. However, the popular Conservative view held that these goods would flow exclusively to the Israelites. By brushing aside Isaiah's recital of "the day of vengeance of our God"—a curse directed toward other nations—Jesus denies his audience the opportunity to savor their popular in-group theology and narrow tribalism. Creatively interpreting the past, he draws examples from Elijah and Elisha, who once snubbed the starving widows and hapless lepers in Israel so they could meet these same needs for two *foreigners*. This affront to nationalism stuns and outrages the hometown folks who turn into a lynch mob—Luke's way of linking Jesus' rejection of national superiority to his eventual crucifixion. The real culprit, however, was not the people, but the popular, ingrained spiritual politics: that Earth's bounty flows to God's "chosen" nation. Even on pain of death, Jesus could not promote such blind patriotism—our nation, number one; our nation, exceptionally blessed; our nation, right or wrong—as political virtues.

Jesus' later actions and teachings will reinforce this inaugural speech. He shows his love for disliked foreigners by healing them and by rebuking his followers for wanting lethal revenge on some hostile Samaritans (Luke 17: 11–19, 9:55). When he heals a Centurion's servant boy, he links it to international unity, declaring, "Many will come from east and west and will eat with Abraham and Isaac and Jacob in the kingdom of heaven" (Matt 8:5–13; also Luke 13:29). Jesus frequently lifts up Gentiles as role models who inherit the Good Government, like the courageous Syrophoenician woman (Matt 12:38–42; Mark 7:24–30). One biblical scholar rightly notes that *every* one of Jesus references to the Kingdom of God implies international cooperation.[4] In the end, the Basileia is *all nations* united under a common covenant that governs with moral strength and nurtures the international biocomunnity's good.

Jesus' internationalism calls attention to the promise that Abraham (meaning "ancestor of a multitude") would be the father of many nations; and through him "all the families of the earth shall be blessed" (Gen 17:5, 12:3). The prophets would describe Israel as a light to the nations, a symbol ("ensign") of servant political leadership, and a force that will bring justice and peace to the whole Earth (Isa 42:1–6, 49:6; Luke 2:32). As a light, Israel will enlighten governments to "offer food to the hungry and satisfy the (subsistence) needs of the afflicted" (Isa 58:10). In order to bring both peace and food, it teaches them to craft their swords into life sustaining farm implements. Jesus sends out his campaign workers with the same message to be the "light of the world" and the "salt of the earth" (Matt 5:13–16). This

---

4. Jeremias, *Jesus' Promise to the Nations*, 70.

deepened view of international service finds its echo today in Progressive ecospiritual politics with its priority of unifying, serving, and preserving the whole human and extra-human family.

Understanding Jesus' international thrust helps us to further appreciate his final political showdown in Jerusalem. The most definitive symbol of Israelite national pride was the Temple, and the Gentiles (under penalty of death) were forbidden to enter its inner areas. The prophets, however, saw the Temple, not only as Israel's rallying point after its exile, but also as benefitting every nation. "All the nations shall stream" to the Temple to learn about the compassionate justice of God and how to eliminate war and bring sustainability as predicted by Isaiah (Isa 2:3–4, 56:7). Jesus' disruptive actions in the Temple carry a similar international role. Quoting Isaiah, he affirms the Temple as a place of "prayer for *all nations*" (italics mine), leading to the suggestion that he meant, among other things, to cleanse it of its "profane" exclusion of Gentiles (Mark 11:17).[5] For Jesus, the rebirth of the true Israel (the reign of God) touches all peoples—the Jewish good news "proclaimed to all nations" (Mark 13:9–10).

The lesson for today is simple and clear: in the spirit of Jesus, peoples and nations must begin embracing an ecospiritual politics of unity that treats other citizens and countries—including those deemed enemies—as equals, even as special. Moreover, international cooperation is critical in dealing with the global crises, since poverty, marginalization, and ecodestruction spill over all borders. Yet, the Conservative morality lodged deeply into America's psyche has dug-in its heels against even modest reductions in world poverty, national vanity, and our part in global pollution, much less taking responsibility for their harmful effects.

Our partisan pride and narrow family loyalty are intensified when yoked to religion. Note the phrase "under God" wedged into the Pledge of Allegiance. Also take the American flag. Many churches have planted the flag within their spaces of worship (often in the place of honor over against the red, white, and blue Christian flag). Most of my Baptist forerunners insisted on the separation of church and state and would be appalled if they knew this symbol of narrow nationalism adorned their sanctuaries. According to one Baptist historian, American flags began appearing in churches during World War I to provide divine sanction for the war effort. During World War II, flags proliferated in worship spaces for much the same reason.[6] Even though the wars ended, the flags remained.

---

5. Jeremias, *Jesus' Promise to the Nations*, 66.

6. Dr. Norman Maring, a Baptist Church historian and colleague of mine at Eastern Baptist Seminary, in private conversations.

If Christians yearn to erect flags in their churches, it seems most appropriate, following the spirit of Jesus, to fly the flags of many countries or the United Nations flag. While people may disagree about the effectiveness of the U.N., displaying its symbol would demonstrate a commitment to internationalism and to the belief that all people stand as children of the divine and thus, belong to one another as brothers and sisters. As Martin Luther King Jr. reminded us, we exist as *citizens of the world*, bonded by our common ancestry that rises above race, class, tribe and nation, yet still loyal to our own country.[7] Extending this truth ecologically, we are citizens of Earth first, bonded to its life-support systems and, by our common ancestry, to its plants and animals. We might call it "internaturism," a further implication of our international consciousness.

ON WAGING PEACE

The greatest plague on humanity is our resort to predatory violence. It devastates our spiritual capacity, human dignity, the quest for unity, and the environment's sustainability (which is why the Bible images the imperial powers as "beasts"). At the local level, the hometown folks' attempt to throw Jesus over a cliff signals a tragic but abiding truth: fervent nationalism evokes collective violence. The imperial ethic, with its in-group honor and national hubris, buttresses a just-below-the-surface rage so that, in a matter of minutes, admiring hometown friends and relatives become a rampaging lynch mob. On a grand scale, nationalism is inevitably linked to militarism, often encouraged by religious fervency, providing Jesus yet another reason to reject a spiritual politics that glorifies and deifies collective egoism.

Militarism, as a major plank in the imperial ethic, had snaked its way through Israel's early history and some parties in Jesus' day believed in armed force as the means to restore Israel. Rebellions occurred before and during Jesus' childhood, noticeably the one that broke out after Herod the Great's death. Rome quickly squashed it, razing the city of Sepphoris (a stronghold of the rebel movement), crucifying nearly two thousand rebels, and enslaving its remaining inhabitants. No doubt the violence impacted Nazareth a few miles away, forcing it citizens to devise strategies to preserve their community from a firestorm of Roman retribution.[8] Jesus, like the prophets, distrusts military might and sees it as unwarranted within the Good Governing. Yet, most violence flowed from the structural brutalities of the Roman imperial system with its countless forms of human degradation.

7. King, "Beyond Vietnam."
8. Horsley and Silberman, *Message and the Kingdom*, 21.

Some suggest that Jesus sympathized with the rural resistance, a claim that deserves a response.[9] When he talks about people breaking violently into the Kingdom, he is not anticipating a literal revolution, but employs political imagery to express desperate peoples' clamor to enter it (Matt 11:12).[10] Although Jesus instructs his supporters to purchase a sword for their campaigns, he speaks to the camping needs of itinerants; he limits the swords to two—hardly enough to stage a revolution (Luke 22:36–38). His remark about not bringing peace but a sword sits couched within a discussion of *family* conflict, reflecting Luke's substitution of "division" for "sword" (Matt 10:34; Luke 12:51).[11] Jesus knows well the fireworks that his peacemaking activities will ignite when he begins assaulting the prevailing assumptions. Although a Progressive ethic always respects differences and seeks common ground, it realistically inflames strong opposition from its Conservative detractors, dividing friends and family. Hopefully, such disputes today will spark only Thanksgiving dinner and water-cooler standoffs.

Conflict escalates for Jesus when he wreaks havoc in the Temple (Mark 11:15–16; John 2:15). Like the prophets of old, he purposes a disruptive assault on the pervasive imperial ethic with its economic props grounded in exploiting Creation (selling animals). In this situation of unjust rule, Jesus stifles the aggrandizing activities and violates the "rights" generated by the official ethic. Similar to blocking downtown traffic in a contemporary example, he renders their supports temporarily nonfunctional, but he does not inflict bodily or property harm. He enters the capitol as a prophetic reformer to rid it of its harsh politics and comes across as *a morally forceful man*, but not as a violent one.

In the Garden of Gethsemane, one of Jesus' supporters pulls a sword and whacks off the ear of a Temple-state servant of the High Priest. This bloody act symbolically blemishes the ruler's religio-political honor and authority, thereby severing his ability to carry on business as usual (Mark 14:47–50). Jesus' non-militaristic ethic surfaces when he shouts, "No more of this!" and heals the official's ear (Luke 22:51). His meaning is clear: all militaristic activity must cease—the clubs of official violence as well as the swords of rebellion. Exiled from the original Garden, Cain struck Abel; in this Garden, and in the new politics, brother and sister shall not raise the

---

9. Brandon, *Jesus and the Zealots*, 358. He believes Jesus had a "bond of common sympathy" with the Zealots. See also Aslan, *Zealot*, 120, who considers Jesus a "zealous revolutionary," but not of the Zealot Party. Though not "bent on armed rebellion," Jesus was not a pacifist. The epigraph of Aslan's book is Jesus' statement, "I have not come to bring peace, but a sword" (Matt 10:34).

10. Clinton, *Pure Kingdom*, 94–96.

11. See Black, "Not Peace, but a Sword," 293–94.

sword against one another. By healing the severed ear, he defuses the *spiral of destructive violence* created by the imperial ethic and the peoples' violent resistance to it. Jesus then voices his most famous comment on militarism: "Put your sword back into its place; for all who take the sword will perish by the sword" (Matt 26:52). These venerable words utter war's pale and futile purpose—simply the digging of graves and the devastation of the environment. Jesus puts to rest, once and forever, any need to be "God's Warriors."

The above saying also addresses the "eye for an eye" law of retaliation (Lev 24:20; Matt 5:38-48). This ancient precept originally arose to limit violence, so that a retaliator could not take a life in exchange for a slight wound. Crumbling farm communities, however, face deadly honor feuds. Treating antagonists with kindness and respect are behaviors considered shameful and dangerous. Jesus eschews the vengeful politics of negative reciprocity— "do back to others what they do to you." Instead, with his Progressive interpretation of retaliation, Jesus delivers his most famous campaign plank of just three words: "love your enemies," a breathtaking mandate unique to him but deeply ingrained by his Jewish faith (Exod 23:4). Standing as the highest expression of universal love, these immortal words provide a sure stratagem for eliminating violence everywhere. It follows from Jesus' view of the Creator God as nurturing-Parent who loves and bestows Earth's favors of sunshine and rain even on enemies (Matt 5:43-48).

For Jesus, then, retaliation means *beneficial reciprocality*—the return of something good for an evil. In a revenge-seeking culture, he rules that when you are insulted, "retaliate" by turning your other cheek; i.e., "cut people a lot of slack." If you are sued for your shirt, it's honorable to hand over your coat as well; possibly he or she needs it. When the Roman authorities disrespectfully force you to carry a burden a mile, counter by going two miles. When fellow farmers you dislike lose their Land and are reduced to begging or borrowing, retaliate by coming to their aid—even praying for their good (Luke 6:28). Clearly, Jesus' activist subsistence reinterpretation of the *lex talionus* (law of retaliation) yields a whole range of safety net policies, in a world where everyone is a potential enemy in the cutthroat game of survival (Luke 6:27-36). His renderings cage the prevailing Conservative ethic and halt the downward spiral. They restructure communities, grounding them in mutual esteem, forgiveness, civic friendship, and sustainability.

Today's Spiritual Progressives similarly reject the role of retaliation in social/political policy, including the death penalty for crimes or as a warrant for engaging in war. We would have done well to reject the ethic of negative reciprocity in American's blind thirst for revenge after the terrorist attacks of 9/11. The nineteenth century Danish theologian Soren Kierkegaard wisely wrote that when we close our eyes to social and political distinctions, we no longer see the other as an enemy, but as a neighbor.[12] We then perceive our *common* humanity, our immeasurable dignity. To love an enemy implies that a person or nation will go to extreme measures to eliminate "enemy-ness" itself. It means not whipping up retaliatory hatred toward adversaries, labeling them as evil, and proudly reaching for the gun—the ingredients of a "crusader ethic" and stand-your-ground laws that seem to have taken hold of America.[13] The community that eliminates enmity and promotes equality and communication reflects the true character of God; its citizens deserve the title "children of God" (Matt 5:9).

In the end, Jesus held firmly to Judaism's most prized virtue, shalom. Rome, however, hijacked the term "peace." Under the *Pax Romana*, Rome slashed its way through the ancient world, conquering at will and crushing all resistance. Roman occupation legions existed only as peace *keepers,* not peace*makers.* Their concept of peace keeping meant rivers of blood, piles of corpses, and crucifying anyone who crosses them. But a new ecospirituality of peacemaking was to emerge from a man sitting on a lowly donkey.

Jesus' ride into Jerusalem during Passover expressly ridicules the recent high-stepping Roman war horses that had entered the capital to keep the peace during the volatile Passover festival—an event that ironically celebrates Israel's liberation from foreign oppressors. The Gospel writers link his entry to Zechariah's prophecy calling for a governing that would "command peace to the nations." This prophet soundly rejects militarism: "War horses, battle chariots, and bows" will be "cut off" (Zech 9:10). This peace is not an abstract ideal, but rather one embodied in a peace-loving ecospiritual politics, a viable legal structure, and a fruitful Land. When this occurs, according to Zechariah, violent international showdowns will cease forever. Jesus' highly volatile "political theater"[14] promotes Zechariah's vision of humble governing inscribed by peacemaking, while unmasking and neutralizing the Conservative hierarchy that relies on naked force.

Other prophets similarly push for a spiritually grounded peacemaking. While the people were declaring military might as "our god," Hosea becomes the first prophet (and perhaps the first person in recorded history) to renounce militarism, calling it a sin—a form of idolatry (Hos 10:13–14, 14:3). Jeremiah states it most eloquently, "Do not let the mighty boast in their might . . . ; but let those who boast boast in this . . . that I am the Lord; I act with steadfast love, justice, and righteousness in the earth, for in these things I delight, says the Lord" (Jer 9:23–24). In the good society, love's

---

12. Kierkegaard, *Works of Love*, 68.
13. Long, *War and Conscience*, 33–40 for a description of the "crusader ethic."
14. Horsley, *Message and the Kingdom*, 72.

sustaining justice triumphs over strong armies. Israel can only fulfill its destiny by waging peace in the face of a culture of violence.[15] Then, Israel will become the impetus and symbol of every nation's ecospiritual destiny—to be united and at peace with one another.

According to Isaiah, all the nations shall stream to the mountain of the Lord's house to learn the ways of God and recast their swords and spears into plows so that "nation shall not lift up sword against nation, neither shall they learn war anymore" (Isa 2:1–4; Mic 4:1–4). This remarkable ecospiritual vision hails an end to the culture of war that feeds on inequality, poverty, marginalization, and Land abuse. The shroud of death cast over all nations will be "swallowed up;" a time of "endless peace" will prevail (Isa 25:7, 9:7). Isaiah's compelling vision of international peace, including its ecological shalom of lions and fearless lambs grazing together, reaches the pinnacle of politics. Its morality of unity has energized peace-loving people and inspired religious art and literature throughout the ages (Isa 11:6–9). The hope of the world rests in learning to farm and subsist together in peace. This breathtaking ideal shaped Judaism and mirrors the Progressive vision of the Good Government Jesus heralded.

The peacemaking of the Governing for the Common Good starts in Galilean villages where people languish in a spiral of self-destructive rage. When Jesus insists that parties of conflicts be "reconciled" and "come to terms quickly . . . or you will be thrown into prison," he is advising not only against the disgrace and torment of imprisonment, but also the danger of prolonging conflicts (Matt 5:23–26). Antagonisms will end by bringing others good things, including fruits from the Land.[16] The peasant sustainability ideal of being a brother and sister's keeper is the strongest guarantee to end war and its destruction forevermore. Blessing the adversary means the less likelihood of being butchered by one. Including all nations into one nurturing family makes that prospect even more unlikely. This is the enduring standard-bearer of the Liberal faith and the morally compelling reason it insists that negotiation and aid pave the road to peace at every level of the human community.

For Jesus, peacemaking goes beyond simply the elimination of conflict. As we have seen, the Hebrew word "shalom" means more than "peace" or "hello," but conveys the broad political meaning of sustainability for the common good. It includes good health, general social welfare, economic prosperity, proper Land use, tranquility of mind, ecospiritual growth, and saving lives. Jesus offers this larger vision when he commissions his followers

15. Kaufmann, *Religion of Israel*, 346.
16. Theissen, *Social Reality*, 124–25.

to establish the coming Compassionate Governing among the families and villages by instructing them to proclaim "shalom to this house" (Luke 10:5–6). In Jesus' Good Government, the banishing of violence against people and Land means sustaining life in all its dimensions; Jesus is radically pro-living, radically pro-peacemaking.

An important lesson from Jesus for building peace looks to his ridicule of imperial tyranny with its "sword and clubs" used to bully others. Even as Jesus eloquently expresses his nonviolent ecospiritual politics, his followers, still seduced by imperial values, jockey among themselves for presumed "power-politics-as-usual" positions in the coming Government. In rebuke, Jesus quotes the reversal notion, rejecting the death-threat power plays of tyrants. Instead, he defines governing as sacrificial service to all citizens (Matt 20:25–28). Unfortunately, our American Conservative streak of militarism and its bed-partner nationalism has wielded its swords and clubs for the flimsiest of reasons and with deadly consequences. Regarding the Vietnam War, one Conservative stated that this war "should have been fought and won," to stop "worrisome Communist expansion."[17] The judgment of history suggests, however, that Vietnamese Communism presented little threat to our national interests, and that the ongoing war was a costly and tragic mistake. In addition to our own military casualties (more than 50,000 killed and 300,000 wounded), a great many Vietnamese perished (more than a million innocent women and children)—dismissed under the euphemism "collateral damage." We must add to this the massive environmental destruction.

A generation later nationalism and militarism again prevailed to push us into the second Gulf War after the 9/11 tragedy. Rather than exhausting all peaceful alternatives to resolve our disagreements with Iraq and without support from the United Nations or even direct negotiations with Iraq's leaders, America's Conservative leaders clamored to invade that country. A devastating assault was launched under the guise of highly questionable charges—that Iraq possessed weapons of mass destruction, along with its supposed ties to the 9/11 terrorists. When these reasons proved false, Conservatives didn't blink. They contrived an after the fact justification for the invasion—the despotic rule of President Saddam Hussein.

The warrant for America's involvement in Vietnam and blitzkrieg-like occupation of Iraq shows disdain for the traditional "Just War Theory," a view championed by St. Augustine and advanced by many theologians and foreign policy theorists in modern times. Just War principles hold that engaging in battle should be a last resort and carried out for strictly

---

17. Bork, *Slouching toward Gomorrah*, 19.

defensive purposes—never preventive. Our government not only violated these moral criteria by invading Iraq, it also breached principles directed toward the *conduct* in war with its inhumane treatment of prisoners and the extraordinarily high number (150,000) of civilian casualties. Tragically, astronomical death counts only reflect the tip of history's iceberg of humiliation, torture, and environmental destruction due to the culture of war. Our invasion and occupation can only be justified by a discredited crusade ethic (with its implied religious fever), as succinctly expressed in the sick parody bumper sticker: "Give war a chance."

To many around the world, America's infamous action in Iraq represents an act of economic and cultural imperialism buttressed by multinational corporations (primarily oil and weapons companies). Here, the parallel with ancient Roman imperialism is striking. Rome saw itself endowed with a natural destiny to "civilize" the world. It conquered to gain access to goods under the brutal guise of *Pax Romana*, or keeping the peace. In their conquered provinces, the Romans permitted only high-positioned wealthy collaborators to rule. Rome occupied the Lands and "supplemented" the local police forces with well-equipped Roman Legions. Using local resources, they developed distinctive Roman-style social and material infrastructures. They ruled by the will of the gods with extreme force, often by terror, as have most imperial powers throughout history. And, like Rome, America assured itself strategic access to vital resources.[18] *Imperialistic wars of aggression remain history's moral pandemic.* That this plague will someday be eradicated is the Spiritual Progressive's most fervent hope, given that a militant leader's nod could mean millions killed and maimed.

From Jesus' perspective, civilization hangs in the balance over whether the nationalistic militancy that plagues our hearts, our halls, and our Planet can be eliminated. This will happen only when we abolish the contaminating culture of violence. This culture begins in the family when a child sees father hitting mother or hunting animals for sport, is slapped by a parent, is cruel to little creatures, bops or bullies another child, becomes saturated with TV and movie savagery, and engages in virtual violence through video games. Then, the child may join a gang or be recruited to fight wars (over which sacred banners often fly) and inflict massive destruction on people and the environment. Violence infects our souls and pummels our ecospirituality. Progressive politics is committed to exorcising this menacing spirit until we no longer croon the discordant notes of war or embark upon its troubling sea of horrors.

---

18. Elliott, *Arrogance of Nations*, 3–16.

Building on nurturing family values, Spiritual Progressives dream that governments will implement strategies of cooperation; that they will, as the Earth Charter mandates: comply with international declarations, covenants and conventions; commit to schedules for eliminating weapons of mass destruction; push for universal disarmament; end the culture of war; and turn the tide of the Planet's woes.[19] The Progressive goal is to create a universal ecospiritual consciousness through programs of peace and justice, knowing that the Planet's macro-plagues of hunger, oppression, poverty, disease, and ecocatastrophe are often a result of, and contribute to, war.[20] By appreciating national differences, Progressives affirm a rational pluralism and diversity—the foundation for a less violent, more unified, and sustainable world. Our vision is roughly equivalent to the ecospiritual politics of the Hebrew prophets, including Jesus of Nazareth and the Judaism he loved. The same hope has stayed alive through the centuries to inspire the Progressive dreams of Martin Luther King Jr., Cesar Chavez, Gandhi, Dorothy Day, Bishop Desmond Tutu, Jim Wallis, Rabbi Michael Lerner, Bill Mckibben, and other great shalom-loving prophets of the modern age. Yet, we always stand at the brink, compelling all peacemakers to remain vigilant.

---

19. Raskin, *Liberalism*, 54.
20. Ibid., 247.

12

What Would Jesus Do in Washington?

> When he entered Jerusalem, the whole city was in turmoil.
> —MATTHEW

MINISTERS REVEL IN THE story about a pastor preaching on Jesus turning water into the most excellent wine at a Cana wedding. After the sermon, a teetotaling deacon rushes up to the minister and grumbles, "Pastor, you know when Jesus turned water into wine? Well, that's the one thing I don't like about Jesus!" The irony of this tale reminds us that the route to Jesus remains perplexing; we meet him not only on familiar turf, but sometimes on strange and rocky paths. Each of us could probably make a whole list of things we don't like about Jesus. That is the nature of ecospiritual growth and our return from any exile.

In these pages we have delved into the heart and soul of Jesus and encountered a Progressive visionary who meant to make a big difference in his world. He teaches us profound ecospiritual truths: the creative God compassionately nurtures and sustains; this God is "imaged" when these values shape our thoughts and actions; and we need to turn from the flawed Conservative values that continually seduce us. Undermining the pieties and rationales of the dominating elites, his ecospiritual politics of "the way"—the way of sustainability—sows seeds that transform. He changes hearts of stone into compassion for all of Creation; the drive for unlimited material gain into equal sharing; social walls into table fellowship; sickness into health care; shame into dignity; revenge into forgiveness; fasting into celebration; militancy into peacemaking; and nationalism into the union of all peoples. These God-given, Earth-keeping, Christ-centered, Progressive values define and deepen our faith and shape our action. They give voice to the billions born to be unheard and doomed to a lifetime of poverty and indignity and to a Planet reeling in its waste. In proclaiming these ideals, Jesus was compelled to travel a turbulent *political* road—a road that eventually led to the seat of power and to his crucifixion. A lofty morality exacts a high price. Yet he never blinked at imperialism's stare down.

Unfortunately, history has often asked, "*Who* was responsible for Jesus' vicious death?" Such posing of the question reflects a certain bias that has, for centuries, pinpointed the Jews and contributed to a ghastly story of bigotry. It reached the most horrible chapter in the Holocaust. And the underlying intolerance slithers on. History's dark past (of which Christianity plays a part) compels a more accurate answer to extinguish all re-igniting sparks of anti-Semitism. Thus, a better framed question is, "*What* killed Jesus?" The correct answer, which lies at the heart of this work, is that Jesus was put to death by *a moral order—the imperial ethic*. As a thoroughgoing, Land-loving Jew, Jesus got caught between competing visions of the nation's future. He was unable to rest beneath the tree of the prevailing spiritual politics and so its morality nailed him to that tree under its shabby veil of justice. Jesus died at the hands of collective egoism, institutionalized greed, onerous Land schemes, toxic creeds, and organized fear—the bloodhounds of a misguided but enduring ethic.

This ethic that began in the Garden of pride with Adam's sinful desire to be high-and-mighty like God, raised its head, struck violently, and has flimflammed its way throughout human history in various crude and subtle forms. It hoped to obliterate such notions as honoring the shamed, positioning the last on par with the first, and loving one's enemies. It has unsheathed itself in the divine right of kings, the institution of slavery, the second-class citizenship of women, discrimination against Jews, Muslims, and people of color, the mistreatment of homosexuals, economic meltdowns, blind nationalism, the causes of climate change, anti-immigrant sentiments, militaristic approaches to solving problems, and the global imperialism of governments and huge unrestrained corporations. In our time we name it "Conservatism" and its media pundits and preachers, slaves to it values, lend their strident voices to its flaws—celebrating the very thing that nailed Jesus to the cross. This ethic is a moral step backwards. To put it in terms of the first-century world view, Conservatism—the nursling of the imperial ethic—rears up as a tormenting spirit. It makes Earth its junkyard

. . . and its slaughterhouse; we stand aghast at the wreckage. This leads to another reason for Jesus' death.

Christians believe that Jesus went willingly to the cross to redeem us from our sins and recover the best in us. Humans have been rendered blind, deaf, and mute, always living somewhere between home and exile. The path to salvation begins when we repent of our sins—our service to flawed values, including those *imperial values* that executed Jesus. These ever-hovering mores settled in my Oregon hometown as group prejudices, sheltered by the "sacred canopy" of my church. From the cradle on, I learned all the "curses" that God rained down on various out-groups—the most famous being the *curse of Ham* that instilled a negative attitude toward African-Americans. The *curse of Eve* also coursed through my small-town veins and affected my perception of women. The *curse of Sodom*, which placed homosexuals under God's wrath, reinforced my initial homegrown disgust of gays and lesbians. The *curse of Onan* intensified my sexual guilt. The *curse of the Jews* nourished my infused fear of Jews. As a child, I was warned to walk near the curb when passing a Jewish owned department store lest one of the Weil brothers reach out and pick my pocket. Yet my small world wasn't finished with me. I learned about the *curse of the ground* in Genesis that declared Nature at war with us, and so needed subduing.

I had been exposed to the worst in Christianity. Over the years, however, and with the insights of wise biblical teachers and scholars, I learned that Jesus never fostered these attitudes. In fact, these beliefs disgrace him. How long will religious communities continue to hold similar prejudices against our out-grouped brothers and sisters? Views like the above, fed by the Conservative ethic, have brought out the worst in our nation as well. As we have seen, Conservatism taints all it touches: morality, law, politics, family, business, culture, community, religion, soil, air, sea, and other creatures. It leaves little unscathed. For the Christian, then, Jesus died to deliver us from, among other things, *the sins of Conservatism* that dwell within us all: the dark spell of excluding others, the avarice of unlimited gain, the pride of status seeking, the violence of anger, and the wanton exploitation of Earth— in all their various manifestations. These "works of the flesh" call for our continual contrition and repentance, in line with the biblical injunction that if we confess our sins, God, being faithful and just, will forgive those sins and cleanse us from all our injustices (1 John 1:9). But being "reconciled" with God implies making peace with others and with Earth.

Furthermore, Jesus died as a suffering Messiah, not only to redeem persons, but governments as well. In his Matthew 25 speech, Jesus spells out in vivid detail what good governing accomplishes and what he expects his followers to establish on Earth. All his examples focus on the most vulnerable: the hungry, the thirsty, the unsheltered, the prisoners, and the socially estranged ones. How the downtrodden are treated is how people and governments treat Jesus. By extension, how Earth, too, is treated is how we regard Jesus. To gas the air is to gas Jesus; to ravage the Land is to ravage Jesus; to extinct a species is to crucify him anew. However, to love this vulnerable Earth and all within it translates to cherishing Jesus. This is the good news of the *whole* gospel, making transformed governing possible. Yet, without decisive action, possibilities remain but dreams.

EVANGELICALS WITH AN UNEASY CONSCIENCE

Over sixty years ago, my beloved neighbor and colleague, Dr. Carl F. H. Henry, wrote about the "uneasy conscience" of conservative Christians who ignore burning ethical issues.[1] Today, most Evangelicals recognize the importance of social action and a considerable number are actively engaged, with many embracing Jesus' Progressive ecospiritual politics. Some call themselves "Red Letter" Christians to hail their commitment to Jesus' words.[2] They have realized that many of the cherished values they had been taught were flawed and actually disdained by Jesus. In fact, they underwrote his death—a death that, ironically, delivers us from those very values. Some Conservative Christians have caught their own reflection in the mirror of the imperial ethic and see that the phrase "politically conservative Christian" is a contradiction of terms, as John Dean, in his book *Conservatives without a Conscience*, forthrightly states.[3] What do we say to these Christians who have become uneasy with Conservative values?

First, Christians need continual reminding that *Jesus is the norm* for everything Christian. This means that the good news (gospel) of Jesus Christ, the living Lord and Savior who resides within us, includes the historical "facts" about him: his life, his teachings, his values, his actions, and the God he lived—the nurturing-Parent/God where compassion reigns supreme. Given these facts, I have tried to locate Jesus more faithfully on the left side of the political spectrum and to stress that his most devoted followers stand committed to his Progressive values. Genuine faith in Jesus Christ means, then, believing in his *alternative* political loyalty and nothing less. His ecospiritual politics must infuse our character and be incorporated accurately into the message we "preach" about him (the *kerygma*). To express the gospel succinctly (as an Evangelical might frame it): "To accept Jesus

1. Henry, *Uneasy Conscience*, 4.
2. Campolo, *Red Letter Christians*, 21–29.
3. Dean, *Conservatives without a Conscience*, 28.

Christ as my personal Lord and Savior means, without the slightest doubt or hesitation, to accept the *Progressive* Jesus into my heart."

To state it negatively: ignoring, rejecting, denying, or working against his ecospiritual politics would be to cheapen God, faith, morality, and Jesus himself and make a mockery of his sacrificial life, his death, and his resurrection. The Christian who does these (and we all do) remains in exile and in need of deliverance. In effect, failing to heed Jesus' Progressive values means rejecting his authority and ultimately casting aside everything about him, including his saving power. His ecospiritual politics must pervade our understanding of the plan of salvation and define what it means to be born again. If not, we risk worshipping a false Jesus—a Jesus who proves in the end to be a figment of our own self-interest, or even an "anti-Christ."[4] I struggle with this daily.

Second, and most importantly, *believing* in the Progressive Jesus is never enough; one must also submit to his Lordship or *live out* those values for which he died. Otherwise we manifest, as Dietrich Bonhoeffer warned, "cheap grace"—accepting what Jesus did on the cross without following him in costly discipleship.[5] A cheapened grace leads to a cheapened ethic. For the serious follower, the pinnacle of an ecospiritual walk means incorporating the mind of Christ, i.e., emulating Jesus' Progressive politics in ways appropriate to our day. Ideally, all Christians will model his love, joy, peace, gentleness, goodness, humility—the costly virtues or implanted fruit of the Spirit—through the political parties, the candidates, and the policies they support. Bearing these Progressive fruits defines and brings out the best in Christianity and America; they stand as the bases and goals of the church. In the end, Christians of all political colors, whether red or blue or green, must strive together to become more Christ-like—become less inclined to gratify ourselves and more open to do political battle on behalf of those who wage daily wars against peril. Jesus' resurrection secures a huge victory over the imperial ethic. The corporate powers can never silence and bury the truth that sacrificial love is God's will for all people in both their personal and political dealings, and that this love will ultimately prevail . . . and forever.

A FINAL CAUTION ON POLITICS AND RELIGION

Even though values are fundamental to all political philosophies, Conservatism talks as if it owns them. Hopefully, this work convinces you that the

---

4. Kasemann, *Jesus Means Freedom*, 38–40. Also Kasemann, *New Testament Questions*, 50, 52.

5. Bonhoeffer, *Cost of Discipleship*, 47.

historical Jesus stands as an important mediator of Progressive ecospiritual values. Therefore, we must reclaim him—in fact rescue him—from the Religious Right that has squeezed him into their imperial-based moral mold. However, unchaining Jesus from Conservatism and displaying his kinship to Progressive ideals is not to suggest that faith-specific beliefs should intrude into America's contemporary political agenda. We must guard against using the Bible as a strictly interpreted legislative handbook in the way that theocratic extremists in other religions and some Christians do. Whereas all political moralities of the ancient world were tied to religious conviction, including Jesus' ecospiritual politics, his Progressive values stand on their own, regardless of their religious garb. These values come down to us independent of, but reinforced by, the highest ideals in the major religions. They do not promote partisan religious dogma, but the common good. Thus, even the nonreligious will revere the values for which, as a lofty example, Martin Luther King Jr. died.

By saying the above, I certainly do not wish to discourage secular Liberals from embracing religion or ecospirituality. In fact, I believe they would find it invigorating, adventuresome, and advantageous to do so. Liberal philosopher Martha Nussbaum notes that all the great religions emphasize compassion for human suffering and have been "powerful sources of protection for human rights, of commitment to justice, and of energy for social change."[6] Some, like the Orthodox, have taken the lead in promoting Creation care. This is the bright side of religion. Yet, all Progressives, whether religious or not, will unite over the same universal values Jesus held—ideals that bring out the best in both Christianity and American democracy. Most of all, we have Judaism to thank for that.

A PROGRESSIVE ECOSPIRITUALITY CALLED COMPASSION

Now, having journeyed with Jesus throughout Palestine, we get a clearer picture of who he was, what it entails to become intimate with him, and thus, how Christian spirituality is defined. According to Jesus, the foundation for an authentic ecospirituality is the *Liberal spirit* that weds compassion with justice and responds appropriately. Some find it difficult to grasp this truth. Once, after my presentation of the Prodigal Son and the Good Samaritan Parables in a Bible study class, someone asked, "Do you see anything spiritual in these parables?" I could tell by her tone that she didn't like my Progressive slant on them. Both parables present a nearly identical story

---

6. Nussbaum, *Women*, 178.

line in which the main characters show *compassion*—the Samaritan toward the man attacked and the father toward his wayward son. I also made it clear that I thought the two heroes model God. She seemed to agree with these elements of the stories.

I responded by asking her, "Do you think the Good Samaritan and the nurturing father come across as highly spiritual persons?"

Her answer took me aback: "Not really."

I thought to myself, "How could she think that the actions of God are not spiritual?"

Of course, many people restrict their understanding of spirituality to acts of prayer and Bible reading, devotion to church activities, and generous giving—all important, but what sociologists call markers of *religiosity*. In my view, the Liberal actions of the Samaritan and the father, by their compassionate response to both misfortune and waywardness, illustrate *spirituality* in its highest and most glorious forms. Our identity as ecospiritual beings unfolds in our empathy with the Other. We continually repent of our stern spirituality represented by the so-called "holy" leaders who passed by the dying man, and by the self-righteous elder son who cold-shouldered his disgraced brother. Lacking compassion, their spirituality was deeply flawed.

Jesus challenges us to be empathic, which mandates we become the undocumented worker, the African-American, the Palestinian refugee, the AIDS victim, the scorned homosexual, the houseless, the gray wolf, and on and on—even though we might be none of these. Our devotion to Jesus means dedication to Godliness/goodness by identifying with and committing ourselves to empower those whom society considers expendable. It assumes that we, like God, are an active presence, and this defines Christ-honoring ecospirituality at its very best. These stories about the Samaritan and the father, however, speak not just about personal compassion. They teach that ecospirituality ripens when compassion moves into *the public sphere*. At the point of compassionate justice, religion most profoundly and legitimately intersects politics. To repeat a theme: being moved with compassion in the *civic/ecological realm* may be the most significant way our devotion to God is expressed, especially in these troubling times.

The compassion modeled in the two parables mentioned above embraces not only the victim, but also the victimizer. The father of the disappointed elder son reaches out and expresses love toward him, hoping to draw him back in. Jesus never demonizes the questioning scribe or the priest and the Levite who passed by a hurting man but exhorts them to go and do as the Samaritan did. Jesus directed God's empathy to all those victimized by the imperial ethic, which includes all of us. This truth needs recovery in today's fractured political arena where lions crouch, eager to tear apart and draw blood.

Jesus leads us from exile and challenges us to grow spiritually within his Progressive politics. Unlike those in some populist movements today, he was no anti-government zealot. He defended the government's role in providing free food as needed, free medical care for those without means, generous doses of dignity for the marginalized, and a renewed Land policy of sustainability. But how would his view of governing impact us today? We have presented him as a prophet/legislator trying to redeem his country in order to save humanity. Given his mission what would Jesus do now if he were to go to Washington? For your meditation, I offer the following suggestions, while you add (or subtract) your thoughts:

1. Jesus would introduce *compassionate, egalitarian* legislation that maximizes the core human capabilities and Earth's integrities and that responds to victims of catastrophe, institutionalized stigma, and structural destitution.

2. Jesus would legislate in ways that honor a reasonable pluralism and guarantees that all marginal and vulnerable minority groups are mainstreamed into society. His policies would not only *tolerate differences* compatible with common values, but *welcome them*. His welcoming would create laws to counter blatant and subtle prejudices against Jews, people of color, women, immigrants, people without homes, prisoners, sexual minorities, Native Americans, Muslims, the differently abled and mentally challenged, nuisance animals, and other historically persecuted groups. He would insist that governing treat all citizens and all creatures as brothers and sisters of one family and would promote *affirmative action* as an appropriate means to redress lingering injustices.

3. Jesus would favor bills that support *the poor*, upholding their interests, empowering them, and insisting that government grant them basic necessities compatible with the environment's well-being. He understands that persistent poverty is both a great political failure and a spiritual matter—a heinous economic sin that even Christians perpetuate. With his ingrained civic affection, he would vote for: a living wage, progressive taxation, enlarged entitlement programs, robust labor unions, Wall Street and corporate accountability, stronger campaign finance laws, reigning in lobbyists, more oversight, and other policies that reduce the extremes between the rich and poor. He would introduce "sin-taxes" (carbon, junk food, luxury) to discourage the ecodestructive vices of over-indulgence, neglect, and just plain laziness.

4. As one who reverences Creation and sees humans as its trustees, Jesus would insist that government guarantee a *clean and renewable environment*,

not subject to consumerism and corporate domination. He would introduce legislation that reflects love for all our neighbors including plants and animals and their ongoing life-support systems. He would propose incentives for people to green their homes and public buildings, while writing strict environmental regulations in line with international protocols. Given the irreversible nature of environmental degradation—especially the climate crisis—he would act with urgency. He would promote educating people and encourage them to embrace the principles within the Earth Charter, the most compelling moral document of this century. He would try to persuade us to live more sustainably and renewably as he did.

5. Jesus would introduce bills to enhance nurturing *family values*. He would strengthen laws that protect women (and men) from male (and female) overreach and from subordinate social and economic roles. He would decry people being defined by society's standards of outward beauty (looksism). His laws would defend children who are vulnerable to abuse, who are raised on junk food, who are bombarded with commercialism and violence by the mass media, and who stand in need of adequate affection for their self-esteem. As a great lover of truth and believer that the higher virtues never ally with ignorance, Jesus would make sure our children are exposed to a nurture-driven public education that instills a love for learning, an intellectual honesty, and how Progressive values contribute to the good of everyone and Earth. Jesus would also write laws that support the *validity of singleness, homosexual marriage,* and other *diverse but loving forms* of family structure. He would also recognize that humans and nonhumans are one large family.

6. If Jesus were to be a Supreme Court Justice, he would hand down *Liberal socio/eco-activist* interpretations of the law, applying it in ways that enhance compassionate justice and sustainability. He would see our Constitution in light of the Progressive ethic (its inner spirit) that created it. His interpretations of the laws would promote fair equality, basic liberty, general well-being, and an ever expanding list of reasoned *civil, human, and Earth rights*.

7. As he did in his day, Jesus would assign top priority to individual, community, and environmental health. He would co-sponsor *holistic, single-payer, affordable, and first-rate health care as a right* for all citizens and the world community. He would make sure laws addressed the mental, emotional, spiritual, and social realities of people, as well as the biological. He would also be a strong advocate for women's health. His platform would also push for prevention through education, exercise, and proper food choices—beginning in childhood.

8. Because Jesus taught that power and authority reside in the compelling truth of one's political vision and in returning good for evil, he would *oppose*

militaristic solutions to solve international problems, and reject retaliation as government policy. His programs would enhance peacemaking through *mutual cooperation*, generally holding other nations in respect. He would support international treaties and protocols and would use force only as a last resort and under the auspices of bodies like the United Nations. He would work to banish all weapons of mass destruction, as well as the social and economic causes of violence. He would introduce strong gun control bills, restrict the hunting animals for sport, eliminate the death penalty, restrain media violence, and stop the spewing of poisons into the air, water, and ground.

9. Jesus would *join and work for* political parties that most closely reflect his political vision and agenda and appear likely to be successful in promoting Progressive ecospiritual values. He would forge a *partnership* with other parties and groups over concerns such as drug and alcohol abuse, child exploitation and molestation, child pornography, inadequate education, the high divorce rate, crime, illiteracy, unwanted pregnancies, natural disasters, the worldwide AIDS crisis, slave trafficking, conservation, recycling, climate change, pandemics, prisoner abuse, substandard housing, torture, governmental and corporate dishonesty, to name some pressing ones. He would also join forces in the spirit of cooperation to solve age-old problems such as poverty, racism, genderism, war, etc. Without abandoning his core Progressive principles, he would see the value of compromise and consensus in the political arena.

10. Jesus would contest Conservatism's vision and agenda for America and show us its flaws and partial truths, leaving us with an *uneasy conscience* when we succumb to it. He would *urge us* to repent from those values and embrace the Progressive message as a dimension of our spirituality and the heart of our political vision. Then we bring that good news to the whole world.

All of these policies follow from a comprehensive understanding of the common good and are not religious specific. They reflect humanity's universal craving for love and dignity through equality—the ground swell of our highest dreams. The Progressive values and policies that Jesus supports serve as guideposts for realizing those dreams. They are the self-same values that have driven America's moral imagination throughout its history—the imagination that envisioned a republic we pledge "with liberty and justice for all."

The Progressive agenda, with its ecological focus, insists on (1) a *comprehensive* compassion that, in addition to personal acts of charity, shapes empathic public policies for a better world; (2) an *expansive* justice that advances an across-the-board equality for everyone, but with a green undercurrent; (3) a *full-blown* freedom that insists, not simply on the freedoms of speech, religion, property ownership, etc., but also on the freedom from want and misery; (4) a *thoroughgoing* pro-family stance that brings dignity to a variety of marriage and extended family structures; (5) a *radical* pro-life position that values the quality of all life, including animals, and cares more for those facing death in wars, on death row, and by death squads than for stem cells used in research; and (6) a *true-blue* patriotism that will, when called for, chasten its beloved country. For these values Jesus lived and died. They remain the pledge of all his followers for a better Christianity, a better America, and a better world.

Unfortunately, even though the Progressive vision for the common good has stamped history, it has never been completely fulfilled. The forces of Conservatism—the ghosts of Rome's ethic that still haunt us—continually wrestle with Progressive ideals, endangering, eroding, or even subverting them. Jesus' Progressive stance dismayed even his first followers. We all can be uppity and self-aggrandizing to the core; we all remain sinners and in need of repentance and restoration. With its half-baked values, Conservatism has hindered our ability to deal with critical global issues. Creating a just and generous society requires an ongoing effort to shake from our feet the Conservative dust that clouds our spiritual politics, thereby shading the achievements of our most noble ideals.

Yet ideals, as ideals, will always struggle to become realities. Theologian and social critic Reinhold Niebuhr reminded us that in the everyday world of practical partisan politics, we never fully actualize our loftiest aims. Policy formation embodies consensus building and the art of compromise. But Niebuhr also taught us that we must never succumb to a cynical realism, but always stretch up toward our guiding ideals, knowing that while we inevitably fall short and reform is piecemeal, we land higher than if we had not reached up at all.[7] In this way, compromise never lapses into moral capitulation. Thus, the Spiritual Progressive's dream must be renewed at all levels of community—family, small town, urban, nation, world body, and planetary. It demands a new spiritual movement—a Transformational ecospiritual politics that deeply connects our souls with nurturing values around which the children of humanity are united. With help from the Jesus tradition, the prophets of the major religions, and all people of good will, our exile can end and our dreams fulfilled.

HABITAT FOR HUMANITY—A MODEL FOR GOOD GOVERNING

We have promoted Progressive ecospiritual values upon which a just society and sustainable Planet are built. But how might these values translate into

7. See Niebuhr, *Nature and Destiny*, vol. 2, 68–90.

personal and corporate actions by non-profits cooperating with government? We touch on two: Habitat for Humanity that addresses human need and ECOFaith that looks to Earth's needs.

One basic human good is suitable shelter which a responsive government should provide as a fundamental right. One of the finest examples of addressing the core values surrounding housing is Habitat for Humanity, a non-profit Christian organization, whose goal is not only to eliminate substandard shelter around the world, but also provide a context so that people and communities might grow in every way, including spiritually. Many of its values reflect those of the Spiritual Progressive and could provide a model for the government in its obligation to provide adequate housing for all its citizens.

Habitat for Humanity, founded upon the vision of Millard and Linda Fuller, but heralded by its most famous volunteers, Jimmy and Rosalynn Carter, aims to express the love of Jesus by building decent homes at affordable prices. It strives to bring hope and dignity to individual families while, at the same time, restoring communities. Searching out and respectfully partnering with those having the greatest need for housing, Habitat gives priority to those whose incomes fall below the medium for any given community but sufficient to pay back an interest-free loan (determined by the cost of building materials). Generally, each adult family member contributes 250 hours of "sweat equity" in constructing the house. They can also earn hours by attending classes on finance, on home repair, or volunteer in other ways for Habitat (especially for those not capable of physical labor). In the Santa Barbara affiliate, if the family should later move away they would be returned all their monthly mortgage payments (plus a slight cost of living adjustment) as their accumulated equity.

Because Habitat's approach is holistic—more than just houses—it creates a partnership with families to ensure shalom. Each qualifying family is appointed a caring partner who respectfully provides support and counsel on becoming better homeowners, members of condo associations, and community participants. This program is designed to be a mutual learning, growing, and empowering experience. Volunteers (along with skilled paid professionals) help in the home construction, creating a sense of civic purpose as well as engaging them with one another and the chosen families (promoting civic friendship). Their labor is holy work; building homes with affection—"love in the mortar joints," as Habitat expresses it. Habitat does not aim to build "projects," but a sacred space called home that helps to restore the dignity of people and neighborhoods. Through its programs, the virtues of respect, self-reliance, love, joy, generosity, cooperation, and community building are enhanced. It also shows love to the environment by building green.

Habitat for Humanity partners with government in a number of ways. It fully complies with non-discriminatory laws in hiring and in determining who receives a home. Government also aids in providing infrastructure (utilities, roads, loans for ground, etc.). Habitat understands that shelter is tied to a living wage, good health care, proper Land use planning, transportation, and a host of issues where public entities (and some private) are better positioned to provide these basic needs. But government could follow Habitat's respectful and holistic example by enhancing the spiritual dimension through love, genuine care, and community building or what Habitat calls "outrageous generosity."[8] Good governing might provide trained care partners (not just caseworkers, but co-workers who supplement the busy bureaucrats), encouraging and supporting families, especially through crises. In this way, both families and communities are transformed. People then feel they are not only served, but also loved by government. On the day a family celebrates taking possession of their home (and if they happen to be religious), Habitat presents them a Bible or the sacred text of their tradition to symbolize the spiritual dimension of the whole process—a ritual beyond government's proper role.

This approach by government might do more to revitalize neighborhoods, reduce crime, eliminate illegal drugs, discourage blight, deal with houselessness, encourage hope, contribute to overall health, enhance the desire for education, create jobs, and decrease poverty than the present piecemeal efforts with their limited success. The key to change is making people feel special and empowered—the thrust of Jesus' spiritual politics and the goal of all good governing. If you decide to volunteer, you will be spiritually transformed and so will your community.[9]

ECOFAITH'S "PATH TO SUSTAINABILITY PROJECT"

Another example of applying Progressive values in partnership with government institutions is ECOFaith, a group of interfaith partners in Santa Barbara, California whose mission is to encourage ecological awareness and action. The underlying philosophy assumes that religious communities have a great influence on governments, businesses, schools, and non-profits when collectively mobilized. An important way to begin engaging people is to bring the Planet's woes face to face with their sacred places of worship and teach the importance of greening their buildings and grounds, as divine mandate. From

---

8. Reckford, *Creating a Habitat*, 26.

9. For more information about Habitat for Humanity and to find your closest affiliate, go to www.habitat.org.

there, they green their homes and their communities. Thus far, four congregations in the Santa Barbara area have completed the pilot project.

ECOFaith, in collaboration with the Bren School of Environmental Science and Management at the University of California at Santa Barbara, has developed a path to sustainability that includes five elements to which congregations commit. First, they assemble a Green Team, composed of members with an Earth conscience and dedicated to preserving and restoring the environment. Providing leadership, they coordinate all the steps and assemble a workbook that includes materials relevant to their congregation. Second, each faith body will develop a comprehensive education program, including worship themes and sermons, study groups of all ages, work days for energy retrofitting, the use of posters, art, music, etc. Excellent launch pads are the Earth Charter and the *Green Bible* with its introductory essays and its Bible study guide, action plans, and green index. Third, an energy audit is required and ECOFaith has developed an online, do-it-yourself website that each congregation could adapt to their context.[10] Fourth, ECOFaith provides a cost-benefit tool that includes, not only the downstream financial benefits to the congregation, but also the benefits to the environment (for instance, in the amount of reduced carbon released into the atmosphere).

Last, members of the congregation pledge to follow the path of sustainability in their own lives. Through the process of religious commitment, education, and action, an eco-consciousness emerges, resulting in changes at home, school, and business. Of equal importance, however, is that their devotion translates into political will, heralding a fire and brimstone ecological message—pressuring local, regional, national, and international communities to consider environmental impacts on all policy decisions. ECOFaith mentors each congregation through the whole process, ending with each developing its own website version of the program as a better fit for like congregations.

Jesus awakens us to see the bigger picture and recognize our political role in the Progressive movement he energized. The values that inflamed him to face the imperial ethic of the past inspire many to stand against the same repackaged ethic today, stirring them to civic action that transforms governing into a more compassionate force. Like the nurturing God whom he loved, Jesus heard the cries of his people and took immediate steps to reverse the misery wrought by self-aggrandizing rulers. The imperial ethic relentlessly re-incarnates itself and continues to haunt. Social pyramids persist with those at the bottom still bearing the brunt of inequality, still being marginalized, still being poor. Jesus promoted everyone's rights to the

---

10. www.ecofaith-sb.org

basic goods of life: health, freedom, self-respect, justice, spiritual development, play, a healthy environment, and love. His insights enhance dignity and rights by placing all races, genders, ages, nationalities, humane religions, and species into one family—a loving and nurturing biocommunity. Because of our faith in God and in Jesus Christ, his moral truths course though our religious and political veins. We can herald them with a hearty, but humble, confidence. An old hymn expresses it: "On Christ the solid rock I stand; all other ground is sinking sand."

This book began with the hypothetical question, "What would Jesus do?" within the American political landscape. Donning the mantle of a spirit-filled prophet/lawgiver, this remarkable Galilean elbowed his way into a world exiled by misery and shame. He brought a message about good governing with consistency and nerve until the very end. After traveling with him on a long campaign trail, we have learned that he took a different political path—one that led to equal respect for all of Creation. We have seen him in action. We heard his first speech in his hometown and saw how badly it went. But he never gave up.

Out of the past, Jesus shows us how to cherish humane values and calls us to achieve them. He offered grandiose standards for our often pragmatic and partial reforms. The Spiritual Progressive's quest for human equality and Earth integrity echoes his longings and dreams, irrespective of political party affiliations. We strive for the day when every person and creature will possess a dignity that has eluded those *under* the social, economic, and ecological table—the dignity of sitting *at* a family table as coequal brothers and sisters. For this treasure all ecospiritual reformers are willing to pay a high price. Jesus certainly did. Yet, if the best in Christianity and America is to prevail, it's worth the cost.

John Wesley, one of the great spiritual leaders of the past and the founder of the Methodist Church summed it all up:

> Do all the good you can,
> By all the means you can,
> In all the ways you can,
> In all the places you can,
> At all the times you can,
> To all the people you can,
> As long as ever you can.

Appendix 1

The Earth Charter

PREAMBLE

We stand at a critical moment in Earth's history, a time when humanity must choose its future. As the world becomes increasingly interdependent and fragile, the future holds at once great peril and great promise. To move forward we must recognize that in the midst of a magnificent diversity of cultures and life forms we are one human family and one Earth community with a common destiny. We must join together to bring forth a sustainable global society founded on respect for nature, universal human rights, economic justice, and the culture of peace. Towards this end, it is imperative that we, the peoples of Earth, declare our responsibility to one another, to the greater community of life, and to future generations.

EARTH, OUR HOME

Humanity is part of a vast evolving universe. Earth, our home, is alive with a unique community of life. The forces of nature make existence a demanding and uncertain adventure, but Earth has provided the conditions essential to life's evolution. The resilience of the community of life and the well-being of humanity depend upon preserving a healthy biosphere with all its ecological systems, a rich variety of plants and animals, fertile soils, pure waters, and clean air. The global environment with its finite resources is a common concern of all peoples. The protection of Earth's vitality, diversity, and beauty is a sacred trust.

THE GLOBAL SITUATION

The dominant patterns of production and consumption are causing environmental devastation, the depletion of resources, and a massive extinction of species. Communities are being undermined. The benefits of development are not shared equitably and the gap between rich and poor is widening. Injustice, poverty, ignorance, and violent conflict are widespread and the cause of great suffering. An unprecedented rise in human population has overburdened ecological and social systems. The foundations of global security are threatened. These trends are perilous—but not inevitable.

THE CHALLENGE AHEAD

The choice is ours: form a global partnership to care for Earth and one another or risk the destruction of ourselves and the diversity of life. Fundamental changes are needed in our values, institutions, and ways of living. We must realize that when basic needs have been met, human development is primarily about being more, not having more. We have the knowledge and technology to provide for all and to reduce our impacts on the environment.

The emergence of a global civil society is creating new opportunities to build a democratic and humane world. Our environmental, economic, political, social, and spiritual challenges are interconnected, and together we can forge inclusive solutions.

UNIVERSAL RESPONSIBILITY

To realize these aspirations, we must decide to live with a sense of universal responsibility, identifying ourselves with the whole Earth community as well as our local communities. We are at once citizens of different nations and of one world in which the local and global are linked. Everyone shares responsibility for the present and future well-being of the human family and the larger living world. The spirit of human solidarity and kinship with all life is strengthened when we live with reverence for the mystery of being, gratitude for the gift of life, and humility regarding the human place in nature.

We urgently need a shared vision of basic values to provide an ethical foundation for the emerging world community. Therefore, together in hope we affirm the following interdependent principles for a sustainable way of life as a common standard by which the conduct of all individuals, organizations, businesses, government, and transnational institutions is to be guided and assessed.

PRINCIPLES

A. Respect and Care for the Community of Life

1. *Respect Earth and life in all its diversity.*
    a. Recognize that all beings are interdependent and every form of life has value regardless of its worth to human beings.
    b. Affirm faith in the inherent dignity of all human beings and in the intellectual, artistic, ethical, and spiritual potential of humanity.

2. *Care for the community of life with understanding, compassion, and love.*
    a. Accept that with the right to own, manage, and use natural resources comes the duty to prevent environmental harm and to protect the rights of people.
    b. Affirm that with increased freedom, knowledge, and power comes increased responsibility to promote the common good.

3. *Build democratic societies that are just, participatory, sustainable, and peaceful.*
    a. Ensure that communities at all levels guarantee human rights and fundamental freedoms and provide everyone an opportunity to realize his or her full potential.
    b. Promote social and economic justice, enabling all to achieve a secure and meaningful livelihood that is ecologically responsible.

4. *Secure Earth's bounty and beauty for the present and future generations.*
    a. Recognize that the freedom of action of each generation is qualified by the needs of future generations.

b. Transmit to future generations values, traditions, and institutions that support the long-term flourishing of Earth's human and ecological communities.

In order to fulfill these four broad commitments, it is necessary to:

B. Ecological Integrity

5. *Protect and restore the integrity of Earth's ecological systems, with special concern for biological diversity and the natural processes that sustain life.*

    a. Adopt at all levels sustainable development plans and regulations that make environmental conservation and rehabilitation integral to all development initiatives.

    b. Establish and safeguard viable nature and biosphere reserves, including wild lands and marine areas, to protect Earth's life-support systems, maintain biodiversity, and preserve our natural heritage.

    c. Promote the recovery of endangered species and ecosystems.

    d. Control and eradicate non-native or genetically modified organisms harmful to native species and the environment, and prevent introduction of such harmful organisms.

    e. Manage the use of renewable resources such as water, soil, forest products, and marine life in ways that do not exceed rates of regeneration and that protect the health of ecosystems.

    f. Manage the extraction and use of non-renewable resources such as minerals and fossil fuels in ways that minimize depletion and cause no serious environmental damage.

6. *Prevent harm as the best method of environmental protection and, when knowledge is limited, apply a precautionary approach.*

    a. Take action to avoid the possibility of serious or irreversible environmental harm even when scientific knowledge is incomplete or inconclusive.

    b. Place the burden of proof on those who argue that a proposed activity will not cause significant harm, and make the responsible parties liable for environmental harm.

    c. Ensure that decision making addresses the cumulative, long-term, indirect, long-distance, and global consequences of human activities.

d. Prevent pollution of any part of the environment and allow no build-up of radioactive, toxic, or other hazardous substances.
   e. Avoid military activities damaging to the environment.
7. *Adopt patterns of production, consumption, and reproduction that safeguard Earth's regenerative capacities, human rights, and community well-being.*
   a. Reduce, reuse, and recycle the materials used in production and consumption systems, and ensure that residual waste can be assimilated by ecological systems.
   b. Act with restraint and efficiency when using energy, and rely increasingly on renewable energy sources such as solar and wind.
   c. Promote the development, adoption, and equitable transfer of environmentally sound technologies.
   d. Internalize the full environmental and social costs of goods and services in the selling price, and enable consumers to identify products that meet the highest social and environmental standards.
   e. Ensure universal access to health care that fosters reproductive health and responsible reproduction.
   f. Adopt lifestyles that emphasize the quality of life and material sufficiency in a finite world.
8. *Advance the study of ecological sustainability and promote the open exchange and wide application of the knowledge acquired.*
   a. Support international scientific and technical cooperation on sustainability, with special attention to the needs of developing nations.
   b. Recognize and preserve the traditional knowledge and spiritual wisdom in all cultures that contribute to environmental protection and human well-being.
   c. Ensure that information of vital importance to human health and environmental protection, including genetic information, remains available in the public domain.

C. Social and Economic Justice

9. *Eradicate poverty as an ethical, social, and environmental imperative.*

a. Guarantee the right to potable water, clean air, food security, uncontaminated soil, shelter, and safe sanitation, allocating the national and international resources required.

b. Empower every human being with the education and resources to secure a sustainable livelihood, and provide social security and safety nets for those who are unable to support themselves.

c. Recognize the ignored, protect the vulnerable, serve those who suffer, and enable them to develop their capacities and to pursue their aspirations.

10. *Ensure that economic activities and institutions at all levels promote human development in an equitable and sustainable manner.*

    a. Promote the equitable distribution of wealth within nations and among nations.

    b. Enhance the intellectual, financial, technical, and social resources of developing nations, and relieve them of onerous international debt.

    c. Ensure that all trade supports sustainable resource use, environmental protection, and progressive labor standards.

    d. Require multinational corporations and international financial organizations to act transparently in the public good, and hold them accountable for the consequences of their activities.

11. *Affirm gender equality and equity as prerequisites to sustainable development and ensure universal access to education, health care, and economic opportunity.*

    a. Secure the human rights of women and girls and end all violence against them.

    b. Promote the active participation of women in all aspects of economic, political, civil, social, and cultural life as full and equal partners, decision makers, leaders, and beneficiaries.

    c. Strengthen families and ensure the safety and loving nurture of all family members.

12. *Uphold the right of all, without discrimination, to a natural and social environment supportive of human dignity, bodily health, and spiritual well-being, with special attention to the rights of indigenous peoples and minorities.*

a. Eliminate discrimination in all its forms, such as that based on race, color, sex, sexual orientation, religion, language, and national, ethnic or social origin.

b. Affirm the right of indigenous peoples to their spirituality, knowledge, lands and resources and to their related practice of sustainable livelihoods.

c. Honor and support the young people of our communities, enabling them to fulfill their essential role in creating sustainable societies.

d. Protect and restore outstanding places of cultural and spiritual significance.

D. Democracy, Nonviolence, and Peace

13. *Strengthen democratic institutions at all levels, and provide transparency and accountability in governance, inclusive participation in decision making, and access to justice.*

    a. Uphold the right of everyone to clear and timely information on environmental matters and all development plans and activities which are likely to affect them or in which they have an interest.

    b. Support local, regional, and global civil society, and promote the meaningful participation of all interested individuals and organizations in decision making.

    c. Protect the rights to freedom of opinion, expression, peaceful assemble, association, and dissent.

    d. Institute effective and efficient access to administrative and independent judicial procedures, including remedies and redress for environmental harm and the threat of such harm.

    e. Eliminate corruption in all public and private institutions.

    f. Strengthen local communities, enabling them to care for their environments, and assign environmental responsibilities to the levels of government where they can be carried out most effectively.

14. *Integrate into formal education and life-long learning the knowledge, values, and skills needed for a sustainable way of life.*

a. Provide all, especially children and youth, with educational opportunities that empower them to contribute actively to sustainable development.

b. Promote the contribution of the arts and humanities as well as the sciences in sustainability education.

c. Enhance the role of the mass media in raising awareness of ecological and social challenges.

d. Recognize the importance of moral and spiritual education for sustainable living.

15. *Treat all living beings with respect and consideration.*

    a. Prevent cruelty to animals kept in human societies and protect them from suffering.

    b. Protect wild animals from methods of hunting, trapping, and fishing that cause extreme, prolonged or avoidable suffering.

    c. Avoid or eliminate to the full extent possible the taking or destruction of non-targeted species.

16. *Promote a culture of tolerance, nonviolence, and peace.*

    a. Encourage and support mutual understanding, solidarity, and cooperation among all peoples and within and among nations.

    b. Implement comprehensive strategies to prevent violent conflict and use collaborative problem solving to manage and resolve environmental conflicts and other disputes.

    c. Demilitarize national security systems to the level of a non-provocative defense posture, and convert military resources to peaceful purposes, including ecological restoration.

    d. Eliminate nuclear, biological, and toxic weapons and other weapons of mass destruction.

    e. Ensure that the use of orbital and outer space supports environmental protection and peace.

    f. Recognize that peace is the wholeness created by right relationships with oneself, other persons, other cultures, other life, Earth, and the larger whole of which all are a part.

THE WAY FORWARD

As never before in history, common destiny beckons us to seek a new beginning. Such renewal is the promise of these Earth Charter principles. To fulfill this promise, we must commit ourselves to adopt and promote the values and objectives of the Charter.

This requires a change of mind and heart. It requires a new sense of global interdependence and universal responsibility. We must imaginatively develop and apply the vision of a sustainable way of life locally, nationally, regionally, and globally. Our cultural diversity is a precious heritage and different cultures will find their own distinctive ways to realize the vision. We must deepen and expand the global dialogue that generated the Earth Charter, for we have much to learn from the ongoing collaborative search for truth and wisdom.

Life often involves tensions between important values. This can mean difficult choices. However, we must find ways to harmonize diversity with unity, the exercise of freedom with the common good, short-term objectives with long-term goals. Every individual, family, organization, and community has a vital role to play. The arts, sciences, religions, educational institutions, media, businesses, nongovernmental organizations, and governments are all called to offer creative leadership. The partnership of government, civil society, and business is essential for effective governance.

In order to build a sustainable global community, the nations of the world must renew their commitment to the United Nations, fulfill their obligations under existing international agreements, and support the implementation of the Earth Charter principles with an international legally binding instrument on environment and development.

Let ours be a time remembered for the awakening of the new reverence for life, the firm resolve to achieve sustainability, the quickening of the struggle for justice and peace, and the joyful celebration of life.

Appendix 2

Reconciling Past and Present

THE SEARCH FOR THE *political* Jesus follows from the quest for the *historical* Jesus. My aim is to provide a clearer picture of Jesus than generally presented—one that has remained somewhat hidden. Our main sources, the four Gospels, were written 40 to 100 years after Jesus' crucifixion and based upon oral traditions. Stories change shape when passed along by word of mouth and can be "spun" according to the concerns and interests of the writers. Nevertheless, I believe that the Synoptic Gospels (Matthew, Mark, and Luke) truly reflect the thrust of Jesus' political vision and program. He emerges "everywhere recognizable" in these texts and they bring an "authenticity" that refuses obliteration.[1] I draw heavily on the so-called "third quest" for the historical Jesus as reflected in the recent writings of New Testament scholars N. T. Wright and Craig S. Keener. They confirm that behind the Gospel texts a reliable picture of Jesus surfaces, especially regarding his Kingdom speeches and parables—which undergird this work.[2]

The purpose of studying biblical texts is to unfold their contemporary relevance. Nevertheless, we must guard against inevitable anachronisms (misrepresenting things as happening at other than their proper time) and clearly demonstrate that close analogies or connections actually exist between the social realities, the opinions, and the ethos of different times and places. The bridge that transports Jesus to the present day is only a footbridge—precarious and shaky, but at least crossable. Thus, we exercise

---

1. Althaus, *Fact and Faith*, 74–75.
2. Wright, *Jesus*, 83–124. Keener, *Historical Jesus*, 196–302.

caution when dragging terms like "ecology," "Liberalism," or "Conservatism" back to a pre-democratic, pre-capitalist, pre-industrial, pre-Enlightenment, pre-technological and pre-literate past. We must be open to the likelihood that our meanings are not perfect, but only rough analogies, always in need of serious examination and update.

Since the best picture of Jesus isn't a photograph but a drawing, interpreters need to apply some "critical imagination."[3] While sketching a reliable account of Jesus, we open our eyes to new lines and shadings under-brushed by sociological, anthropological, economic, and ecological realities. For instance, research on present and ancient Mediterranean peasant culture helps to understand the patronage system, honor/shame codes, Land policies, purity dynamics, the peasant subsistence ethic, and the dining regulations of Jesus' time. These factors are especially insightful for identifying ancient values that drive contemporary societies as well. Understanding the impact of both empire and resistance traditions also aids in fathoming Jesus. As we imaginatively incorporate these new insights and relate them to emerging contemporary concerns (especially given the magnitude of social and ecological disaster), we enter an ever expanding circle of enlightenment—a "hermeneutical circle"—in which the past and present worlds shed light on one another. In so doing, they bring new meaning and insight into both worlds. In my opinion, this new approach to times past, not only tends to confirm the reliability of the Gospel records about Jesus, but also builds moral and spiritual equivalencies to the present. Yet, we always guard against the possibility that the tentative notions we bring to a text could harden into unexamined prejudices.

Despite the immense differences in human cultures and historical eras, the past and present are linked by (1) the common human condition and (2) the core human capabilities. For example, a large portion of the world's population today live in conditions much like first-century Palestinian peasants—shot through and through with poverty, disease, starvation/malnutrition, Land exploitation, and fear. Blighted urban areas, the catastrophe of Hurricane Katrina, and large-scale homelessness and hunger have awakened America to pockets of misery that exist even here. Moreover, wherever people live and whatever the historical era, they all pursue the core capacities of good health, adequate nourishment, appropriate clothing and shelter, control over their bodies, a sense of fairness, the care for Nature and others, joy, and greater freedom.[4] They also try to avoid the negative sides of these that cause humans and Earth to suffer (the reason the seven

---

3. Gottwald, *Politics of Ancient Israel*, 158.
4. Nussbaum, *Women*, 78–80.

deadly sins are just as relevant today as they were in ancient times). These basic human quests and obstacles, dignities and indignities vary in degree, but undergird politics in every culture and every age, and thus, provide meaningful connections between space and time.

It seems quite appropriate, then, to apply the modern terms "Liberal" or "Progressive" and "Conservative" to the past since they describe particular political *moralities* that embrace *enduring* values such as fairness, compassion, Earth integrity, hierarchy, unlimited gain, militarism, etc. Much of history reflects the struggle between the imperial ethic that wantonly appropriates Earth's goods and an opposing ethic grounded in egalitarian sharing and sustainability. Jesus became ensnared in this ongoing clash of political moralities. With all its nuanced faces, it still remains one that challenges America and the world today, and is most appropriately billed: "Conservative vs. Liberal." The ultimate question, however, remains the same in every age and place, "What comprises good governing?" Jesus spent and gave his life providing us the answer.

APPENDIX 3

Jesus Speaks at Different Moral/ Spiritual Levels

JESUS' POLITICAL MORALITY FOLLOWS a pattern technically referred to as the "levels of moral discourse."[5] These levels create a funnel effect where the most abstract and universal aspects of moral reflection at the top, or wide end, give life to the more concrete and specific rules, laws, and policies relative to changing conditions flowing out the bottom's narrow end. The following list describes eight levels of *political* ethics from top to bottom and they dictate the internal structure of this book:

1. *Religio-political and cultural traditions.* At the top level of a political ethic are the "pre-ethical" traditions and beliefs that shape a political morality. Jesus believed in a creating and nurturing God expressed in Jewish written and oral traditions, the peasant subsistence economy, the regional "little" traditions of Galilee, and his family lore. In Jesus' world, separating religion, morality, economics, legality, and the Land was unthinkable; to distinguish public from private morality was impossible. Jesus lived as a first-century peasant, Jew, and Galilean, and his historical legacy includes a unique blend of these social realities and their memories.

2. *Core political values.* A second level of political moral discourse ranks the core priority values. Many political conflicts can be traced back, not to any differences in values, but rather to how they are defined and which are considered most important. For instance, Jesus assumed that political love (compassion) stood above the purity codes, the honor codes, or economic gain.

---

5. Aiken, *Reason and Conduct*, 65–87.

3. *An ultimate political guide.* The next level assumes an ultimate guide that reflects value priorities and informs specific laws and policies. Jesus affirmed the peasant moral universe that promoted reciprocality as expressed in the Golden Rule and in the Mosaic Charter, which stipulated that community members ought to love and care for their neighbors as themselves. On this ultimate moral guide hangs every principle, virtue, institution, moral rule, law, policy, and specific action. All the major religions embrace the Golden Rule.

4. *General political principles.* This dimension of political ethics enumerates universal principles that flow from the core values and the ultimate moral guide. Jesus expected good governing to uphold compassionate justice (*sedeq*), freedom, and general well-being (shalom). The great political conflicts in Jesus' day, and throughout human history, have been fought over the meaning, application, and priority of these universal moral guides.

5. *Political virtues.* Virtues, which comprise character, also flow from the principles and values mentioned above. They reside within both the human heart *and* good governing. Jesus would focus mainly on civic love and its nuances: compassion, generosity, joy, dignity, freedom, humility, wonder, tolerance, fairness, caring, integrity, nonviolence, and trust. These virtues constituted the spiritual and political dimensions of the Basileia of God.

6. *Political goods and services.* The next dimension lists the primary and secondary goods (material and nonmaterial) that the community believes are worth pursuing. These include universal human necessities like food, shelter, health, spiritual growth, and affection—items from Creation that enhance all our primary human capacities and are compatible with the above levels of moral reflection. Grounded in the subsistence ethic, Jesus renounced wasteful living and affirmed the importance of meeting basic needs, while criticizing the ruling powers that withheld or suppressed them.

7. *Basic structures and the general rules that create them.* This level of political morality refers to the basic social, political, economic, and ecological structures that spring from all the previous dimensions of moral discourse. These arrangements entail rules that create functioning institutions like marriage and family, education, village assemblies to national governments, and the economy. For Jesus and most of those within the Israelite traditions, the Ten Commandments functioned as basic political guidelines for creating and defining community life.

8. *Specific laws and policies.* All the general institutions need good laws and regulations to govern everyday life—the last and most detailed level of moral discourse. With changing times, the Constitutional commands were reinterpreted and concretely applied. The conflict between Jesus and his

opponents arose over issues of daily living tied to Land policy, each applying the law as they saw fit for viable family, village, and national life.

Although Jesus debated abstract levels of moral discourse (such as the role of political compassion and restorative justice in the peasant moral economy), he mainly looked to specific legal stipulations for stopping the downward social, economic, and psychological spiral of Galilean life (and beyond) due to imperial values.

Bibliography

Aburdene, Patricia. *Megatrends 2010: The Rise of Conscious Capitalism.* Charlottesville, VA: Hampton Rds., 2005.
Aiken, Henry D. *Reason and Conduct.* New York: Alfred A. Knopf, 1962.
Althaus, Paul. *Fact and Faith in the Kerygma of Today.* Translated by David Cairns. Philadelphia: Muhlenberg, 1959.
Arendt, Hannah. *On Revolution.* New York: Viking, 1965.
Aristotle. "Nicomachean Ethics." In *Introduction to Aristotle.* Translated and edited by Richard McKeon, 300–543. New York: The Modern Library, 1947.
Aslan, Reza. *Zealot: The Life and Times of Jesus of Nazareth.* New York: Random House, 2013.
Bartchy, Scott. "Table Fellowship." In *Dictionary of Jesus and the Gospels*, edited by Joel B. Green, et. al., 796–800. Downers Grove, IL: InterVarsity, 1992.
Batey, Richard. *Jesus and the Poor: The Poverty Program of the First Christians.* New York: Harper and Row, 1972.
Becker, Ernest. *Escape from Evil.* New York: Free Press, 1975.
Bernstein, Ellen. "Creation Theology: A Jewish Perspective." In *The Green Bible*, edited by Michael G. Maudlin and Marlene Baer, 51–57. New York: HarperOne, 2008.
Beyerhaus, Peter P. J. *God's Kingdom and the Utopian Error: Discerning the Biblical Kingdom of God from its Counterparts.* Wheaton, IL: Crossway, 1992.
Black, Matthew. "'Not Peace, but a Sword': Matt. 10:34ff; Luke 12:51ff." In *Jesus and the Politics of His Day*, edited by E. Bammel & C. F. D. Moule, 287–94. Cambridge: Cambridge University Press, 1985.
Bonhoeffer, Dietrich. *The Cost of Discipleship.* New York: Macmillan, 1963.
Borg, Marcus. *Conflict, Holiness and Politics in the Teachings of Jesus.* New York: Edwin Mellen, 1984
———. "From Galilean Jew to the Face of God: The Pre-Easter and Post-Easter Jesus." In *Jesus at 2000*, edited by Marcus J. Borg, 7–20. Boulder, CO: Westview, 1998.
———, and N. T. Wright. *The Meaning of Jesus: Two Visions.* San Francisco: HarperSanFrancisco, 2000.
Bork, Robert H. *Slouching towards Gomorrah: Modern Liberalism and American Decline.* New York: Regan, 1996.
Boswell, John. *Christianity, Social Tolerance, and Homosexuality: Gay People in Western Europe from the Beginning of the Christian Era to the Fourteenth Century.* Chicago: University of Chicago Press, 1980.

Brandon. S. G. F. *Jesus and the Zealots: A Study of the Political Factor in Primitive Christianity.* Manchester: Manchester University Press, 1967.

Brueggemann, Walter. *The Land: Place as Gift, Promise, and Challenge.* Minneapolis: Fortress, 2002.

Buchanan, Patrick J. *State of Emergency: The Third World Invasion and Conquest of America.* New York: St. Martins, 2006.

Buckley, William F. Jr. "Credenda and Statement of Principles." In *Conservatism in America Since 1930*, edited by Gregory L. Schneider, 201–6. New York: New York University Press, 2003.

Campolo, Tony. *Red Letter Christians: A Citizen's Guide to Faith and Politics.* Ventura, CA: Regal, 2008.

Carter, Jimmy. *Our Endangered Values: America's Moral Crisis.* New York: Simon and Schuster, 2005.

Carter, Warren. *The Roman Empire and the New Testament: An Essential Guide.* Nashville: Abingdon, 2006.

Chadwick, Douglas H. "Wolf Wars." *National Geographic*, March 2010, 34–55.

Chilton, Bruce. *Pure Kingdom: Jesus' Vision of God.* Grand Rapids: Eerdmans, 1996.

Clark, Kenneth. *Dark Ghetto: Dilemmas of Social Power.* New York: Harper Torchbooks, 1965.

Crossan, John Dominic. *God and Empire: Jesus against Rome, Then and Now.* San Francisco: HarperSanFrancisco, 2007.

———. *Jesus: A Revolutionary Biography.* San Francisco: HarperSanFrancisco, 1995.

———. *The Historical Jesus.* San Francisco: HarperSanFrancisco, 1991.

Davis, Karen, et al. "Mirror, Mirror on the Wall: An International Update on the Comparative Performance of America's Health Care." Commonwealth Fund (May 16, 2007) N. P.

Dean, John W. *Conservatives without Conscience.* New York: Viking, 2006.

Domhoff, William G. "Power in America." No pages. Online: sociology.ucsc.edu/whorulesamerica/power/wealth.

Dugger, Celia W. "Big Reduction in Extreme Poverty 'Utterly Affordable.'" *San Francisco Chronicle* (January 18, 2005). N. P.

Earth Charter (2000). No pages. Downloaded on 6/4/12 from http://www.earthcharterinaction.org/content/pages/Read-the-Charter.html.

Eichrodt, Walther. *Theology of the Old Testament.* Vol. 1. Translated by J. A. Baker. Philadelphia: Westminster, 1961.

Elliott, Neil, *The Arrogance of Nations: Reading Romans in the Shadow of Empire.* Minneapolis: Fortress, 2008.

Epstein, Helen. "Enough to Make You Sick?" In *Annual Editions*, edited by Eileen L. Daniel, 18–25. Dubuque: Dushkin, 2005/6.

Families USA Report. "The Clock Is Ticking: More Americans Losing Health Coverage," July 2009, 1–5. Online: http://www.familiesusa.org.

Fanon, Frantz. *The Wretched of the Earth.* Translated by Constance Farrington. New York: Grove, 1963.

Finley, M. I. *Politics in the Ancient World.* Cambridge: Cambridge University Press, 1983.

Fiorenza, Elisabeth Schüssler. *In Memory of Her: A Feminist Theological Reconstruction of Christian Origins.* New York: Crossroad, 1984.

Frankfort, Henri, et al. *Before Philosophy.* Baltimore: Penguin, 1949.

Franzen, Aaron B. "A Left-leaning Text." *Christianity Today*, Oct. 2011, 32–33.
Freyne, Sean. *Galilee: Jesus and the Gospels*. Philadelphia: Fortress, 1988.
Fried, Charles. "An Analysis of 'Equality' and 'Rights' in Medical Care." In *Ethical Issues in Modern Medicine*, edited by John Arras and Robert Hunt, 527–32. Palo Alto, CA: Mayfield, 1983.
Funk, Robert W., Roy W. Hoover, and the Jesus Seminar. *The Five Gospels: The Search for the Authentic Words of Jesus*. San Francisco: HarperSanFrancisco, 1993.
Furnish, Victor Paul. *The Love Command in the New Testament*. New York: Abingdon, 1972.
Galbraith, John Kenneth. "Stop the Madness." Interview with Rupert Cornwell. *Toronto Globe and Mail*, July 6, 2002.
Goldhagen, Daniel. *Hitler's Willing Executioners: Ordinary Germans and the Holocaust*. New York: Vintage, 1997.
Gottlieb, Roger S. *A Greener Faith: Religious Environmentalism and Our Planet's Future*. New York: Oxford University Press, 2006.
Gottwald, Norman K. *The Politics of Ancient Israel*. Louisville: Westminster John Knox, 2001.
———. *The Tribes of Israel: A Sociology of the Religion of Liberated Israel 1250–1050 B.C.E.* Maryknoll, NY: Orbis, 1979.
Green, Douglas J. "When the Gardener Returns: An Ecological Perspective on Adam's Dominion." In *Keeping God's Earth: The Global Environment in Biblical Perspective*, edited by Noah J. Toly and Daniel I. Block, 267–75. Downers Grove, IL: InterVarsity, 2010.
Guijarro, Santiago. "The Politics of Exorcism." In *The Social Setting of Jesus and the Gospels*, edited by W. Stegemann et al., 159–74. Minneapolis: Fortress, 2002.
Hansen, Jim. "The Threat to the Planet." *New York Review of Books* 53, June 15, 2006, 12–16.
Hanson, K. C., and Douglas E. Oakman. *Palestine in the Time of Jesus: Social Structure and Social Conflict*. Minneapolis: Fortress, 1998.
Hardin, Garrett. "The Tragedy of the Commons." *Science* 162, Dec. 13, 1968, 1243–48.
Hendricks, Obery M. Jr. *The Politics of Jesus: Rediscovering the True Revolutionary Nature of Jesus' Teachings and How They Have Been Corrupted*. New York: Doubleday, 2006.
Henry, Carl F. H. *The Confessions of a Conservative: An Autobiography*. Waco, TX: Word, 1986.
———. *The Uneasy Conscience of Modern Fundamentalism*. Grand Rapids: Eerdmans, 1947.
Herzog, William R. II. *Parables as Subversive Speech*. Louisville: Westminster/John Knox, 1994.
Hoffman, Martin L. "Empathy, Role Taking, Guilt and Development of Altruistic Motives." In *Moral Development and Behavior*, edited by Thomas Lickora,124–43. New York: Holt, Rinehart and Winston, 1976.
Horsley, Richard A. *Galilee: History, Politics, People*. Valley Forge: Trinity, 1995.
———. *Jesus and Empire*. Minneapolis: Fortress, 2003.
———. *Jesus and the Spiral of Violence: Popular Jewish Resistance in Roman Palestine*. Minneapolis: Fortress, 1993.
———. "Introduction—Jesus, Paul, and the 'Arts of Resistance': Leaves from the Notebook of James C. Scott." In *Hidden Transcripts and the Arts of Resistance:*

Applying the Work of James C. Scott to Jesus and Paul, edited by Richard A Horsley, 1–26. Atlanta: Society of Biblical Literature, 2004.

———, and Neil A. Silberman. *The Message and the Kingdom*. Minneapolis: Augsburg Fortress, 2002.

Humphrey, Hubert. "The Enduring Principles of Liberalism." In *The Political Spectrum: Opposing Viewpoints*, edited by David L. Bender and Bruno Leone, 90–95. St. Paul: Greenhaven, 1986.

Jacob, Edmond. *Theology of the Old Testament*. New York: Harper and Row, 1958.

Jeremias, Joachim. *Jesus' Promise to the Nations*. London: SCM, 1958.

———. *The Parables of Jesus*. New York: Scribner's Sons, 1963.

Jones, James. *Jesus and the Earth*. London: SPCK, 2003.

Kasemann, Ernst. *Jesus Means Freedom*. Translated by Frank Clarke. Philadelphia: Fortress, 1969.

———. *New Testament Questions of Today*. London: SCM, 1969.

Kaufmann, Yehezkel. *The Religion of Israel*. Chicago: University of Chicago Press, 1960.

Keener, Craig S. *The Historical Jesus of the Gospels*. Grand Rapids: Eerdmans, 2009.

Kekes, John. *A Case for Conservatism*. Ithaca: Cornell University Press, 1998.

Kelsey, George. *Racism and the Christian Understanding of Man*. New York: Scribner, 1965.

Kierkegaard, Soren. *Works of Love*. Translated and edited by V. Hong and Edna H. Hong. Princeton: Princeton University Press, 1995.

King, Martin Luther Jr. "Letter from Birmingham City Jail." Philadelphia: American Friends Service Committee, n. d., 14.

———. "Beyond Vietnam." Address at Riverside Church, April 4, 1967. Online: www.africanamericans.com.

Kirk, Alan. "Love Your Enemies, The Golden Rule, and Ancient Reciprocity (Luke 6:27–35)." *Journal of Biblical Literature* 122/4 (2003): 667–86.

Kirk, Russell. *The Politics of Prudence*. Bryn Mawr, PA: Intercollegiate Studies Institute, 1994.

Kristol, William and Donald Kagan. "National Interest and Global Responsibility." In *The Neocon Reader*, edited by Irwin Stelzer, 55–78. New York: Grove, 2004.

LaFraniere, Sharon. "Africa's World of Forced Labor," *New York Times News Service*, quoted in *The Santa Barbara News Press*, Oct. 29, 2006, B1, B4.

Lakoff, George. *Moral Politics: How Liberals and Conservatives Think*. Chicago: University of Chicago Press, 2002.

Landsberg, Mitchell. "In Poorest Schools, Fear, Despair Rule." *LA Times*, April 26, 2008, sec. B.

Lasswell, Harold. *Politics: Who Gets What, When, and How?* Cleveland, OH: World. 1958.

Lebacqz, Karen. "Justice, Economics, and the Uncomfortable Kingdom: Reflections on Matthew 20:1–16." In *The Annual of the Society of Christian Ethics*, edited by Larry Rasmussen. (1983): 27–53.

Lerner, Michael. *The Left Hand of God: Taking Back Our Country from the Religious Right*. San Francisco: HarperSanFrancisco, 2006.

Long, Edward Leroy Jr. *War and Conscience in America*. Philadelphia: Westminster, 1968.

Love, Stuart L. "Jesus Heals the Hemorrhaging Woman." In *The Social Settings of Jesus and the Gospels*, edited by W. Stegemann et. al., 85–101. Minneapolis: Fortress, 2002.

Mack, Burton L. *The Lost Gospel: The Book of Q and Christian Origins*. San Francisco: HarperSanFrancisco, 1993.

Malina, Bruce J. *The New Testament World: Insights from Cultural Anthropology*. Louisville: Westminster/John Knox, 1993.

———. *The Social Gospel of Jesus*. Minneapolis: Augsburg Fortress, 2001.

May, Rollo. *Love and Will*. New York: W. W. Norton, 1969.

Meadows, Donella H. et al. *The Limits to Growth: A Report for the Club of Rome's Project on the Predicament of Mankind*. New York: Universe, 1972.

Meier, John P. *A Marginal Jew: Rethinking the Historical Jesus*. Vol. 2. New York: Doubleday, 1994.

———. *A Marginal Jew: Rethinking the Historical Jesus*. Vol. 3. New York: Doubleday, 2001.

Mendenhall, George. *The Tenth Generation*. Baltimore: John Hopkins University Press, 1973.

Michel, Otto. "Faith," in *The New International Dictionary of New Testament Theology*. Vol. 1, edited by Colin Brown, 593–606. Grand Rapids: Zondervan, 1986.

Miller, Douglas J. "Civil Rights." In *Evangelical Dictionary of Theology*, edited by Walter A. Elwell, 250–52. Grand Rapids: Baker, 1984.

Moo, Douglas J. "Jesus and the Authority of the Mosaic Law." In *Journal for the Study of the New Testament* 20 (1984): 3–49.

Mowinckel, Sigmund. *He That Cometh*. Translated by G. W. Anderson. New York: Abingdon, 1954.

Myers, Ched. *Binding the Strong Man: A Political Reading of Mark's Story of Jesus*. Maryknoll: Orbis, 2000.

Niebuhr, Reinhold. *The Nature and Destiny of Man*. Vol. 2. New York: Scribner's, 1964.

Nisbet, Robert. *Conservatism: Dream and Reality*. Minneapolis: University of Minnesota Press, 1986.

Nussbaum, Martha C. *Hiding from Humanity: Disgust, Shame, and the Law*. Princeton, Princeton University Press, 2004.

———. *Sex and Social Justice*. Oxford: Oxford University Press, 1999.

———. *Upheavals of Thought: the Intelligence of Emotions*. Cambridge: Cambridge University Press, 2001.

———. *Women and Human Development: The Capabilities Approach*. Cambridge: Cambridge University Press, 2000.

O'Reilly, Bill. *Culture Warrior*. New York: Broadway, 2006.

Pannenberg, Wolfhart. *Theology and the Kingdom of God*. Philadelphia: Westminster, 1969

Pathauri, R. K., and A. Reisinger. *Climate Change 2007: Synthesis Report Contribution of Working Group I, II, III to the Fourth Assessment Report of the IPCC*, 1–104. Geneva, Switzerland, 2007. Online: http://www.ipcc.ch/publications_and_data/ar4/syr/en/contents. html.

Pelevnik, Joseph. "Honor/Shame." In *Handbook of Biblical Social Values*, edited by John J. Pilch and Bruce J. Malina, 106–15. Peabody, MA: Hendrickson, 1998.

Perrin, Norman. *The Kingdom of God in the Teachings of Jesus*. Philadelphia: Westminster, 1963.

Phillips, Kevin. *American Theocracy: The Peril and Politics of Radical Religion, Oil, and Borrowed Money in the 21st Century*. New York: Viking, 2006.

Putnam, Robert D., and David E. Campbell. *American Grace: How Religion Divides and Unites Us*. New York: Simon & Schuster, 2010.

Rad, Gerhard von. "Israel." In *Theological Dictionary of the New Testament*. Edited by Gerhard Kittel and Gerhard Friedrick, translated by Geoffrey W. Bromiley, 3:356–59. Grand Rapids: Eerdmans, 1965.

———. *Theology of the Old Testament*. Vol. 1. Translated by D. M. G. Stalker. New York: Harper and Row, 1962.

Rawls, John. *A Theory of Justice*. Cambridge: Harvard University Press, 1971.

———. *Justice as Fairness: A Restatement*. Cambridge: Harvard University Press, 2001.

———. *Political Liberalism*. New York: Columbia University Press, 1993.

Reckford, Jonathan T. M. *Creating a Habitat for Humanity: No Hands but Yours*. Minneapolis: Fortress, 2007.

Regan, Tom. *All That Dwell Therein: Animal Rights and Environmental Ethics*. Berkeley: University of California Press, 1982.

Rengstorf, Karl. "*Hamartolos*." In *Theological Dictionary of the New Testament*. Edited by Gerhard Kittel and Gerhard Friedrick, translated by Geoffrey W. Bromiley, 1:317–35. Grand Rapids: Eerdmans, 1965.

Rescher, Nicholas. "The Canons of Distributive Justice." In *Justice: Alternative Political Perspectives*, edited by James P. Sterba, 33–40. Belmont, CA: Wadsworth, 1980.

Rice, Condoleezza. "The President's National Security Strategy." In *The Neocon Reader*, edited by Irwin Stelzer, 79–87. New York: Grove, 2004.

Robinson, James M. *Jesus: According to the Earliest Witness*. Minneapolis: Fortress, 2007.

Sachs, Jeffrey D. *The End of Poverty: Economic Possibilities for Our Time*. New York: Penguin, 2005.

Safire, William. "Bleeding Heart." In *Safire's New Political Dictionary*, 61. New York: Random House, 1993.

Sanders, E. P. *The Historical Figure of Jesus*. New York: Penguin, 1993.

Schnellnhuber, Hans J. et. al. "Solving the Climate Dilemma: The Budget Approach." German Advisory Council on Global Climate. Berlin, 2009, 13. Online: http://www.wbgu.de/en/special-reports/sr-2009-budget-approach/.

Scott, James C. *The Moral Economy of the Peasant: Rebellion and Subsistence in Southeast Asia*. New Haven: Yale University Press, 1976.

Sideris, Lisa H. "Religion, Environmentalism, and the Meaning of Ecology." In *The Oxford Handbook of Religion and Ecology*, edited by Roger S Gottlieb, 446–64. New York: Oxford University Press, 2006.

Sleeth, Matthew J. "Teaching on Creation through the Ages." In *The Green Bible*, 98–114. New York: HarperCollins, 2008.

Stephenson, Wen. "Thoreau's Radical Moment—and Ours." *The Nation*, May 27, 2013, 11–15.

Storkey, Alan. *Jesus and Politics: Confronting the Powers*. Grand Rapids: Baker, 2005.

Theissen, Gerd. "The Political Dimension of Jesus' Activities." In *The Social Settings of Jesus and the Gospels*, edited by W. Stegemann et al., 225–50. Minneapolis: Fortress, 2002.

———. *Social Reality and the Early Christians*. Translated by Margaret Kohl. Minneapolis: Fortress, 1992.

———, and Annette Merz, *The Historical Jesus: A Comprehensive Guide*. Minneapolis: Fortress, 1996.

USDA Hunger Report. Online: ers.usda.gov.briefing/foodsecurity/stats_graphs.htm.

Vaux, Roland de. *Ancient Israel: Social Institutions*. Vol. 1. New York: McGraw-Hill, 1965.

Wallis, Gerhard. "*Ahabh*." In *The Theological Dictionary of the Old Testament*, edited by G. Johannes Botterweck and Helmer Ringgren, translated by John T. Willis, 1:105–7. Grand Rapids: Eerdmans, 1974.

Walsh, J. P. M. *The Mighty from their Thrones: Power in the Biblical Tradition*. Philadelphia: Fortress, 1987.

Weissenrieder, Annette. "The Plague of Uncleanness? The Ancient Illness Construct 'Issue of Blood' in Luke 8:43–48." In *The Social Setting of Jesus and the Gospels*, edited by W. Stegemann et al., 207–22. Minneapolis: Fortress, 2002.

White, Lynn. "The Historical Roots of our Ecological Crisis." *Science* 155, March 10, 1967, 1203–7.

Wilder, Amos. *Jesus' Parables and the War of Myths*. Philadelphia: Fortress, 1982.

Will, George F. "The Slow Undoing: The Assault on, and Underestimation of, Nationality." In *The Neocon Reader*, edited by Irwin Stelzer, 127–39. New York: Grove, 2004.

Wink, Walter. *The Powers That Be*. New York: Doubleday, 1998.

Wolfson, Adam. "Conservatives and Neoconservatives." In *The Neocon Reader*, edited by Irwin Stelzer, 215–31. New York: Grove, 2004.

Wright, N. T. *Jesus and the Victory of God*. Minneapolis: Fortress, 1996.

Yablonsky, Lewis. *Robopaths: People as Machines*. Baltimore: Penguin, 1972.

Subject Index

Adam and Eve, 10, 14; imperial temptations of, 31–34, 58, 102, 170
adultery, 100, 138
affirmative action, 89–91; ecological; 100–104; economic, 106–14, 122, 126; Jesus and, 91–104
anger: form of murder, 139–40
animals: human connection to, 13, 30; rights of, 30, 33, 68, 149, 161, 176
antitheses, 138
anxiety, 153–54
apocalyptic, 46
Aristotle, 18
authority: Jesus,' 17–19, 43–45
awe, 29, 33, 157

baptism: Jesus,' 37; meaning of John's, 37, 143
Beatitudes, the, 120–22
Bible: as political document, 24; proper interpretation of, 38, 82, 96, 101, 135, 174
bigotry, 59
biocommunity, 5, 15, 33, 82, 137, 149
Bonhoeffer, Dietrich, 173
born again, 173
brothers and sisters: keepers of, 30–33, 55, 74, 80, 97, 99
Buckley, William F Jr, 158

Caesar, Augustus: divine status of, 21, 43, 47, 62, 127, 149; imperial policies of, 61–62, 115
Caiaphas, 60, 69
Cain and Able, 32, 162

capabilities approach, 51–52, 141, 176
capital punishment, 178
capitalism, 28, 72
Cardinal Earth Virtues, 33–34
child abuse, 98, 167, 177
Child of God: designation of kings, 47; Jesus as, 47
Child of Humanity (Son of Man); as human being, 43; Daniel's vision, 43; Jesus' use of, 28, 43–44, 85
children: of God, 14, 161, 164; model of Kingdom, 97
Christian, Christianity; Conservative, 37, 40, 172; Fundamentalist, 3, 5, 38, 96; Progressive, 33, 55, 85, 118, 126, 173–79
civic friendship, 53, 91, 112–13, 163, 180
civil disobedience, 144
civil rights, 54, 75, 90, 177
climate change, 5, 26, 100, 147, 177
community, 29–31, 47, 49, 89, 91, 99; beloved, 19; building of, 120, 150, 179–80; of equals, 97–98; law and, 137, 145
community organizing, 46
common good, 3, 19, 53, 128, 144, 174; as content of the Kingdom of God, 43, 55, 116, 142; as shalom, 8, 49, 165; subsistence values of, 36, 52
Communion (Lord's Supper, Eucharist), 131–32
compassion, 74–87; as essence of God, 25, 42; Jesus on, 16, 77–86, 123;

Subject Index

as holiness, 74; lack of, 66, 86–87, 102; love and justice word, 44–45, 113, 116, 118, 174–75; politics of, 49, 53, 79–85, 108–10, 128
conscience, 12, 15, 114,
Conservatism, 2, 40; echo of imperial ethic, 69, 72, 95, 103; principles of, 70–71, 129, 179; as political ethic, 69, 81, 85, 96, 171; self-interest and, 132, 135, 142, 150; values of, 98–99, 142, 158, 160, 164
conspicuous consumption, 62, 108
Constitution: of Israel, 26–27, 32, 67, 81; Jesus' renewal of, 36, 50, 74, 116, 121, 136–43, 177; as living document; 135, 144; subsistence notions within, 44, 59. *See also* Ten Commandments
Creation: care of, 7, 13, 15, 26, 30–31, 43–44, 102–3; Intrinsic value of, 28, 123, 176; politics of, 32–33, 43, 100; principles embodied within, 28–34
Credo, the, 26, 47
cross, crucifixion: media event, 61; political meaning of Jesus,' 15, 97, 132, 170–72; salvation by, 131, 170, 173
Crossan, John Dominic, 25
cultural warriors, 22, 67, 72, 80, 90

Dean, John W., 172
demons, demonic, 148, 150
destitute, 120–22; honoring of 45
difference principle, 53, 113, 133
dignity: Declarations of, 121–22; as honor and worth, 30, 34, 90, 164, 180; Jesus brought, 45, 47, 66, 132, 141, 153; politics and, 25, 54, 84, 93–104, 113, 176
discrimination, 89, 91, 170
diversity, 30, 177
divorce, 99–100
downtrodden, 13, 34, 59, 90, 172

Earth/Land: its integrities and worth, 5, 12, 28–30, 53–54 121; our bond to it, 8, 14, 29, 136, 161; our love and upkeep of, 11, 91, 101, 131–32; our mother, 30; its sustainability, 13, 18, 30, 37, 117, 125; woes of, 1–2, 32, 46, 58, 75, 101–4, 170–72
Earth Charter, 1, 12, 29, 31, 33, 74, 90, 105, 152, 177; summary of, 54
ecodestruction, 86, 160
ECOFaith, 181–82
ecojustice, 26, 53, 67, 91, 104
ecological crisis, 9, 28, 39, 81
ecology, 31, 33, 39
economics: inequalities and, 2, 53, 62, 69, 70, 90, 92; of Jesus, 105–17, 120–32, 176; justice and, 45, 105, 118; linked to Land, 8; linked to religion, 16
ecospirituality, 7–19. *See also* spirituality
ecospiritual politics, 7–23; of affirmative action, 96–97, 113; for the common good, 55; of compassion, 80–84, 136; of health care, 147, 152–53, 155; of international peace, 160, 164, 166, 168; and Jesus, 37, 41, 44, 46, 129, 131, 144; and moral values, 19, 23, 26, 35, 45, 67, 93, 121; of restoration, 27, 45, 47, 49, 116, 126; reverses inequalities, 93–94, 104, 109, 118–19; of subsistence/sustainability, 68, 154, 169. *See also* politics
elderly, 138–39
elites, 60, 86, 105, 115, 169
empathy: basis of compassionate justice, 53, 74, 86, 113, 136–37, 175; essence of God, 25, 27, 34, 55, 80
equality, egalitarian, 89, 133, 136, 158; basis of Liberalism, 52–54, 104, 141, 176–78; brings dignity, 19, 27, 66, 93, 132, 164; economic, 75, 90–91, 131; social, 55, 96, 99–100
eternal life: inheriting, 8, 81, 125; as Kingdom of God, 42, 49, 159
ethics: Christian, 12, 33–34, 89, 176–79; Conservative, 69–71;

imperial, 58–62; Land, 28–34; Liberal, 51–55; 176–79; subsistence/sustainability, 18–19
Evangelicals, 10, 39–40, 172–73
exile: Earth's, 9, 144; Israel's, 8, 31, 60, 64–65, 74, 85, 158; personal, 3–4, 75; return from, 42–43, 48–49, 77–81; social/political, 10, 14
Exodus, 25, 33, 80, 151
exorcism, 148; politics of, 150–52
exploitation, 149, 162

faith: greening of, 2, 30, 60; in God/Jesus, 15, 26, 170, 172, 183; In Israel's future, 17, 26; politics of, 38, 55, 82, 153–54, 165
family: of the biocommunity, 19, 30, 91, 104, 183; of God, 11, 14, 153; of all humankind/nations, 47, 76, 84–85, 115, 165, 176–78; Jesus' definition of, 98–100; values of, 50, 71–72, 141, 167–68
fasting, 16; social/ecopolitical meaning of, 35, 68
father: Abba, 110, 159; Caesar as, 115–16; call no man as, 98–99; God as, 11, 74, 79–81, 84–85, 115, 175
food/eating: distributing it, 36, 49, 110, 154, 159, 176; importance of, 9, 49, 113, 117; politics of, 31, 37, 49, 66, 85, 94, 96, 123–25; purity and, 67–68
forgive, forgiveness: debts, 91–92, 117, 119; God's 24, 78, 171; politics of, 48–49, 170
freedom: civil liberties, 51; as moral principle, 26, 36, 54, 96, 100, 127, 158; politics of, 52, 54; from want and misery, 54, 147, 170

Galbraith, John, K., 132
Galilee, 41, 65, 123, 127, 158
Garden of Eden, 18, 31–33, 44, 55, 170
Garden of Gethsemane, 162
generosity, 24; politics of, 45, 53, 89, 106, 114
generous justice. *See* justice
Gentile, 159–60

global warming, 9
God: as Creator, 7, 27–34, 115, 127; empathic/loving essence of, 13, 25–26, 76, 79–80; goodness of, 26, 36, 42–43, 158; justice of, 26, 35, 59, 101, 133, 115–16; liberating presence of, 25–27, 94, 175; as nurturing/sustaining, 11–13, 24–35, 123, 125, 135, 152; as Yahweh (Lord), 25; Kingdom of. *See* Good Government
Golden Rule, 137; as interpretive norm, 138–42
good, goodness: intrinsic, 29, 33; moral pursuit of 43–44, 132, 177. *See also* common good and God, goodness of
goods: basic human, 8, 52, 55, 147, 154, 180, 183; redistribution of, 106–7, 126, 136, 165
Good Government, Governing: as translation of "Kingdom of God," 42–43; as the common good, 36; features of, 43–49, 116–17, 148–49, 176–78; subsistence rights of, 83–84; 112–13, 121–26, 131–32, 146, 152–54; values of, 55, 75, 77, 80, 97–98, 118, 148
gospel, 97, 172
grace, 11, 135, 173
greed, 31, 48, 102–3, 106, 108, 138
grief, 154–56

Habitat for Humanity, 179–81
Hansen, Jim, 9
Hardin, Garrett, 142–43
hate crimes, 139–40
healing/health care: Jesus and, 146–54; politics of, 147–50, 152; universal, 149, 152, 177
heart: seat of values, 13–15, 34, 67, 83, 122; "bleeding hearts," 76; change of, 122, 125, 169, 178; hardness of, 38, 81, 85, 87, 91, 99, 106, 110, 138, 155
heaven, 115–16, 143, 150
Henry, Carl F. H., 172
Herod Antipas, 37, 41, 60, 150

Herodian Party, 64, 127
hierarchy: imperial value, 62, 70; Jesus undercuts, 94, 96, 98–100, 116, 125, 132–33, 164
holiness: as compassion, 74–87; God's 65; politics of, 65, 138; purity and, 65
Holy Spirit, 11, 13, 37, 43, 47, 150, 173
homelessness, 176, 195
homosexual, 66, 140, 170–71, 175, 177
honor/shame: dignity and, 78, 100, 103, 121–23, 137–38; in Jesus' day, 45, 60, 65–66, 81, 106, 125, 162–63; politics of, 93–104, 118, 151–52
hope: anticipating Good Governing, 3, 77, 92, 95, 133, 154–55, 165; for humanity/Planet, 4, 11, 27, 29, 103, 118, 120, 168
hospitality, 85, 1, 124
humans: bond to Earth, 14, 25, 29–30, 91, 155, 177; bond to one another, 18, 34, 100, 165; creation of, 29–30; dignity of, 29, 30, 47, 49, 53–54, 89, 121–22; 164; missteps of, 27–28, 31–32, 58, 132
humility: basis of spirituality, 16–17, 66; basis of leadership, 47, 59–60; vs. exalted, 67, 91–94, 98, 122; politics of, 79, 94, 97, 122, 129, 143, 164
hunger, 49, 60, 68–69, 84, 86, 92, 99, 108, 122–23
hypocrisy, 65, 142

ideals: Liberal/Progressive, 33, 53–55, 176–78; Roman/Conservative, 62, 70–71
immortality, 49
imperial ethic: crucified Jesus, 170–71, Jesus opposed, 43–44, 46–47, 97–98, 115–18, 128–30, 150–51, 166; precursor to Conservatism, 71–72, 142, 149, 172, 174, 182; principles of, 62
imperialism: ancient 23; Egyptian, 26–32; Israelite, 36, 58–59, 161; modern, 14, 34, 46, 167; Roman. *See* Rome
integrity: Earth's, 12, 21, 29, 33, 53, 100; human, 142
internationalism, 53, 157–68
Israel: blessing to nations, 20, 44, 73, 82, 96, 158–60; 165; exile of, 34–35, 48, 60, 77; restoration of, 17, 19–20, 49, 63–64, 78 116, 152–53

Jeremias, Joachim, 77, 112
Jerusalem, 63, 129, 155, 164
Jesus: on affirmative action. *See* affirmative action; campaign slogan, 41–43; crucifixion of, 133, 179; compassion of. *See* compassion; vs. Conservative/imperial ethic, 60–63, 71, 80, 83, 85–87, 115–18, 122, 126, 128–30, 171; divinity of, 5, 21, 37, 47, 51, 149, 151; to emulate, 4, 37, 172; first/last sayings, 27, 93–94, humanity of, 21; as healer. *See* health care; as Jew, 64, 69; Kingdom message. See Good Government; Liberal ethic of, 18–19, 31, 33, 50–56, 84, 125–33, 164; as Lord and Savior, 5, 171–75; non-violence of, 162–64, 176–78; opponents of, 64–69, 74; as politician, 16–23, 28, 38, 149; as prophet/lawgiver, 36, 134–43; resurrection of 173; saves marginalized, 78, 91–104, 108–14, 121, 126; spiritual way of, 10–19, 38; titles of. *See* Child of God, Child of Humanity, and Messiah
Jews, Judaism: legacy of, 64, 81, 87, 96, 135, 164–65, 168, 174; prejudice against, 64, 66, 139–40, 170–71, 176. See also Jesus, as Jew.
John the Baptist, 36–37, 129, 143
joy, 12, 68; politics of, 49, 76, 78, 95, 122, 155
Jubilee, 13, 31, 91–92, 112, 119
judges: activist, 71, 135; disciples as, 47, 137; Jesus as, 37, 129, 135

judgment: political nature of, 48, 63, 84–85, 107
justice: ecojustice, 26, 33, 42, 58, 67; essence of God, 25–26, 35; as generous and compassionate, 44–45, 54, 113, 116, 137, 144, 147, 160, 174, 178; rectifying. See affirmative action; social/economic distributive, 52–53, 69, 89–91, 118, 132, 136, 138, 143, 154, 176
Just War theory, 166

Kasemann, Ernst, 50–51
Kelsey, George, 139
killing, 59, 77. See anger, murder
kindness, 19, 38, 45, 59
King, Martin Luther Jr, 53, 144, 161, 168, 174
Kingdom of God. See Good Government

Land. See Earth
Lasswell, Harold, 17
Last Supper. See Communion
law, 17, 26, 31, 42, 44, 47–48, 76, 82, 91, 135: the breaking of, 144; Jesus' authority over, 143–44; Jesus fulfills, 136, 176–78
leader, leadership, 47–48; of bad, 35, 60–63, 83, 101–2; 123, 130, 167; of good, 60, 85–86, 96–98, 129, 159
Liberalism: Christian embracing, 40–41, 100, 170, 172–78; Jesus and, 50–51, 84, 100, 104, 110, 113, 124, 135, 163, 176–78; meaning of 51–52; principles of, 53–54, 76–77, 111–13, 167–68, 176–78; third-stage, 51–53
liberty, liberation. See freedom
lie. See truth
limits to growth, 31–32, 34
living wage, 110–13, 117–18, 176
Lord. See God
Lord's Prayer, 114–19
Lord's Supper. See Communion
love: to enemies, 163–64; to Earth, 13, 32–33, 39, 91, 172, 177; to God/neighbors, 81–84, 136, 147; of God, 11, 26, 29, 38, 43; linked to justice, 136–37; politics of, 19, 34, 45, 86; supreme virtue, 11–12; universal, 12

Magnificat, 92
marriage, 99–100, 177
material sufficiency, 18, 54
materialism/luxury, 62, 72, 106, 108, 110, 159, 169, 178
May, Rollo, 86
Messiah, 20–21, 47, 92, 172
militarism, 32, 56, 158, 161–64, 166–67
money, 105–7, 124, 148
morality. See ethics
murder, 139–41, 155
Muslims, 140, 170, 176

nations: Israel to honor, 20, 28, 43; united, 158–61, 178, responsibility of, 84–85
Nature. See Earth
Niebuhr, Reinhold, 179
nonviolence, 37, 54, 77, 141, 161–68, 178
nurturing: Earth as, 30; family/community as, 44, 50, 74, 98–99. 157, 165, 177; God as, 24–26, 29, 53, 78–80, 115, 117, 153, 163, 172
Nussbaum, Martha C., 51, 174

O'Reilly, Bill, 57, 72–73
originalism, 71, 136

parables: as empowerment, 77; as weapons of resistance, 77
parables of the Hebrew Scriptures: The Lamb, 58–59; The Trees, 59; Unfruitful Vineyard, 101
parables of Jesus: Fig Tree, 103; Friend Awakened at Midnight, 124; Good Samaritan, 82–83; Laborers in the Vineyard, 111–12; Great Banquet, 94–95; Mustard Seed; 93–94; Pharisee and Tax-collector, 67–68; Plundered

House, 151; Prodigal Son, 78; Rich Fool, 107; Rich Man and Lazarus, 108–9; Sheep and Goats, 84–85; Talents, 126; Wicked Tenants, 102; Yeast, 94
patriotism, 157–59
patron/client system, 60, 62–63, 79, 98–99, 115
peace: expansive definition of, 165–66; keeping vs. making, 62, 71, 122, 164; message of, 20, 32, 44, 54, 178; the waging of, 161–68
peasants: Jesus as, 106; Roman oppression of, 18, 61; subsistence ethic of, 18, 37, 55, 79, 117, 124, 136
Pharaoh, 26–27, 31–32, 151
Pharisees, 64–69
Planet. *See* Earth
pluralism, 54, 168, 176
political correctness, 140
political ethics: of Jesus, 43–51; 176–78; Liberals and Conservatives, 53–54; of peasants, 18; of Rome, 62
politics: definition of, 16–19; Jesus and, 11, 19–23, 68, 91, 96–97, 176–78; religion and, 11, 17, 19, 38, 173–74
pollution, 65, 100, 160
poverty, poor, 105; as destitute, 121; caused by evil, 76, 106, 120, 122, 176; God cares for, 27, 94; honoring of, 106–14; Jesus' program for, 92, 120–32
power, 17–18, 37, 42, 46, 62
prayer. *See* Lord's Prayer
prejudice, 75, 139–41
pride, 31–32, 67
Progressive. *See* Liberal
pro-living, 166
Promised Land, 37, 42
prophets: Constitutional defenders, 35–36; guardians of political morality, 31, 58–60, 85, 101, 161, 164; hope of restoring Israel, 43, 45, 226, 247, 158–59; Jesus as, 35, 55, 129–30, 134, 152, 162, 176; John as, 36–37, 144

prostitutes, 37, 66, 96
purity codes: Jesus on, 67, 99–100, 122; misuse of, 65–66; value of, 65
race, racism, 71, 86, 88, 139, 178
Rawls, John, 52, 133
reform, 52: Jesus on, 20, 69, 77, 96, 114, 117, 129–30, 162
respect: for Creation, 8, 12, 29–30, 68; for others, 45, 75, 89, 95, 133, 141, 178
restoration: of Earth/Land, 18, 33, 91, 100–101; of good governing, 35, 44, 66, 126, 149; of Israel, 28, 60, 64, 69, 116, 161
restorative justice. *See* affirmative action
retaliation: Jesus' redefinition of, 139, 163, 178
reversal, as affirmative action, 27, 92, 95–96, 121–22, 133; Jesus' sayings on, 45, 91, 111, 166
Rice, Condoleezza, 157
rights: 29, 33; Earth's, 30–31, 91, 101, 104; expanding civil, 54, 135, 138, 177, 182–83; human, 51–52, 54, 70, 90, 96, 100; to subsist, 18, 44, 81–83, 121–22
Rome: its imperial ethic, 62; Jesus' opposition to, 43, 96, 103, 115–17, 127–29, 150–51, 164; ruinous rule of, 43, 60–63, 78, 96, 106, 120

Sabbath: rest for animals/Land, 30–31; people, 68, 136, 149, 153
Sachs, Jeffrey D., 98
Sadducees, 22, 64
safety net, 47, 51, 163
salvation: Earth's, 5; expanded view of, 4, 7, 44, 176; personal, 22, 131, 171, 173; political, 48, 126
science, 9, 33, 38–39
Scripture. *See* Bible
selfishness, 11, 31–32, 72, 124, 138, 149, 179
Sermon of the Mount, 121, 136–42
service: essence of Good Governing, 38, 74, 85, 131, 144, 158, 166

sex, 100, 141, 171
sexism, 71, 86, 91, 99, 141
shalom. *See* common good, peace, welfare
sin, 14, 32, 45, 76, 106, 120, 148–49, 164, 171, 176
"sinners," 37, 65, 69, 80, 95–96, 126
slavery, 61, 66, 98, 170
species, 54, 101, 172, 183
speciesism, 30
spirituality: eco-, 4, 11, 16–23; nature of, 1–16; political ethics of, 11–14, 16–19
Spiritual Progressives, 52. *See also* Liberalism
stewardship, 28–29, 103
strict-parent: of family, 98; of God, 24–25, 67, 115; politics of, 71
subsistence ethic. See ethics, political ethics
Suffering Servant, 132
sustainability: God's essence rooted in, 26; new ethical paradigm, 1, 18, 26, 80, 84–85, 110, 120–32, 165; path to, 10–16; 28–29, 31–33; pillars of 12, 33, 55–56, 176–78
swords: beating into farm implements, 159, 165–66; Jesus opposed to, 162–63

taxes, 61, 68, 105, 127–28
Temple, Roman Temple-state, function of, 63, 95, 105, 127; Jesus' cleansing of, 129–30, 132, 144, 160, 162
temptations: Adam and Eve's, 31; political, 117
Ten Commandments, 44, 125, 137–43
Theissen, Gerd, 16, 20
tithe, tithing, 61, 68, 127–28, 136
tolerance, 140–41, 176
Torah, 19, 65, 84, 135
tradition, 24, 57–73, 141

Transfiguration, 134
transformation: of self, 10–11, 15, 172–74; socio-political, 3, 5, 15, 20, 42–43, 176–78
truth-telling, 142
twelve disciples, 47–48, 131, 137

United Nations, 158, 161, 166, 178

values: changing of, 2, 11, 172–73, 178; Conservative, 53, 58, 62, 71–72, 99, 103, 171; family, 98–100, 141; Liberal, 50–52, 77, 98, 116, 122, 126, 141, 170, 176–78; struggle over, 2, 15, 135, 172, 182
violence: beginning of, 32, 102; downward spiral of, 84, 98, 139, 151, 161; Jesus opposed, 161–66, 178. *See also* non-violence
virtues, 16, 19, 33–34, 159, 164
war: Crusader Ethic, 167, elimination of, 31, 160, 162–65; environmental destruction of, 168; futility of, 168; Iraq and Vietnam, 166–67; Just War theory, 166–67; weapons of mass destruction, 166, 178
Way, the, 11, 169
wealth, 14, 31, 62; redistribution of, 53–54, 125–26; as sin, 106–10; 113–14, 122, 132, 137
welfare, 54, 123, 146, 165; Conservative opposition to, 70–71, 75
"What would Jesus do?" 4, 183
White, Lynn, 28, 33
women: equality of, 92, 95–98, 99–100, 153, 176–77; war on, 97, 139 141
wonder, 12, 34, 141
Wright, N. T., 21, 41

Yablonsky, Lewis, 86

zeal, proto-Zealots, 18, 64

www.ingramcontent.com/pod-product-compliance
Lightning Source LLC
Chambersburg PA
CBHW070315230426
43663CB00011B/2145